Jean Renoir

MANCHESTER
UNIVERSITY PRESS

FRENCH FILM DIRECTORS

DIANA HOLMES and ROBERT INGRAM *series editors*
DUDLEY ANDREW *series consultant*

Luc Besson SUSAN HAYWARD

Robert Bresson KEITH READER

Claude Chabrol GUY AUSTIN

Diane Kurys CARRIE TARR

Georges Méliès ELIZABETH EZRA

Coline Serreau BRIGITTE ROLLET

François Truffaut DIANA HOLMES AND ROBERT INGRAM

Agnès Varda ALISON SMITH

forthcoming titles

Jean-Jacques Beineix PHIL POWRIE

Bertrand Blier SUE HARRIS

Jean Cocteau JAMES WILLIAMS

Marguerite Duras RENATE GUNTHER

Jean-Luc Godard STEVE CANNON AND ELIANE MEYER

Bertrand Tavernier LYNN A. HIGGINS

André Teclimé BILL MARSHALL

Jean Vigo MICHAEL TEMPLE

FRENCH FILM DIRECTORS

Jean Renoir

MARTIN O'SHAUGHNESSY

Manchester University Press

MANCHESTER AND NEW YORK

distributed exclusively in the USA by St. Martin's Press

Copyright © Martin O'Shaughnessy 2000

The right of Martin O'Shaughnessy to be identified as the author of this
work has been asserted by him in accordance with the Copyright, Designs
and Patents Act 1988.

Published by Manchester University Press
Oxford Road, Manchester M13 9NR, UK
and Room 400, 175 Fifth Avenue, New York, NY 10010, USA
http://www.man.ac.uk/mup

Distributed exclusively in the USA by
St. Martin's Press, Inc., 175 Fifth Avenue, New York,
NY 10010, USA

Distributed exclusively in Canada by
UBC Press, University of British Columbia, 2029 West Mall,
Vancouver, BC, Canada V6T 1Z2

British Library Cataloguing-in-Publication Data
A catalogue record for this book is available from the British Library

Library of Congress Cataloging-in-Publication Data applied for

ISBN 0 7190 5062 6 *hardback*
    0 7190 5063 4 *paperback*

First published 2000

07 06 05 04 03 02 01 00   10 9 8 7 6 5 4 3 2 1

Typeset in Scala with Meta display
by Koinonia, Manchester
Printed in Great Britain
by Bookcraft (Bath) Ltd, Midsomer Norton

Contents

List of plates

Series editors' foreword

To an anglophone audience, the combination of the words 'French' and 'cinema' evokes a particular kind of film: elegant and wordy, sexy but serious – an image as dependent on national stereotypes as is that of the crudely commercial Hollywood blockbuster, which is not to say that either image is without foundation. Over the past two decades, this generalised sense of a significant relationship between French identity and film has been explored in scholarly books and articles, and has entered the curriculum at university level and, in Britain, at A-level. The study of film as an art-form and (to a lesser extent) as industry, has become a popular and widespread element of French Studies, and French cinema has acquired an important place within Film Studies. Meanwhile, the growth in multi-screen and 'art-house' cinemas, together with the development of the video industry, has led to the greater availability of foreign-language films to an English-speaking audience. Responding to these developments, this series is designed for students and teachers seeking information and accessible but rigorous critical study of French cinema, and for the enthusiastic filmgoer who wants to know more.

The adoption of a director-based approach raises questions about *auteurism*. A series that categorises films not according to period or to genre (for example), but to the person who directed them, runs the risk of espousing a romantic view of film as the product of solitary inspiration. On this model, the critic's role might seem to be that of discovering continuities, revealing a necessary coherent set of themes and motifs which correspond to the particular genius of the individual. This is not our aim: the *auteur* perspective on film, itself most clearly articulated in France in the early 1950s, will be interrogated in certain volumes of the series, and, throughout, the director will be treated as one highly significant element in a complex process of film production and reception which includes socio-economic and political determinants, the work of a large and highly skilled team of artists and technicians, the mechanisms of production and distribution, and the complex and multiply determined responses of spectators.

The work of some of the directors in the series is already known outside France, that of others is less so – the aim is both to provide informative and original English-language studies of established figures, and to extend the range of French directors known to anglophone students of cinema. We intend the series to contribute to the promotion of the informal and formal study of French films, and to the pleasure of those who watch them.

DIANA HOLMES
ROBERT INGRAM

Acknowledgements

I would like to thank the following: the series editors for their patience and advice; Roger Viry-Babel whose help was vital at an early stage of this project; Trevor Pull for his technical support; colleagues at Nottingham Trent for their ongoing support and encouragement; staff at the BIFI and Arsenal libraries in Paris and at the BFI in London whose help has proved invaluable. A special thanks to my students who have helped me clarify my ideas over the years.

To Gloria, Ana, John and Kay

1

An uneven career

This first chapter introduces Renoir's life and highly uneven career. It demarcates his vision of his films, craft and ideological evolution, indicating, in the process, the shape of this book and some of its main lines of inquiry. It draws substantially on his writings and interviews he gave at various times but it does so with a degree of scepticism. Much of what we know of him derives from his own accounts. It would be naïve not to expect him to have shaped his version of his life and career to fit the particular directorial persona he wished to present at a given time. Rather than taking biographical details as a somehow full and objective account, it is better to view them in terms of the retrospective importance Renoir grants them, an importance that can provide insights into his outlook at the time of writing. Of this, more later.

His life and films

Born in 1894 in Paris, Jean Renoir was the son of the Impressionist painter Auguste Renoir and Aline Charigot, a woman with peasant origins. His childhood was divided between three locations: Paris, or more specifically, Montmartre, which at the time was a semi-rural suburb of Paris; Essoyes, in Burgundy, where his mother's wine-growing family lived; Provence, and more specifically *Les Colettes*, the property where the old Renoir painted in his last years surrounded by olive trees.

There is some suggestion in Renoir's accounts that his home environment was overprotective. One key bone of contention was Auguste's insistence that his son should keep his long blond locks. The only adult male in a house otherwise full of women seemed intent on preventing him from asserting his masculinity. Jean was repeatedly mistaken for a girl and saw anything overtly masculine, especially anything military, as an escape into a more male world. Thus his passion for Dumas's stories of the musketeers and for Napoleonic toy soldiers, his interest in one of the servant's soldier boyfriend, and his hatred for ribbons and satin. Jean calls himself a *froussard*, a coward, telling how he was frightened by the noisy play of the boys in the street. This story of a young man having enormous difficulty negotiating his way between a 'feminine' domestic space and the world of adult masculinity is banal. What is of interest however is to what degree it seems to have haunted him, to the extent that it is a running theme of his book about his father (Renoir 1981b). It is also striking that when the young Renoir sought for role models in the broader culture, what was most immediately at hand were real or fictional military images. This was a highly gender-demarcated world.

If in some ways Jean had a particularly bourgeois lifestyle, in others his childhood was very unconventional. He was certainly relatively privileged, being part of a family with servants and more than one home. But on the other hand, his artist father was very unlike the other parents at his bourgeois school. Auguste's friends, people such as Zola, Cézanne or Toulouse-Lautrec, were predominantly drawn from a world of art and literature which tended to define itself by rejection of the very bourgeoisie with whom its education and lifestyle might otherwise seem to align it. His Montmartre home is also indicative of a degree of marginality, for the area was classically associated with prostitution, crime, artists and the entertainment industry, all a far cry from bourgeois respectability.

Formative cultural experiences that Jean retrospectively cites are Guignol (the French equivalent of Punch and Judy), the adventure stories of Dumas *père*, the music hall and the popular melodramatic plays shown on the *boulevard du crime* in Paris. It was Gabrielle, his main carer, nurse and playmate who took him to see his first film at a Paris department store, an experience which apparently overwhelmed the young boy. His second exposure to film was at school where he laughed at the antics of *Automaboul*, a comically uncooperative car. Despite his exposure to an eclectic range of cultural forms, the dominant influence was surely high cultural. Jean grew up in a household which revolved around the needs of a great painter and was a centre for discussion between prominent artists and writers (Renoir 1974b: 31–2). His account of a young man growing up between élite and popular culture is particularly apt for a director whose work had to find a space for itself between 'high' and 'low' cultural forms.

To escape the shadow of his artist father, Renoir initially sought a career diametrically opposed to creative art, becoming an officer in the French cavalry, one of the most traditional and aristocratic branches of the military, only to find himself thrust into the trenches in 1914. Wounded and rescued from no-man's land, he was saved from gangrene and the amputation of his leg by innovative treatment. His sick mother, who had rushed to his bedside, died soon after in 1915. Jean re-enlisted, this time in the airforce. Aerial reconnaissance gave him his first experience of using a camera, but a bad landing put him out of action, this time permanently. This was not the last time war would turn his life upside down.

His recuperation afforded him a period of enforced idleness in Paris, during which he became steeped in the American cinema which was then assuming the unchallenged domination of world cinema screens that it has never relinquished. He had a particular passion for Chaplin. Later, he was given a desk job that enabled him to be beside his father, with whom he was now able to have long discussions. Auguste died in 1919 and soon after Jean married Andrée Heuschling, the artist's last model and an aspiring actress. She adopted the professional name of Catherine Hessling.

It was, he tells us, to help launch 'Catherine' that he decided to become involved in film-making (Renoir 1974b: 47–53). For his first project, *Catherine ou une vie sans joie* (1924), he hired Albert

Dieudonné (famous for his role as Napoleon in Abel Gance's film) to direct his wife. Having agreed to restrict himself to providing the story, he apparently made Dieudonné's life unbearable by interfering in the filming. He then donned the mantle of director himself to make the low-budget *La Fille de l'eau* (1924), which again centred on his wife. It seemed destined to be a complete flop but its dream sequence was projected at an avant-garde venue and achieved a success that convinced Renoir to continue in film-making. His next venture was a costly adaptation of Zola's celebrated novel, *Nana* (1926). Despite co-financing from a German production company, the film ate deep into Renoir's fortune, forcing him to sell some of his father's paintings. Almost at the same time, he shot *Sur un air de Charleston* (1926), a short avant-gardist science fantasy film designed to show off Catherine's dancing ability. Most of his subsequent silent works were paid for by others ranging from wealthy lovers of aspiring actresses to the *Société des Films Historiques*. In among these commercial ventures, Renoir made *La Petite Marchande d'allumettes* (1928), an adaptation of the Hans Christian Andersen story, in a small studio in the Vieux Colombier theatre. For this do-it-yourself production, Renoir and Jean Tedesco turned their hand to everything from lighting and special effects to developing.

It is astonishing to consider the diversity of this early work. Ranging from prestige literary adaptation to popular melodrama, from vaudeville to avant-garde experiment, and from costume drama to colonial propaganda, it certainly did not suggest someone who knew which way he wished to develop, or if he did, someone who was able to choose which films he would make. Looking back on it, Renoir picked out certain films which he felt to be important for different reasons, but the period seems to have been dominated by an interest in visual invention and technical innovation. Here was a director ready to experiment with film stocks, lighting, camera movements and scale models, someone who was ready, if need arose, to draw on his own cavalry skills and take the camera on horseback to film a desert chase.

The coming of sound at the end of the 1920s changed the context for Renoir and others. Films became much more expensive to make so that commercial considerations discouraged innovative productions. The heroically mobile camera of the silent era was now tied down by microphone placements and bulky soundproofing. Stagebound, dialogue-dominated and highly derivative filmed theatre became the dominant form in the French industry, although adaptations of novels offered an alternative and increasingly important direction of development. Sound was not the only novelty in the period. With the collapse of the French majors in the mid-1930s, productions were increasingly *ad hoc* for single films. While some people suggest that this fragmentation held back the development of French cinema, others maintain that it made possible a diversity of film-making that a more structured system would not have allowed. Certainly, Renoir lived from hand to mouth with each project representing a new departure. On the other hand, he was able to work repeatedly with people he was close to, thus creating the tight-knit crews that he preferred. Jacques Becker, later a considerable director himself, became his assistant in 1932. Claude Renoir, his nephew, became his cameraman in the same year, while Marguerite Renoir, his companion in the 1930s (and who adopted his name), was his editor from 1931 onwards. His brother, the actor Pierre Renoir, played star roles in two films while other actors repeatedly appeared.

Renoir's initial forays into sound followed a conventional pattern, with three adaptations of successful theatrical comedies and three of novels to his credit between 1931 and 1934. While the theatrical adaptations were predominantly studio shot, the films taken from novels encouraged location shooting which permitted the close companionship, communal meals and single-minded concentration the director preferred. Perhaps because of the more uniform literary sources for all these films, it is much easier to discern shared characteristics than it is for the more diverse silent cinema. All the films can be seen as portraits of sectors of French society, usually the bourgeoisie, and most if not all share a satirical tone that ranges from the gentle to the acerbic. Moreover, in the tension between theatre and novel, and between studio and location shooting, one can suggest a Renoir struggling to escape from the predominant theatricality of early sound cinema and develop a realist mode of filming. Renoir's final film of the early 1930s, *Toni* (1934), shot on location in the south of France, can be seen as a pursuit of such a quest. Breaking free from his literary moorings, Renoir made a film more closely rooted in contemporary issues and, for the first time, put ordinary workers and peasants on the screen. The key question that hangs over this period of Renoir's film-making is whether the early sound films' greater thematic consistency and new-found critical edge derives from directorial intent or from shared tendencies of their literary sources.

The year 1933 saw the coming to power of Hitler. Having visited Germany with his producer friend Braunberger, himself a Jew, Renoir witnessed an old Jewish lady being forced to lick the footpath by some of Hitler's brown-shirts. Closer to home, he stood out against a petition asking for foreigners to be excluded from the French film industry (Renoir 1994: 25–6). His hostility to racism was the first sign of overt politicisation of his outlook. Another potential factor is the largely unexplored influence of Marguerite, his companion and editor. Coming from a committed family as she did, she helped to expose Renoir to left-wing ideas and activists. Although the precise motives and circumstances are unknown, the fact that he became politically involved is neither surprising nor exceptional. Like many other French intellectuals of the 1930s, he was faced with an increasingly polarised and dangerous political context that encouraged involvement. Clearly too, after *Toni*, he must have been an obvious candidate for recruitment by the left, and especially by the Communist Party (PCF), which traditionally sought to associate artists and intellectuals with its cause.

Whatever the roots of his engagement, Renoir's next two films located him very firmly on the left of the political spectrum. *Le Crime de Monsieur Lange* (1935) brought him into close collaboration with the Groupe Octobre, the most celebrated left-wing theatre troupe of the period, while for his next venture he supervised a team of younger film-makers to produce a propaganda film for the French Communist Party in the run-up to the 1936 elections that would bring the Popular Front to power. Willy-nilly, he was now a figurehead, the major left-wing film-maker of his day. He was a leading voice in Ciné-liberté, an ambitious attempt to bring together film workers and cinema viewers to create a radical alternative to commercial cinema and to ensure an audience for left-wing films outside of normal distribution circuits. The showpiece of Ciné-liberté was to be his *La Marseillaise* (1937).

Renoir's involvement did not stop there. He contributed a regular column to *Ce soir*, the Communist-affiliated daily, from the spring of 1937 till the autumn of 1938. He visited the Soviet Union in 1936 and wrote glowingly of his experiences in the Communist newspaper, *l'Humanité*. He also found time to make three other less obviously partisan films (*Une Partie de campagne* (1936), *Les Bas-Fonds* (1936), and *La Grande Illusion* (1937)). As the Front unravelled, Renoir made two dramatically different films, the dark, doom-laden naturalistic *La Bête humaine* (1938), and his final film of the 1930s, *La Règle du jeu* (1939), which shifted decisively away from naturalism by drawing on classical French theatre for inspiration. The latter's run was cut short by the approach of war, but not before it had provoked some violently hostile reactions. The challenge with these Frontist and immediately post-Frontist films is to trace the contours and evolution of their political commitment, considering them as interventions in a broader struggle but simultaneously investigating their specific need to invent modes of film-making that matched the demands of the time.

La Règle du jeu was followed by a curious and highly ambiguous episode. By this time working for the army film service, Renoir was invited to go to Italy by none other than Mussolini himself, to work on a film inspired by Puccini's *Tosca*. His acceptance, under apparent pressure from a French government determined to keep Italy friendly, dismayed his erstwhile allies on the left. While he only managed to shoot a small part of the film before the outbreak of hostilities forced him to leave Italy, the adaptation by a renowned French director of a prestigious Italian opera may be seen as a propaganda *coup* for the Fascist regime. However, the film's story of heroic self-sacrifice in the cause of liberty and in the face of a tyrannical police chief is a strange one for the Fascists to have commissioned.

The rout of France in 1940 turned Renoir's life upside down. Accompanied by Dido Freire, who would become his second wife, he took to the roads along with millions of his compatriots. His flight came to a temporary halt at *Les Colettes*, his father's old house in Provence, only to restart again when he took up the invitation of the great documentary maker, Robert Flaherty, to go to the United States. His journey took him on a roundabout route through North Africa and Portugal. While in the latter location, he proposed the development of a 'Latin cinema' (Renoir 1994: 85–6) As the countries presumably to be involved were extreme right-wing or Fascist regimes, this was again an astonishing move, whatever his underlying intentions may have been. It was at this time that he developed the outline of *Magnificat* that was to have been the story of a group of French missionaries in Latin America and their self-sacrifice in the cause of the faith (Renoir 1981a: 79–83). The story is not overtly political but comes close to some key themes of the undemocratic Pétainist régime. The only existing article that Renoir wrote after the fall of France is similarly ambiguous. He castigates the French cinema of 1939 as selfish and frivolous, calling for a renewed industry that would demonstrate more fraternal attitudes (Renoir 1989a: 41–4). Although the sentiments expressed would not seem out of place in a Pétainist article, there is again no overt political stance.

How Renoir might have developed had he stayed in occupied France is sheer speculation and the existing evidence is so thin that no defensible hypothesis could be built on it. What we do know is that he arrived in the USA where he had to rebuild a career from scratch. Not only did he not speak the language, but Hollywood production practices and modes of filming and editing were radically different and unaccommodating to the artisanal practices and very personal style that he had developed in the 1930s in the relatively unstructured French industry. He expected to have a degree of control over almost all stages of the film-making process, from writing the screenplay, through casting and rehearsal, to the *mise-en-scène* and editing. His practice was to work with a tightly knit team but within a loose framework that allowed for constant revision when faced with the concrete realities of filming. The Hollywood studios had evolved a system that depended on division of labour and a high level of specialisation so that the director's control tended to be concentrated on the *mise-en-scène*, and even then limited by highly routinised practices and tight planning. Whether Renoir was engulfed by Hollywood, merely accommodated to it, or indeed transcended the limitations it imposed upon him is clearly a key question.

Renoir made six films in the United States with very varying degrees of directorial control. His first American production, *Swamp Water* (1941) brought him face to face with the Hollywood studio system and the dictatorial power wielded by Zanuck, the studio boss at Twentieth Century-Fox. Renoir wanted to do as much of the film as possible on location. Fox only let him do a few exteriors, preferring the security of studio shooting to the vagaries of location work. Renoir's taste for long takes and a mobile camera that allowed the actors' performances to develop and to be followed through the set came up against the much more fragmented Hollywood style of analytical editing. The multiple shots from different angles that analytical editing produced allowed the same sequence to be put together in very different ways and made editing a vital area of control. Renoir found to his chagrin that Fox had no intention of letting him edit the film as he saw fit. He and they parted company by mutual accord.

His next American film, *This Land is Mine* (1943), was financed by the RKO studio and shot using the American style of analytical editing with shots and counter-shots, master shots and medium shots rather than in Renoir's flowing French style of the late 1930s. In an interview in 1954, Renoir said that he filmed this way in order to be able to remake at the editing stage what was a propaganda piece with a very sensitive message (Renoir 1989b: 17). One might alternatively suggest that he had altered his style to suit Hollywood. He none the less reports enjoying complete freedom while shooting his next three films. The first, *The Southerner* (1945), his own favourite among his American output is set, like *Swamp Water*, in a rural community. Renoir reworked an original screenplay with the help of the great American novelist, William Faulkner, hiring his old set-designer Eugène Lourié and a French cameraman, and shooting on location in his favoured communal atmosphere. *The Diary of a Chambermaid* (1946) was shot in a small, independent studio with considerable room for improvisation (Renoir 1989b: 25). *The Woman on the Beach* (1946), was shot for the RKO studio which apparently let Renoir work as he wished. The film was not a success. RKO bought Renoir out of his contract, bringing his Hollywood period to a close.

His American output is decidedly varied with no clear evolution or thematic consistency. Two films look back to France but only one of them can be definitely attached to the present. Two films are rural dramas which clearly feed off American myths of small towns, settlers and wilderness. One (*The Woman on the Beach*) is a *film noir* that deals with the scarring effects of the war. Should we bracket off Renoir's American production from the rest of his work, seeing it simply as the floundering about of an exile? Is it a mere interlude, or can we link it to what came before or after? One of his films is an overtly propagandistic piece, but to what degree were the other films also tailored for a wartime context? Was Renoir seeking to express some personal vision or making conventional products in a bid for acceptance (in which case his degree of freedom during shooting becomes somewhat irrelevant)? To what degree were myths of America or American genres simply voicing themselves through his films?

It is not really clear why Renoir turned his back on Hollywood. The decision seems to have been an initially tentative separation that hardened into a divorce. In an article which Gauteur dates as 1946 but which simple mathematics locate as 1948, Renoir speaks of enormous difficulty adapting to working in America but adds that he now feels enthusiastic about working there and will be able to express himself as well as in France. He even adds that America is the only place where he can easily finance the projects that he has in mind (Renoir 1974a: 54–9). However, in an interview from 1954, he recounts how American banks refused to finance the innovative low-budget independent productions he then wanted to embark on (Renoir 1989b: 31). Unable to function within the studios or finance ventures outside of them, there were few avenues left to him.

The inevitable question is why France's most famous film-maker did not return sooner to the country where he had made his most celebrated films. Again, no clear answer arises. One problem was that Renoir's divorce from Catherine was not valid in France, so that he might be liable to charges of bigamy if he arrived with his second wife. In addition, his American output was generally very badly received in France, especially *This Land is Mine* which came in for savage attack for what some felt to be an offensively false image of occupied France. At a deeper level, there was clearly a risk that the director who had felt he had his finger on a nation's pulse in 1939 would simply be out of touch with a country that had gone through so much in his absence.

Renoir's next film and his first in colour, *The River* (1950), was shot in India. Because of its concentration on an English family and the twilight of colonialism, it helped bring him closer to Europe again. *Le Carosse d'or* (1952) completed the journey. This Franco-Italian co-production continues *The River*'s critique of European civilisation and opens a tryptych of historical costume dramas that are deliberately anti-realist in their theatricality. *French Cancan* (1954) saw Renoir return at last to film-making in his native country.[1] Set in the *belle époque*, it can be seen as a celebration of French popular culture designed to help the director to re-establish himself in his homeland. *Eléna et les hommes* (1956), an uneasy mix of light comedy and dark satire, is set in the same period.

The last four films were relatively low-key ventures. *Le Testament du Docteur Cordelier* (1959) and *Le Déjeuner sur l'herbe* (1959), shot using the same multi-camera technique, form a deliberate if contrasting pair. *Le Caporal épinglé* (1962) is, on the surface, the

---

1 Renoir began to talk of returning to France to direct from 1949 (see Renoir, J. 1994: 220). The emergence of a European art cinema, the adulation heaped on him in the influential French journal *Cahiers du cinéma*, and the difficulties he was experiencing making films in Hollywood are all factors which may have pushed him back towards France.

story of French prisoners of war in the Second World War, while
Le Petit Théâtre de Jean Renoir (1969), a consciously valedictory
work, is a collection of four short pieces shot in a range of styles
that evoke different aspects and periods of the director's output.
All these late films pursue a critique of the false priorities and
repressive attitudes of modern technological and consumerist
society. Renoir's post-war cinema, even when in apparently realist
mode as in *Le Caporal épinglé*, is predominantly a didactic cinema
of ideas in which characters encapsulate values or attitudes to life
rather than being rounded, socially embedded individuals.

The United States remained Renoir's permanent home in the
post-war period although he no longer made films there. Some of
his later output, because of its transnational production or
themes, positioned him on the international art-house circuit. His
specifically French films seemed to avoid engaging with contemporary issues. He seemed strangely semi-detached. It is easy to
understand why some critics felt he was simply out of touch. This
study will need to justify its identification of a sustained critique of
the West in the later films while at the same time explaining why
other critics read them so differently.

The shape of a career

When one attempts to give a shape to Renoir's career, one is
struck by the difficulty of the endeavour. He made films addressing different audiences with varying degrees of freedom in
shifting production and socio-historical contexts. Rather than
seeking any overall coherence or consistency, it makes more sense,
initially at least, to identify periods when one or more contextual
factors remained relatively stable. Such an approach leads me to
identify the following stages as the basis of my analysis. First, the
silent period which is marked predominantly by Renoir's fascination with technique and shows no consistent sense of artistic
development and no clear ideological stance. Second, the early
sound period which is dominated by adaptations of plays and
novels. Third, The Popular Front period when Renoir's cinema

was engaged fully with contemporary struggles and his realist aesthetic was put at the service of a clear ideological commitment. Fourth, the American period when, against a background of war, the exiled Renoir struggled to establish a sense of direction. Finally, the post-war period when his films turn away from realism and engage in a critique of dominant values and traditions of western societies in general and France in particular.

Renoir's writings

The place of the director in our interpretation of films has been one of the central sites of conflict in film criticism. Those who wish to establish film's credentials as an art form need a central originating genius, an *auteur*, to set it on a par with novel, poetry, music or painting. The director is perforce their central candidate for this role, being the obvious potential link in the various stages of the creative process from scriptwriting, through *mise-en-scène* to editing. Such *auteurism*, undoubtedly the dominant public form of reception of 'art' or 'serious' cinema, is embedded in the way film is presented, viewed and reviewed. *Auteurism* has dominated Renoir criticism, constantly seeking to privilege links between the thoughts expressed by the director outside the films and themes and patterns identified in the films themselves. One cannot engage with the existing body of criticism without considering Renoir's writings and interviews.

Any adequate consideration of Renoir's utterances would consider when they were produced and in what specific institutional and ideological contexts. More specifically, it would consider whether they were produced by the politically committed director of the later 1930s or the politically disengaged figure of the post-war era. It would also consider whether the texts were contemporary to the period they described or whether they were retrospective accounts that imposed a particular slant on previous films in order to bring them into line with the attitudes of a later Renoir. All too often, however, they have been used uncritically and selectively to support a particular interpretation of the films.

Pierre-Auguste Renoir, mon père (Renoir 1981b) is the text most frequently drawn upon to fill in Renoir's early years and to suggest what influence his artist father may have had upon him. The problem with it is that it was published in 1962 when Renoir himself was an old man. Rather than giving a simple account of his father, it repeatedly contrasts his era with the time when the book was written, broadly suggesting how the world has changed for the worst and what role an artist can play in modern society. Some critics (notably Gauteur) have suggested that this text plays a key role in Renoir's denial of his previous political commitment (Gauteur 1980). By creating a father in his own image, Renoir is able to suggest a smooth transition of values that neatly hides his own ideological about-turn. While one may use this text as a source of basic biographical information, it is unwise to take its ideological or aesthetic positions at face value and important to remember that Renoir needed to produce a childhood to account for his adult directorial persona.

Renoir on Renoir (Renoir 1989b) contains a series of key interviews that Renoir gave to the *Cahiers du cinéma* critics for whom he was a totemic figure, the model French *auteur*. *Cahiers* played a key role in the propagation of *auteur* theory in the 1950s and first half of the 1960s. Its interviews with Renoir, which date precisely from this period, provided him with the sort of sustained platform to talk about his outlook and his films that he had never previously enjoyed. *Cahiers* looked positively upon all aspects of his career and invited him to review his previous films in terms of a developing personal style and philosophy, or, in other words, to view himself as an *auteur*. *Cahiers* was not alone in promoting Renoir as an *auteur* at this time. The re-release of key films, television showings, the appearance of the first book-length studies of the director's works and the emergence of a flourishing network of *ciné-clubs* where 'great' directors were adulated, all helped to ensure that Renoir's films were increasingly viewed in a context of personal development and detached from broader socio-historical contexts. However, *Cahiers* undoubtedly played a key role, and its own decided leaning towards formalism and ahistorical humanism tended to create a Renoir in its own image.

My life and my films (Renoir 1974b) builds upon the *auteurist* account of his work that Renoir and *Cahiers* had connived to generate. It gives an evolutionary account of the director's life and work tailored to account for the emergence of his mature outlook and style. The films are seen as the product of personal experiences and of the influence of other artists, usually consecrated cinematic *auteurs*, such as Chaplin (famous for his participation in all aspects of his own films), Griffiths (credited with the almost single-handed invention of the 'grammar' of narrative film and notoriously unable to fit his artistic creativity into the Hollywood mould) and Pagnol (who resolutely maintained his status as an independent film-maker in the 1930s). Although the broader historical and political context is not entirely absent, the text focuses resolutely on individuals and personal contexts. Famously, Renoir glosses over the Popular Front period, the time of his most fertile film-making, in just a few pages, almost completely erasing his own deep involvement in the politics of the period and its decisive influence on some of his most celebrated films.

Claude Gauteur wanted to restore some balance to our vision of Renoir and to show the complexity of his evolution. In *Jean Renoir: Ecrits, 1926–1971* (Renoir 1974a), he assembled a diverse collection of texts which had been unavailable to or neglected by those who had produced overviews of Renoir's work in the previous twenty years. Most notably, he brought together the journalistic writings from the Popular Front period, the majority of which appeared in Renoir's weekly column in *Ce soir*, the Communist daily. These reveal a partisan figure, engaged fully in the quarrels of the period, and happy to bend his language to fit the discourse of the Popular Front or the Communist Party. This political Renoir was, of course, responsible for many of what are conventionally seen as the greatest films. *Auteurists*, who by rights should use these texts to produce political readings of the films, rather unsurprisingly prefer the retrospective and apparently apolitical comments of the later Renoir.

Gauteur's second collection, *Le Passé vivant* (Renoir 1989a), contained neglected texts generated between 1933 and 1978. It was far less polemical than the first, seeming to be motivated more by a desire for completeness than by the earlier wish to correct a distorted view of the director. With his previous volume, it does however demonstrate how little Renoir wrote about his films, his art or his outlook before 1936 and indeed during the 1940s. The two volumes of Renoir letters which are now available can, to a degree, fill the gap for the latter period, although their general focus on day-to-day issues of film production or on private and interpersonal issues prevents them from being an adequate substitute for more considered articles or interviews (Renoir 1984 and 1994). The Renoir of the earlier period is largely unavailable to us except through the films.

While we might seem to have a remarkably rounded picture of the director stretching from his father's youth to his last years, the available texts come largely from an intense burst of activity in the later 1930s and a more sustained period from the 1950s onwards. In both cases, as we have shown, these texts were produced to respond to specific expectations. A key question facing those who work on Renoir is how we should relate them to each other and beyond that to the films. One solution is to contrast the 1930s writings with the later output to show a man who turned his back on progressive politics. Another is to use the later writings to over-write the earlier ones and to reorientate the films, thus producing an 'authentic' and self-consistent Renoir whose commitment was only on the surface. A more judicious approach is to use texts from a period to cast light on the films from that same period while remembering that, although they may provide important insights, they are also part of the production of a directorial persona.

We can now turn to Renoir's versions of his past, his craft and his philosophy of life. I hope it is now clear why we will always need to contextualise his comments and be tentative in any conclusions we draw from them. We will begin by considering the political and ideological stances that he adopts at different stages of his career, showing how these provide an essential context for his comments on his films and his craft.

Committed and uncommitted Renoir?

Renoir's journalistic writings of the later 1930s illustrate his evolving outlook and how he articulates the personal, the professional and the political. The piece that he wrote for the first number of *Ciné-liberté* shows his great enthusiasm at the time of the 1936 elections. After locating himself with a group of *camarades* (comrades) around an editing table, he uses a review of Chaplin's *Modern Times* to launch an attack on capitalism's devastation of the landscape. He presents this 'cinematically' through a succession of shots, beginning with a close-up of an apple tree that has never blossomed more beautifully, tracking back to show spring bursting forth with unknown splendour in the garden, before focusing on the backdrop of hovels and factory chimneys created by the greed and stupidity of industrialists and landowners. He finishes the piece by praising the popular audience's receptivity to innovative cinema and looks forward to the time when the masses will sweep away those who seek to seduce it with the conformism of commercial cinema (Renoir 1974a: 79–81). This blending of a personal voice, a professional viewpoint and a polemically leftist stance sets the pattern for the journalism of the period, although the tone will darken markedly as the Front crumbles and the international situation worsens.

The dominant themes of the Frontist writings are as follows: an attack on the rich and powerful; a satirical assault on Nazism specifically and Fascism in general; a condemnation of the global aggression of Germany, Italy and Japan; praise of the popular classes; a celebration of France accompanied by an attack on the right's betrayal of the nation. While these themes are largely predictable for anyone familiar with the Popular Front, Renoir's writings do help pinpoint his ideological evolution in the enormously complex political landscape of the 1930s.

It is worth noting that he repeatedly expresses anti-racist attitudes which, at a time when even the left was far from immune from pervasive xenophobia, were surely indicative of a clearly held personal principal. His suggestion that racism is a bourgeois vice to which the working class are immune smacks considerably of

Communist Party dogma (Renoir 1974a: 107). A later anecdote in which he describes seeing a Jewish friend knock out a French anti-Semite has a more personal ring to it. After the Munich agreement, by which France and Britain abandoned Czechoslovakia to Nazi aggression, Renoir drew specific attention to the acts of anti-Semitism that would follow (Renoir 1974a: 176–8). Significantly, Jewish characters are located at the heart of *La Grande Illusion* and *La Règle du jeu*, two key films from the period.

Renoir's comments on war illustrate the complexity of his pacifism in this era of intense international tension. Pointing out that it is the common soldier who suffers in war, he mocks the hollowness of apparent heroism (Renoir 1974a: 103). Yet later he celebrates the popular commitment that led to the victory of the revolutionary armies against the Prussians at Valmy and comments that France should be defended to the end by all her children (Renoir 1974a: 128 and 267). His pacifism, a familiar variant of a diverse phenomenon, blends anti-militarism with the need to oppose Fascism with military force if necessary. This position will be usefully borne in mind when we try to understand how the same man could have made, back to back, an apparently pacifist film (*La Grande Illusion*) and one that celebrated the armies of the French Revolution (*La Marseillaise*).

Celebrating France's language, countryside and capital, Renoir's writings are perfectly in tune with the Popular Front's attempt to reclaim nationalism and its symbols from the extreme right. Evocations of a shared cultural heritage become a polemical tool as capitalism is castigated for its damage to the French landscape and to the nation's food and wine. Yet at the same time there are clear hints of a personal appropriation of a collectively generated stance in Renoir's warmly expressed appreciation of the gastronomic marvels of the French regions and the pleasures of sharing wine (Renoir 1974a: 171–2).

In the summer of 1938, well after the replacement of the Popular Front government by Daladier's centre–right coalition, Renoir penned an account of a drive southwards through France. Almost his last contribution to *Ce Soir*, this drive takes on a strong symbolic dimension. He described a storm that ravaged the countryside and blocked roads, leading to confrontation between lorry drivers and the policemen who close a bridge over the Rhône. As the situation turns ugly, the engine of a petrol tanker catches light, threatening to blow up the little town where they are gathered. The driver keeps his calm and with the help of his fellow drivers puts the fire out (Renoir 1974a: 173–5). This picture of workers' solidarity fending off disaster strongly suggests that Renoir clung onto his Frontist faith in the proletariat even as the internal and international situation grew gloomier. His comments on *La Bête humaine* in *Ce Soir* provide further evidence that his political commitment was alive even as his contributions to that paper, already down to a trickle, finally ceased towards the end of 1938 (Renoir 1974a: 261–2). Precisely how and when his allegiance to the left in general and the Communist Party in particular came to an end has never been established. As a result, the evolution of his politics as he made his most celebrated film, *La Règle du jeu*, can only be a matter of speculation.

His politics are also desperately difficult to trace from 1939 to 1946, although it is clear that by the late 1940s his commitment is definitively over. Letters from that period show that material progress has come to be his chief concern. In 1946, we find a reference to 'the horrible development of machines' (Renoir 1994: 174). In 1947, he expresses his concern at the impersonality of a civilisation, whose pre-packaged products are expressions of a general levelling tendency (Renoir 1994: 205). At about the same time he writes, 'There is one thing about which I'm pretty sure: that "progress" has been an error, and that the more material things that we possess, the more our situation on earth becomes complicated' (Renoir 1994: 206). One of the very few articles from this period repeats and amplifies fears expressed in the letters. Renoir expresses his dislike of a massified society, whose symptoms are opinion polls, an administered world and technology and whose cause is science, the new God. He suggests that while dispensing fridges and televisions, this God may steal part of our spiritual heritage. Looking around himself at anonymous, machine-produced goods and blended wines, he regrets a world where objects bore the mark of individual producers. Only a few

creators – painters, chefs or film-makers – keep personal expressivity alive (Renoir 1974a: 191–6). Abandoning his Frontist attacks
on capitalism's destructive effects on the national cuisine, he now
celebrates the French art of cooking as a remaining area of
individual creativity and, moreover, one in which the senses
prevail over the intelligence (Renoir 1989b: 159–60).

Looking back to the Popular Front from 1974, he condemns
both Communism and Fascism for their belief in progress.
Progress is now seen as the true enemy, not because it doesn't
work, but precisely because it does. He recounts how he had
believed that the working class would save western societies from
their destructive selfishness, but he now considers that it has been
corrupted by material prosperity (a very commonly held belief in
the post-war period) (Renoir 1974b: 125). Moving away from a
hope that a specific progressive class might drive social change, he
none the less retains a sense that people may revolt. He writes,
'from time to time, people get fed up, they've had enough of being
martyred or bored or bullied or scorned, and so in one way or
another, they try to put an end to it. They revolt. But my revolts are
not necessarily grand revolts. They're small revolutions, revolutions in a fishbowl' (Renoir 1989b: 112) These comments were
made at the time he was hoping to make a film called *C'est la
Révolution* which was to have featured five sketches showing
revolts against everything from moral convention to war (Renoir
1981a: 341–98). These revolts are all against something rather
than for something. They have no shared political project and no
sense of how an alternative society might be organised.

Renoir's post-war critique of progress is accompanied by a
belief that the world order is changing. He refers repeatedly to a
new Middle Ages that will sweep aside the world of nation-states
that was born when the Renaissance replaced Latin and the
Church with national languages and cultures and secular power.
In the first of his celebrated interviews with Truffaut and Rivette
in *Cahiers du cinéma* in 1954, he suggests that the war has brought
about an uncontrolled reshaping of the world which means that
people will be separated more by civilisation than by nation. He
sees the persistence of nationalist manifestations as the last signs

of a dying phenomenon (Renoir 1989b: 21–2). In an article significantly entitled 'Ce bougre de monde nouveau' he expresses a strong desire that internationalism will replace nationalism in a world where science and money but also cinema are the new universal languages. He is, however, very conscious of the potentially negative consequences of these changes. In a world where revolutions in transport and communications allow for the circulation of people and of cultural objects, there is a danger of a loss of personality through an international levelling of diversity (Renoir 1974a: 64–70). Similar ideas are expressed in *My Life and My Films* (1974b) but with a distinctly more pessimistic tone and a new-found nostalgia for a vanishing nation-state whose cultural diversity is giving way to internationalised uniformity. Even as he attempts to recreate Provençal surroundings in his Californian home, the places he grew up in are changing irrevocably. The only salvation is to plunge into the hell of the new world (Renoir 1974b: 279–82).

Far from taking refuge in artistic detachment or nostalgia, the later Renoir is still a bitter critic of the social order, although his criticism takes a very different form from that of the Popular Front period. In the 1930s, his ideal society is most definitely located in the future and is to be brought about through a political struggle led by the working class. The post-war period, despite some initial optimism about a new internationalism, is marked above all by a critique of progress that essentially looks back to earlier social forms for a better alternative. Revolt, where it still seems possible, is no longer associated with organised politics or a specific Utopian project.

In some ways, it may seem strange to give equal importance to views Renoir expressed during the four years or so he was associated with the Popular Front and the post-war period of about twenty-five years when, despite some changes, he expressed broadly consistent views. Yet we should not forget that in terms of cinematic output, these two periods are of equal importance, each producing eight films. Bearing this important point in mind, let us now turn to a consideration of Renoir's comments on filmmaking, again concentrating primarily on these two key periods.

Renoir's vision of his craft

Renoir's discussions of cinematic creativity during the Popular Front period are an intriguing blend of left-wing collectivism and inherited definitions of the creative process. In a piece from 1936, he stresses the primary need for a good technical and artistic team, suggesting that once it is formed, ideas will flow simply from its being together. Each member must contribute to the shooting script (Renoir 1974a: 90–1). References to 'great writers' and to the director as author show that he also sees his craft in more traditional terms. However, in a political climate that discouraged artistic introspection, it is unsurprising that the bulk of his comments focus on the state of the cinema industry rather than on the creative process.

The main targets of his wrath are the financiers and speculators who dominate an industry whose chaotic state is typical of capitalism (Renoir 1974a: 92). French cinema can only envy the great leap forward that has taken place in the Soviet Union. Nationalisation being impracticable in a capitalist society, the best way forward is cooperative ventures which would unite the workers (a term which clearly embraces technicians, actors and director), and exclude the capitalists from the industry (Renoir 1974a: 48). Renoir's sights are also levelled on right-wing cinema audiences, especially those of the fashionable cinemas along the *Champs Elysées*, where films usually had their first showing and thus where their fate was often decided (again, one senses a coming together of strong personal feelings with political ideology). Renoir laments a situation whereby the direction of popular art is decided by a bourgeois public and decadent, bourgeois directors. Control of the cinema must be given back to the people (Renoir 1974a: 81–2).

Even when the Popular Front government is in power, the state comes in for repeated criticism from Renoir. First, for the political censorship of films (Renoir 1974a: 85). Second, for the failure to defend the French industry sufficiently against foreign penetration and against unscrupulous producers (Renoir 1989a: 35). He laments the fact that French films have to be made using foreign film-stock and sound equipment. He complains too that French directors have to work for American- or German-owned production companies and accuses the state of failing to recognise the propaganda value of a medium which was restoring prestige to the French language on the international stage. French directors who have chosen to work abroad are called to return to a national industry that needs them, which in turn is enjoined to put internecine quarrels behind itself and unite (Renoir 1974a: 151–2). Although he speaks from a resolutely nationalist position, Renoir does not call for the exclusion of foreign films but rather for a tax to be levied upon them to generate revenue to support national production. He takes a similar line with regard to foreign technicians, welcoming the cross-fertilisation that they bring about, but suggesting that they should be the object of a levy which could then be used to support unemployed French cinema workers (Renoir 1974a: 82–6).

Renoir produces a version of himself fully in line with the left's shift of emphasis from internationalism to nationalism. In a celebrated piece entitled 'Mes années d'apprentissage' (My formative years), published by *Le Point* in December 1938, he says that to reach out to people from other nations, he must first of all work in an absolutely national way (Renoir 1974a: 38–46). In another piece from 1938 he declares his total inability to make a film outside of France, while reiterating his refusal of any racialised definition of Frenchness. Love of the French is the stepping stone to love of citizens of other countries. Films must thus be national before they can be international (Renoir 1989a: 33–4).

Post-war Renoir no longer developed his vision of cinema within an overtly political framework. Collectivism gave way to individualism as Renoir the committed film-maker became Renoir the *auteur*, someone who talked about his craft primarily in terms of a personal style that was a vehicle for the expression of an individual outlook.

Renoir's *auteurism* was at times very different from the fetishisation of the individual artist of which the more extreme *auteurists* were guilty. It did not, for example, coincide chronologically with the polemical variant expounded by *Cahiers du cinéma* in the 1950s and 1960s. Renoir had indeed made his own contribution to an earlier polemic about the locus of cinematic creativity by arguing for the centrality of the director in his pre-Frontist writings of the 1930s (Renoir 1989a: 15). Traces of the individually creative 'I' were never completely incorporated by the collective 'we,' even in the period of the Front but, following its failure and his flight from France, Renoir defended his independence against the Hollywood machine in distinctly *auteurist* tones. He writes

> I am much more an author of films than a director ... I do not pretend to be able to do in English what I have done in French: that is, the adaptation of a story (which often was my own, as in the case of *La Grande Illusion*), the screenplay, the dialogue, and everything except the production, in which I do not claim to be a master. But there would be an advantage for the producer in allowing me at least to collaborate. (Renoir 1994: 99–100)

This determination to express his personality by participation in every stage of the creative process hardens after the war, partially in response to the explosion in consumption that was generated by the rapid economic growth of the period. A cinema of (personal) expression is a means to resist the anonymity generated by the uniformity of consumer goods (Renoir 1974a: 195–6). In 1974, he summarises the history of cinema as the struggle of the individual creator against the industry (Renoir 1974b: 11) thus locating it as part of a broader resistance to massification. He is highly aware that his own and others' *auteurism* is a reaction against certain specific features of modern societies, and that individualism is thus a relative not an absolute value. He tells Jacques Rivette, for example: 'We live in a time when we have ten thousand cars on a road, a little red light flashes on, and everyone stops ... What is the reaction to this? It's a wild, exaggerated trend for the *auteur*. I neither approve nor disapprove of it, I observe it, that's all' (Renoir 1989b: 258). The same deliberate distanciation from the cult of the artist's personality prefaces his autobiography where he attributes the fetishisation of the individual to our pride and states that people are largely products of their environment (Renoir 1974b: 12). This distanciation is, however, counterbalanced by the work's narrative of personal evolution and references to individual influences.

In 'On me demande', an important article from 1952, he maintains that although the director is the strongest influence, cinema is a collective production. His own evolution cannot therefore explain the changing nature of his work. Faced with the impossibility of tracing the trajectory of all those who contribute to a film, he simplifies matters by saying that people evolve in groups and not individually and that the role of the work of art is to clarify this collective transformation (Renoir 1974a: 59–62). He adds yet one more dimension to his already complex exploration of authorship by acknowledging the role of the public in creating a film (Renoir 1974a: 66). However, this multifaceted and nuanced account does not render him immune from the excesses of *auteurism*. In a piece published in *Cahiers* in 1964, he said, 'I've basically shot one film, I've continued to shoot one film, ever since I began, and its always the same film' (Renoir 1989b: 250).

Renoir's book on his father confirms a distanciation from the cult of authorial expressivity by suggesting that art is inseparable from the broad historical contextualisation that gives it meaning. Renoir *père* straddles and responds to two completely different phases of history, before and after the transformation of the world by technology. The modern world is described in terms of productivism, mechanisation and an ever-increasing uniformity brought about by revolutions in transportation and communications. The world that began to disappear at the end of the nineteenth century is that of local diversity, of *flânerie*, of a certain carefree attitude to life which the artist celebrated in his paintings of the Paris entertainment industry, and of an easy-going leisure along the banks of the Seine that has since been replaced by factories and pollution (Renoir 1981b: 227). Renoir recounts his father's early attempt to compete with uniform, factory-produced porcelain by high-speed hand-painting. Later, as he recounts his father's last days, he compares the artist to the scientist. While both are engaged in a search for the secrets of nature, artists celebrate it and 'persuade' it while scientists violate it as they seek to satisfy ever-growing material demands which always outrun them. Auguste's last paintings, celebrations of women's and nature's beauty, and a lesson in the 'eternal equilibrium' of our universe are set against the background of the Great War which shows twentieth-century man setting about his work of destruction (Renoir 1981b: 493–4). The artist's detachment suggests that the wars and revolutions which punctuate his life are absurd, fratricidal and pointlessly destructive.

As seen by his son, Renoir *père*'s art is always personal but never introspective nor disengaged from its socio-historical context. It is made into a lesson in sensual enjoyment and pleasurable contemplation for a world torn asunder by political division and driven destructively forward by science and technology. Nostalgic his account certainly is, but its nostalgia is polemical not escapist. Celebrating the lost world of his father's paintings becomes a means of criticising the present. In the end, Renoir's portrait of his father, which is clearly also a self-portrait, suggests a moral role for the artist, an anti-political engagement that replaces the political commitment of the 1930s. It is usefully borne in mind when one considers the later films.

Although the artistic mantle passes from father to son, following the male line, women are far from absent from Renoir's narrative, even if their presence as model, wife or servant follows entirely stereotypical lines. While the artist may wish to detach himself from a history torn by struggle or driven relentlessly forward by progress, he still engages with it. The women of the household simply devote themselves to facilitating his work. Their 'noble' domestic and maternal 'destiny' denies them the possibility of participating in public affairs. Their bodies are an expression of eternal humanity and God's finest creation, but it is the male artist who determines the meaning of their beauty and who makes it part of his own self-expression (Renoir 1981b: 435–6). The artist's sensual encounter with the world is a sexual encounter in which he plays the active and dominant role. His brushstrokes are round, as if they were following a young breast. He seeks to 'penetrate' the subject, but ultimate 'possession' does not come without a struggle. It must be 'caressed and beaten' to express itself fully (Renoir 1981b: 218).

Women are objectified and excluded from the public space of history. None the less, when Renoir seeks to evoke the passing of his father's world after 1914, he sums up his sense of disarray by evoking the 'new woman'. New because of her appearance, short hair and short skirt. New also because she had shown that she could do the work of absent men (Renoir 1981b: 30). This passing recognition of the historical variability of gender does not cause him to reconsider the prevailing essentialism of the rest of the text. It seems that, faced with a tormented and changing world, Renoir needed the stability of a naturalised gender order.

What Renoir writes about his painter father provides insights into his conception of the social role of the artist but unsurprisingly tells us little about his approach to film-making. For this we have to return to his other writings and interviews and primarily to those from the post-war period, when in response to his consecration as a great director, he reflected increasingly upon his work. We will also draw on what he wrote before the war. At times and somewhat surprisingly considering the dramatic ideological shift he underwent, Renoir's comments from the two periods coincide considerably. But style or technique cannot be considered independently from the representations they are used to generate and which transform their significance.

One apparently consistent feature is the preference for a flexible structure. Writing in 1936, Renoir talks of his habit of dividing a shooting script into several self-contained scenes or sequences with independently numbered shots so that each can be modified in response to the coming together of actors and set, without in the process disturbing the rest of the film (Renoir 1974a: 91). Looking back to the same period, thirty years later, he writes:

> There is a world of difference between the original concept and the final result ... To me a script is simply a vehicle to be modified as one draws nearer to the real intention, which must not change. The intention is something that the film-maker has at the back of his mind, often without knowing it ... The film-maker establishes his characters by making them speak, and creates the general ambience by building sets and choosing locations. His own inward conviction only gradually appears. (Renoir 1974b: 128)

The process is substantially the same. What has been added of course is the affirmation of authorial expressivity that was absent from the earlier text.

Renoir consistently expressed the need to place technique in the service of the actors. When *Toni* is released in 1935, he is already clear that camera angles and shots have to be worked out only after performances have been rehearsed on set (Renoir 1989a: 18–19). The increasingly bravura camera movements of his films of the 1930s and the characteristic long takes have their root in the need to follow actors as they move about the set without breaking their flow with repeated cuts. The very different multi-camera shooting of a film such as *Le Testament du Docteur Cordelier* is in part a means to the same end. It gives the director the range of shots he needs while allowing the actors to develop their characters. Renoir's preference for direct sound recording and his abiding hostility to dubbing can also be linked to a belief in the integrity of an actor's performance.

Renoir remained faithful to what he termed the Italian method of rehearsal. He required actors to read the script repeatedly to rid themselves of clichés and to ensure that they acted the character and not the moment. In a short piece written in 1956, he insists that actors must fully internalise the role before they develop the external part of it, the gestures and the movements (Renoir 1974a: 229). In a much earlier piece from 1933, he is already clear that the actors must 'live' their roles for a film to take on the spark of humanity which will bring it alive (Renoir 1974a: 223–4).

One can draw a parallel between this belief in the internalisation of a role and the contrast Renoir often makes between internal and external reality. The anti-realist Renoir of the post-war period repeatedly tells how he has moved from an interest in external reality to a focus on inner truth. It is more surprising when the Renoir of 1936 says something very similar. Explaining the distinctly non-Russian feel to his version of Gorki's *Lower depths* he states that he has always believed that exterior reality does not count in the cinema (Renoir 1974a: 238–9). He adds, however, that it is essential to study and assimilate the relevant milieu even if one must then go beyond its purely external features. He was insisting at about the same time that the lead actors of La Bête humaine (1938) learn how to handle a locomotive so that they would be able to act out their roles on a real train and understand the work of those they were representing (Renoir 1974a: 258–60). The apparently consistent emphasis on human responses should not hide the post-war abandonment of the earlier commitment to exploration of specific social contexts.

Renoir's *mise-en-scène* must be contextualised. The staging in depth which was so characteristic of his work of the 1930s was not simply an aesthetic choice. It was mobilised for the exploration of relationships within and between social classes while a realist aesthetic placed the material consequences of class inequality on the screen. The prowling camera that tracked the actors also pulled spectators into the cinematic space favouring their engagement in the action. Actors were used to embody characters with specific class and ideological positions whom we respond to in far from uniform ways.

Renoir explained his move from exterior to interior realism by an embrace of classicism which began with La Règle du jeu and dominated his post-war films. Classicism signified a critical distance between public and character (Renoir 1974a, 227–8). It also implied a complexity of *mise-en-scène* allied with an evenness of interest, a refusal to privilege a particular detail or individual. Finally, it was associated with a restrained and discrete mode of filming, summed up when Renoir says that for Le Carosse d'or he simply put the camera in front of the scene and shot it (Renoir 1989b: 48). If, at the risk of oversimplification, one were to try to extract from this a politics of form, one might suggest that Renoir's classicism was a translation of his post-war political disengagement. Pulling back from individual characters, no longer plunging us into the space of the films, he asks us to judge behaviour patterns and attitudes rather than participate in a collision of classes or ideologies.

Conclusion

Renoir's writings and interviews need to be used with considerable care. If it is a mistake to accord them analytical priority over the films, it is also absurd to discard them entirely. They can afford precious insights into the director's film-making practice or philosophical and ideological evolution. But they need, at the same time, to be read as productions of self that responded to particular cinematic, political or historical contexts and which fed in turn into the reception of the films. We must recognise too that their apparent completeness, their ability to give a full picture from the director's early years to his old age, is deceptive. The great bulk of Renoir's public pronouncements comes from two periods, one long, one short, when he was under great pressure to present himself and his films in certain ways.

There are remarkably few articles or interviews from before 1936. If this were a Renoir who had a clearly thought-out personal philosophy that he sought to express through his films, he certainly did not put it down in writing. In contrast, the committed Renoir of the Popular Front era expressed himself abundantly, reimagining himself in terms of collectively generated ideological positions in such a way that it is impossible to separate out the individual artist. The American period produced countless letters but little that helped to follow the director's evolving outlook. The post-war period is a time of sustained comment in book and interview when, under the compelling influence of *auteurism* (a very different collectively generated outlook), Renoir reinvented himself and his career in the mould of an expressive artist who none the less refused introspection and engaged fully with his era.

It is hoped that our brief consideration of Renoir's writings and career has shown that there are compelling reasons to periodise his output. This was a film-maker whose work was caught up in half a century of turbulence and traumatic change, a man who knew war, exile, commitment and disengagement, a Frenchman who saw his country rent by divisions, humiliated by war and then transformed by prosperity. His work cries out to be read in terms of its complex and varying engagement with shifting historical, social and cinematic contexts. There is nothing in what we have looked at so far that undermines the initial division of the work into five periods and a lot to support it. The Popular Front and post-war periods clearly stand out due to the evidence of a consistent outlook or set of concerns. There is no evidence of the same consistency during the other periods identified (the silent era, the early 1930s, Hollywood exile) but there are ample reasons for considering them separately due to very different film-making conditions and contexts.

One particular item that should be carried forward into the next chapter is Renoir's uneven and inconsistent, but also, subtle, nuanced and contextualised response to *auteurism* as a mode of viewing films. His account is an essential corrective to the reductionist *auteurism* of a number of critics.

References

Gauteur, C. (1980), *Jean Renoir, la double méprise, 1925–1939*, Paris, Les Editeurs Français Réunis.

Renoir, J. (1974a), *Ecrits, 1926–1971* (ed. Claude Gauteur), Paris, Belfond.

Renoir, J. (1974b), *My Life and My Films*, (trans. N. Denny) London, Collins.

Renoir, J. (1981a), *Œuvres de cinéma inédites*, (ed. C. Gauteur), Paris, Gallimard.

Renoir, J. (1981b), *Pierre-Auguste Renoir, mon père*, Paris, Gallimard.

Renoir, J. (1984), *Lettres d'Amérique*, Paris, Presses de la Renaissance.

Renoir, J. (1989a), *Le Passé vivant*, (ed. C. Gauteur), Paris, Editions de l'Etoile/ Cahiers du cinéma.

Renoir, J. (1989b), *Renoir on Renoir*, (trans. C. Volk), Cambridge, Cambridge University Press.

Renoir, J. (1994), *Letters*, (eds L. LoBianco and D. Thompson), London, Faber & Faber.

2

Renoir and the critics

Criticism is actively productive. Its interpretative schemata and ideological stance interact with a given corpus of films to produce a meaning that was not simply there waiting to be discovered. Sometimes this construction is open and dialectical so that the analytical frame is modified by the readings which it generates. In others cases, it is more rigid and reductionist. Rather aptly for a director whose composition was at times so mobile, Renoir is a challenge to constricting frames.

Because he is widely seen as the greatest French director and one of the major figures of world cinema, Renoir has become a plum prize for critics (especially French ones) to fight over. The principal combatants have been critics of the left and *auterists*. Yet each camp has difficulty with Renoir because of the discontinuities and shifting contexts that we have identified. His challenge to critics of the left comes from his move in and out of commitment. How can they deal with his cinema before the Popular Front except by seeing it, perhaps in somewhat simplistic terms, as a discovery of social reality that paves the way for political involvement? How can they deal with his post-commitment work except by seeing it in reductionist terms as a betrayal? His more specific challenge to those leftist critics with strictly determinist models of artistic production is that his career has no settled national or ideological context and thus no simple explanatory model can account for it. He is likewise a challenge to *auteurists* first, because of his commitment (when his individual voice merged inextricably with collectively generated views) and second, because of his many changes of direction. Trying to explain his work with reference to a single, self-transparent and consistent consciousness is, to say the least, difficult.

Critics have too often dealt with the complex discontinuities of Renoir's output by forcing it into reductionist moulds, making the object of analysis fit the analytical frame. One symptom of this is to use one particular period of his career to cast light on and to (re)interpret all the others. *Auteurists* almost invariably use the politically non-aligned, post-war Renoir to rewrite the pre-war politically committed films to make them fit better into a model of a unified authorial consciousness. Critics of the left may use the later films as the 'true' image of the director, and then set out to demonstrate that the later Renoir's 'reactionary' ideas were always lurking beneath the surface, or, alternatively, they may take the committed films of the 1930s as the ideal by which to judge the shortcomings of the later films. Another symptom of reductionism is the imposition of pre-established narratives that provide an implied interpretative framework even before the films are examined. Apprenticeship leading to maturity, revolt giving way to wisdom, vigour followed by senility, commitment and betrayal – the models vary, but all push us to read the films in certain ways and none is exempt from value judgements.

Renoir and the *Cahiers* critics

Cahiers was a polemical journal, not a centre of detached academic debate. Its adoption of Renoir as an *auteurist* talisman drew him into the heart of broader struggles within French film criticism, struggles which have indelibly marked subsequent interpretations of his work.

The *Cahiers* critics were far from uniform in their general outlook or their specific response to Renoir. Their interpretations of his work did however share certain tendencies. One was a humanism that preferred a moral to a political reading of Renoir and overwrote his partisan commitment with a benign, relativist tolerance. Another was to see the work as an organic whole so that the Frontist films were depoliticised by linkage to those that came before and after. A third tendency was a cinephilic focus on style and technique which produced a Renoir designed for the delectation of film *aficionados* and not one who sought to engage in contemporary struggles. A final, shared feature (one amply considered in the first chapter), was a fetishisation of the individual creator that related the films to their director rather than their broader context.

Some of these tendencies are illustrated when we turn to the *Cahiers* critics response to *La Marseillaise*, one of Renoir's most obviously partisan films. Truffaut asserts that an objective and generous Renoir rises above the struggle and treats all the characters even-handedly (Bazin 1989: 240). Schérer (aka Eric Rohmer) refers, in passing, to the film in the celebrated article where he defends Renoir's American output. Denying that Renoir's cinema was ever polemical, he maintains that apparent attacks on particular groups are always tempered by admiration and that, were he so minded, he could clearly reveal the signs of Renoir's later quiescence in his supposedly radical films (Schérer 1952: 36).

Renoir was an active and consenting partner in *Cahiers'* depoliticisation of his committed work. Particular reference was made to *La Marseillaise* in the interview he gave to two *Cahiers* critics, Delahaye and Narboni, in 1967. The interviewers suggest various causes for the film's failure in 1938, noting its extremely realistic soundtrack, mixing of genres and parallel narration of different episodes. Constructing the film (stereotypically) as a work of art for which the audience were not yet ready, they signally fail to consider that hostile reaction to its committed politics may have influenced its reception (Renoir 1984: 124–6). Renoir does not disabuse them. When he mentions those who influenced the film, he conveniently forgets the role of the trade union confederation and the Communist Party. Rather breathtakingly, he expresses his distaste for sectarianism and characters with clear-cut opinions (Renoir 1984: 129). He later seems to revert to a more political reading of his film when he describes the Revolution as a stage in 'this immense enterprise of liberation that is taking place – the destruction of the class system' (Renoir 1984: 137). However, given that he has just discussed class in terms of people within the same profession and not of antagonistic social groups, and considering too that he says that material differences between people have no spiritual importance and therefore do not count, his approval of the Revolution would seem to stem from a humanist belief in the equal value of individuals rather than a return to a left-wing vision. The interview in question coincided with the writing of *C'est la Révolution*, an initially unrealised project which would have dissolved political revolution into various spontaneous revolts and continued Renoir's ongoing reorientation of his earlier output by overwriting *La Marseillaise*.

The director's later films, interviews and writings worked with the *Cahiers* critics' analyses to tame the Renoir of the Popular Front. The Front was a mythical era for the French left and Renoir's Frontist films the pinnacle of committed feature film. His connivance with *Cahiers*' retrospective depoliticisation of his work infuriated left-wing critics and indelibly marked their response to him.[1]

The Renoir of the left

Premier Plan's *Jean Renoir* (Chardère *et al.* 1962) initially seems to locate itself above and outside the struggles over his work. Its originality is to bring together a range of criticism from different periods, basing its selection on historical and present interest, the importance and ideological stance of the journal where the article appeared, the way in which the articles help to bring a context to life and how they illustrate the evolution of film criticism itself. Rather than promising a definitive Renoir, it offers multiple takes on him, suggesting that each point of view will produce a different object of study. Refusing the fiction of a coherent *œuvre*, it treats the films as separate units and emphasises how they have been

1 Keith Reader provides an excellent diachronic analysis of critical responses to Renoir's Frontist films in Vincendeau and Reader (1986).

read differently at different times. It treats the director's own interpretations with ironic scepticism.

While the conception of the volume helps to unmask the unchallenged assumptions that produce a picture of a coherent and self-contained work that expresses the world-view of a great artist, its execution follows less challenging patterns as it becomes clear that the editors take a familiar, polemical line. A clear preference is expressed for the old Renoir of the Popular Front and open hostility and disrespect are shown for the 'senescent' Renoir of the 1950s and 1960s. This later Renoir is described as a chameleon, a man with no profound convictions, one who is building his own legend and who, by adopting the persona of a tolerant old man, refuses to choose between oppressor and oppressed (Chardère *et al.* 1962: 336–7). Despite their sometimes polemical tone, the strength of the *Premier Plan* critics is to show an awareness of the historical and ideological contingency of the act of criticism while still demonstrating clearly their own political commitment.

Premier Plan contains a piece by Marcel Oms which is a striking example of how criticism may be influenced by its moment and its ideological position. Oms's violent polemic is written from a radical leftist position of hostility to the Communist Party and to the Gaullism that is newly dominant under the recently instituted Fifth Republic (Oms 1962). His anti-Communism pushes him beyond the conventional contrast between a progressive Frontist Renoir and the conservative and politically demobilising post-war figure. He suggests that beneath his superficial radicalism even the committed Renoir had a reactionary attachment to the very French values (work, family, nation, valorisation of the rural) that came to the fore under the Vichy regime. *La Grande Illusion*, for example, is a fundamentally nationalist film which ends with an escapist and reactionary return to the land despite its apparent internationalism and class consciousness. Oms writes while wearing a French military uniform, one presumes with extreme reluctance, in soon-to-be-independent colonial Algeria. He is clearly indignant when he perceives Renoir to be turning his back on the misery of colonised peoples in *Le Carosse d'or* and *The River* and recommending charity within the established social order as preached by the church. He finds the same political quietism in *La Règle du jeu,* where Renoir is seen to suggest that as masters and servants are fundamentally the same, a little less selfishness would be enough to reconcile their differences.

It is deeply ironic that starting from a radically different political position to many *auteurist* critics, Oms goes through a similar process in his construction of an essentially unchanging Renoir. Ignoring the politico-historical context of the earlier films, he interprets them in the light of the later ones, attributing any genuine radicalism he finds to Renoir's collaborators. Although Oms's piece is clearly polemical, we can take some important points from it. First, the critic's refusal to simply take the progressive nature of the Popular Front films for granted and his consideration of nationalism within them. Second, his refusal to see later Renoir films as simply celebrations of art and spectacle and his insistence on considering them in the light of contemporary political contexts and struggles over decolonisation. Third, and most originally, his brief but interesting consideration of the portrayal of women by Renoir, which suggests a pattern of traditionalist attitudes and misogynistic stereotypes.

Francis Poulle (1969) is another left-wing critic who turns his attention to Renoir at a time of particular historical interest. In the period following the events of May 1968, he looks to Renoir, particularly the Renoir of 1936, for a lesson in progressive and non-commercial cinema, only to be disappointed. He accuses Renoir of conniving with the critics to erase the traces of political commitment from his life and works and to hide the often virulent nature of his political opinions at the time of the Popular Front. Poulle considers Renoir to have remade himself in the image of his painter father in the 1950s, using the apparent smooth continuity of ideas between father and son as a smokescreen for this disavowal of a key part of himself.

Poulle attaches great value to Renoir's work of the 1930s seeing it as a valiant but ultimately failed quest for a genuine realism that could have set French cinema on a new and progressive path. He distinguishes sharply between authentic and distorting forms of realism. For him, a genuine realism implies not only an ethnographic description of the poor and downtrodden but the capacity to represent their lived everyday experience, to see them as subjects not as objects of curiosity, and to treat all characters as of equal value. At the start of the 1930s, in *La Chienne* (1931) for example, Renoir tries to speak for the downtrodden but inherits a *petit-bourgeois* literary realism that focuses voyeuristically on the gloomy spectacle of the lower classes, suggesting that although the world may be grim it cannot be changed. As the decade goes on, he gets closer to a genuine realism, through the naturalism of *Madame Bovary* (1933) and the social realism of *Toni*. Making such films in turn sharpens his understanding of the social world. However, he regresses markedly with *Les Bas-fonds* which offers up its grotesque and completely unrepresentative characters as a picturesque tableau. Poulle considers this film to have begun French poetic realism, a style of film-making for which he has great distaste because it offers up the popular as gloomy spectacle and declines to engage with the social (Poulle 1969: 102–3). However, Renoir's ultimate failure to develop a new progressive realism is brought out by *La Bête humaine* wherein he betrays Zola by emphasising the poetic side of the story at the expense of its social realism, and thus generates another example of poetic realism.

Poulle considers Renoir to have allied himself with the Front out of a long-standing desire for human communion but never to have been personally involved in working-class struggles because his motivation was idealistic and not derived from real material needs. As a result, when the Front disintegrated, Renoir could easily detach himself from its cause and seek communion elsewhere. Coinciding with this detachment, *La Bête humaine* is at once cause and symptom of it. While making it, Renoir realised that a desire to be near to the working class was not enough if one did not share their struggle. He thus failed to provide a realistic portrayal of them in a film which is at the same time indicative of the Front's failure. He abandons one of the principal tenets of a progressive realism by showing characters that are victims of fate rather than of a class society created and thus alterable by human action (Poulle 1969: 24–64). Because his successful portrait of the upper bourgeoisie in *La Règle du jeu* drew on an insider's knowledge of that class, it only served to underscore the reasons for his failure to create a cinema that realistically depicted the struggles of the downtrodden. Thereafter, uprooted from a world he knew by his period in the United States, he failed to re-establish contact with French society in the 1950s, abandoned a cinema of social criticism and went back to painting the France of before 1914, eschewing the contemporary for the 'timeless' values of bourgeois art.

Poulle eschews the polemical condemnation that others reserve for late Renoir. He allows that the films may still have interest and value but considers that Renoir no longer has anything to teach those who, in the aftermath of 1968, sought a socially committed cinema that broke with the norms of commercial film-making. Poulle looks back to Renoir's Popular Front films and finds, like Oms, that the roots of his subsequent betrayal were already visible in *La Grande Illusion* and *La Marseillaise*. The former set out to recount class solidarity but ended up excusing the militarism of the career soldiers of the aristocracy and promoting nationalism while the latter individualised revolutionary struggle, making it a question of temperament not of class interest, and treated the motives of each side with non-committal even-handedness (Poulle 1969: 104–10).

One can criticise Poulle's Renoir on various counts. Perhaps surprisingly for a critic of the left, he seems to wish to blame Renoir personally rather than socio-historical or institutional factors for his failure to create an alternative cinema. Likewise, when he criticises Renoir for the nationalism he finds in *La Grande Illusion*, he fails to recognise that nationalism was part of Popular Front strategy and not an individual decision. He is also guilty of an *a priori* workerist judgement that middle-class intellectuals can never engage truly with the struggles of the working class. He fails to dig far enough into the idea that Renoir carried forward the values of 1914 and of his father in his later films and thus failed to engage with post-war society. This is certainly a useful approach in that it suggests possible ideological roots for the later Renoir, but it fails to explain how the director could have come through two world wars, major socio-political conflict and profound social change with such values intact. Poulle does not consider the possibility that Renoir used inherited values tactically in order to provide a grounding for his critique of contemporary French society.

Poulle's book does open some very interesting avenues. He suggests an evolving, complex and at times contradictory Renoir who genuinely works towards commitment to the struggles of the working classes while bearing a social background and inherited attitudes that work against that commitment. He reads films like *La Grande Illusion* as sites of complex ideological struggle rather than as simple expressions of an univocal philosophy, even if that struggle then tends to be collapsed into the character of the director rather than linked to a socio-historical context. His belief that Renoir always sought a community to speak for and to belong to suggests a way we might look for both continuity and contrasts between different stages of the director's career. Continuity in terms of the underlying desire but contrasts in the form of its realisation. He also, very importantly, dissects the notion of realism and how it portrays a social context. It is too easy to suggest, as more than one critic including the director himself has done, that Renoir simply moves from an emphasis on external realism in the 1930s to a commitment to a more profound internal realism in his later films. Such a categorisation groups all the films of the 1930s into one bundle. Poulle usefully suggests ways of unpacking that bundle and looking at the different forms of realism employed by Renoir during the period in question. His insistence on the importance of portraying the day-to-day lived experience of material oppression suggests how we could pinpoint what was lost when Renoir moved to an anti-realist aesthetic in the post-war period.

Poulle, like Oms before him, addresses the issue of gender but, very frustratingly, uses it only to underscore his main point about a dishonest and self-deceiving Renoir. He suggests that Renoir, like Zola, had enormous difficulties dealing with women but would not face up to or admit them. Women in Renoir's films are seductively adorable and threateningly destructive creatures which one cannot do without but which one cannot master. He suggests that Renoir developed what he calls 'donjuanism' (the wish to seduce women and then move on) as a way of dealing with this problematic duality (Poulle 1969: 28–9). Unfortunately, he does not pursue these insights with a serious analysis of gender in the films.

While Poulle writes during the time of crisis and mobilisation of 1968 and Oms during a period of polarised and violent political oppositions, Christopher Faulkner's book on Renoir comes from the more quiescent 1980s and from across the Atlantic. The two former criticise Renoir for his political choices, believing that in a world shaped by human actions, individuals are accountable for their decisions. As an avowed structuralist Marxist, Faulkner is much more interested in what external conditions produce the ideology that Renoir bears.

His book, *The Social Cinema of Jean Renoir* (Faulkner 1986), is probably the most important left-wing analysis to date. Although he echoes the belief that the later Renoir sought to erase his earlier political commitment, his account of Renoir's evolution seeks to move us away from the individual-centred story of commitment, betrayal and denial that we have considered up to now. He works within an Althusserian frame that denies the existence of '"pure" consciousness or "pure" structures unmediated by social structures and social practices' (Faulkner 1986: 6). Because consciousness is constituted within ideology, *auteurist* readings that centre on a lucid creator and a coherent *œuvre* are themselves ideological mystifications that help to hide the social production of the individual. For Faulkner, the correct interpretative frame is the history of class struggle not the *œuvre* of Renoir.

Faulkner focuses on Renoir's sound films, attaching little importance to the work of the silent era. The important films of the early 1930s, *La Chienne, Boudu sauvé des eaux* (1932) and *Toni*, form a prelude to the committed works by taking Renoir down the path of a social realism that demonstrates the alienation of people under capitalism, recognises that society is produced by human activity, and illuminates 'the relationship between social being, conditions of work, and the private passions of people' (Faulkner 1986: 55). These works, which Faulkner sees as disparate and with no clear common intellectual attitude, are politically flawed in that they fail to show how positive actions can transform the oppressive social frame. They do, however, reveal how the pressure of events has pushed Renoir's work to take up the concerns of the left, so that it only remains for him to be given political direction by commitment to the French Communist Party.

At this stage we are told, in suitably depersonalised structuralist terms, that Renoir's consciousness is constituted in the ideology of the Popular Front and that themes such as the fraternity and internationalism of *La Grande Illusion* are authored by history not by any individual. The Frontist films are the director's key works due to their political commitment, but they are also ideologically disarming in that they mask the shortcomings of the Front's reformist project by offering fictional resolution to real social contradictions. Faulkner suggests that Renoir's writings for the Communist newspaper *Ce Soir* are more radical because he is addressing a proletarian public and not the bourgeois audience of the cinema.

Upon the collapse of the Front, Renoir is 'displaced from the site of meaning' of his previous films and regresses with *La Bête humaine* to individualist psychology and fatalism (Faulkner 1986: 12–13 and 101). *La Règle du jeu* however is doubly radical. It is an assault on the upper echelons of French society who betrayed the Popular Front and capitulated to Hitler at Munich and a modernist undermining of ideologically charged narrative convention. Whereas Renoir's other fiction films, including the apparently committed ones, lull the spectator into ideological acquiescence by sucking them into the story and presenting them with an illusion of reality, *La Règle du jeu* demonstrates that form itself is ideological by subverting its norms and thus 'signals ... the interrogation of an ideological mode of perception' (Faulkner 1986: 111). The film is the swansong of Renoir's radicalism. His subsequent exile in the USA is a time of disarray, confusion and transition as indicated by a disparate and relatively unimpressive output. Any coherence the American period may have is an invention of the *auteurists* as they struggle to force recalcitrant material to fit a model of a coherent *œuvre* as expression of a unified authorial consciousness.

Renoir emerges from this confusion into what Faulkner calls a second maturity in the post-war period when his consciousness is reconstituted in a new 'ideological perspective' so that his films offer new fictional solutions to the contradictions of lived experience (Faulkner 1986: 13–14). The shift from a period of confusion is complete with *The River* which symptomatically refuses to engage with the social, political and economic struggles of newly independent India by dissolving concrete historical struggles into 'natural' cycles of life and death. The film achieves ideological closure by offering aesthetic consolation for the miseries of existence. Moving away from a realist aesthetic and from art with a socially interrogatory function, Renoir turns towards deliberately artificial period recreations that occlude history as process and promote essentialist, universalised values (Faulkner 1986: 186). Faulkner is essentially agreeing here with Poulle about the nature of the later films, but instead of suggesting that the director is falling back on a value system inherited from his father, he explains this 'reconstitution' of Renoir's consciousness by locating it in a socially conservative era which he signally fails to analyse. Noting the predilection of 1950s cinema for art and artifice, he writes, somewhat lamely:

> Authors, positioned as subjects, are constituted in the ideological currents of their day. The larger historical context is so broad however, that it would require a separate study to determine fully the impact of the post-world war II economic boom, the Cold War, and the competition from television (to mention some crucial forces) upon the ideological shape of this genre of fifties film production. (Faulkner 1986: 167)

Faulkner's book marks some important advances on what has gone before. He moves away from the assumption that an individual consciousness generates the films, instead foregrounding their ideological nature and consequent collective authorship. He recognises too that they must be interpreted within a historical context. He suggests, importantly, that some of Renoir's American output should be seen as a reworking of national myths and narratives rather than as personal statements. Furthermore, he maintains that at certain stages of his career (the early 1930s, the American period), Renoir's work is an inconsistent amalgam rather than a coherent *œuvre*. Finally, his ideological readings of the films, especially those of the 1930s, are rich, persuasive and challenging. However, the Althusserian analysis which helps to generate these readings is also at the root of some of the main inconsistencies within them.

Althusserianism came to the fore at a time when it appeared that French and other western societies had been substantially pacified through the dramatic post-war economic boom, the Fordist involvement of the working class in the benefits of prosperity and the inclusive security offered by the welfare state. It seemed that the working class's potential for revolution had been successfully nullified by a combination of material advantages and ideological incorporation while at the same time bourgeois democratic politics and consumer choice gave those subjected to capitalism the illusion of freedom. It was thus not surprising to see an essentially static and determinist model of ideology achieving dominance. However, it is hard to see how such a model can deal adequately with Renoir's complex trajectory through a turbulent history.

Perhaps recognising the inherent incompatibility between his analytical system and a recalcitrant object of analysis, Faulkner at times hints at a more complex model. He writes, for example, that Renoir's 'private, material history acts with – interacts with – public history (social, cultural) to produce the work we know and admire' (Faulkner 1986: 15). He goes on to suggest that Renoir is the 'site' for tensions that produce a rich and varied corpus. Unfortunately, such a reading in terms of ideological tensions and historical contextualisation that might have coped better with the complexity of Renoir's career and output is not pursued. Instead, Faulkner seems to alternate between and at times combine two incompatible modes of analysis, the individual–biographical and the socio-structural. He identifies two apprenticeships, the silent era and the wartime period, when Renoir is looking for a direction and learning or relearning his trade. He also identifies two maturities (the Popular Front and the post-war period) when Renoir's subjectivity is constructed by ideology. Seeming to suggest that Renoir passes through stages of conscious disarray before becoming a complete ideological puppet, he does not satisfactorily explain how the director moves from one period to the next. One might accept for the sake of argument that there was a conservative dominant ideology that emerged in the West with the post-war political settlement after 1945 and which 'reconstituted' Renoir's consciousness (even if one might wonder how). But trying to accept that Renoir's post-1935 consciousness had simply been constituted by Popular Front ideology stretches credulity.

It is hard to argue that any ideology achieved dominance during a period marked by ideological polarisation, competition and interpenetration. One certainly cannot argue that any ideology managed to maintain social or political quiescence. Nor can one assume that the Popular Front had a monolithic ideological stance. Representing as it did a tactical coming together of three main political parties with different doctrines and different priorities, its position can perhaps better be seen as a (failed) attempt to negotiate a hegemonic consensus around the centre–left. If no ideology was dominant, why should Renoir have been constructed by one rather than others and if the Popular Front was based on conscious ideological negotiation, why should he not have been able to negotiate to some degree his own ideological engagement with it? Faulkner does seem to grant the director a degree of ideological awareness when he suggests that he was able to adopt a more radical position when writing for a committed public, yet this does not lead him to rethink his determinist starting position.

The confusion deepens when one examines Faulkner's analysis of key films where Renoir is seen to challenge the 'illusionist' practices of conventional cinematic forms, thereby jolting the spectator into an active awareness of the process of meaning creation. If Renoir is capable of making spectators actively aware, it would seem hard to maintain an image of him as merely the site where ideology creates meaning. While the move from the purely individual generation of meaning to the social production of consciousness is a welcome step, Faulkner's replacement of the full consciousness of the *auteurists* with complete evacuation of individual subjectivity is a move from one extreme position to another. Some intermediary position, however messy it may seem, might ultimately prove more fruitful.

A further problem with Faulkner's position is his reductive reading of all forms of oppression in terms of class and capitalist social relations. Whereas the earlier left-wing critics suggested, independently of the rest of their analysis, that Renoir promoted traditional and stereotypical images of women, Faulkner never considers gender in its own right. Similarly, because he perceives that later Renoir films no longer challenge the established social order, he is unwilling or unable to see their critical edge. Moreover, he would seem implicitly to reduce history to the history of class struggle as carried out within national boundaries. Thus, when he suggests, as we saw, that Renoir's American films reiterate ideologically charged generic codes that help to maintain the social status quo, he fails to consider how those forms may have been actively reworked to suit a wartime context. Ironically for a Marxist critic, Faulkner perhaps pays too little attention to history, always judging the films by how much they preach proletarian revolution, rather than considering whether they take up a relatively progressive stance in the ideological struggles of a particular historical conjuncture.

The Renoir of the *auteurists*

If left-wing criticism of Renoir has been indelibly marked by a reaction to the *auteurism* of *Cahiers*, then subsequent *auterist* analyses have had to respond to the Renoir of the left. *Auteurists* come in all shapes and sizes even if ideological and methodological individualism and the cult of 'great' directors pull them together. In the pages that follow, I will first linger on the rich and challenging existential *auteurism* of Serceau before exploring a more typical essentialist variety.

Existential *auteurism*

Daniel Serceau's monumental two-volume analysis (Serceau 1981 and 1985b) represents perhaps the most detailed, coherent and persuasive *auteurist* reading of Renoir.[2] In true *auteurist* fashion, he places a supremely conscious creator figure at the centre of a work which is seen as the univocal expression of a coherent but evolving world view. He asserts thematic and philosophical continuity from the 1920s to the late films and identifies a clear progression in Renoir's thought from revolt to wisdom. The consistency and rigour of his analytical framework enables him to draw out powerful readings of films such as *On purge bébé* (1931) which others simply gloss over. Unlike some *auteurists*, he does not assert that the director simply carried on restating an unchanging world-view. He prefers the notion of a philosophical quest that keeps the same underlying aims but goes through different stages and produces responses to varying situations. Responding to and outflanking critics of the left, he does not simply try to downplay or ignore Renoir's political engagement in the 1930s, suggesting indeed that his Dionysian revolutionary urges were restrained by the conservatism of the French Communist Party. Renoir's political involvement is none the less relativised by incorporation into a narrative that sees it as one stage in a quest for human happiness and fraternity.

Serceau's analysis draws on an eclectic but effective combination of Freudianism, existentialism and Dionysian vitalism. Central place is given to the consciousness's management of the libido's search for pleasure through sensual contact with the physical world and especially through communion with other human beings. There are many barriers to libidinous satisfaction. Pleasurable communion can only be enjoyed by free and equal individuals because oppression or domination will lead inevitably to revolt or conflict. The human spirit which allows us to absorb the world also tries to strait-jacket it and deny its movement and diversity by the imposition of dogmatism and uniformity. The

2 Serceau usefully summarises his analysis of Renoir in the much more compact *Jean Renoir* (1985a).

intellect works against the senses rather than facilitating their pleasurable contact with the world. The law, public opinion and a repressive culture, be it in the form of Christian morality or capitalist productivism, can all prevent the pursuit of pleasure. Furthermore, people are often prisoners of images of themselves, others or the world which prevent them acting upon the real to bring about their pleasures. Pursuit, for example of idealised, everlasting and disembodied romantic love prevents sensual enjoyment of a concrete partner in the present.

Serceau divides Renoir's work into four periods, each one representing a stage in a process of enlightenment. The first, the silent period, only produces one film of real importance, *Tire-au-flanc* (1928). The second period, the 1930s, is treated significantly as a block and not split into a pre-political and a political phase. The third, the American period, is seen as a part of the same ongoing philosophical project which produced no outstanding films. The final period, the 1950s and 1960s, is a peak and a summing-up of Renoir's philosophical quest. Far from accepting any notion of decline, Serceau is convinced that Renoir was prevented by the reluctance of a short-sighted cinema industry from producing further masterpieces.

Serceau identifies two main features of the first period, the first being a passing fascination with technical innovation but the second, of much more lasting significance, being the realisation that a director must have a personal philosophy. *Tire-au-flanc* is seen as an initial statement of key directorial themes such as a critique of Christian values, the refusal of the mind–body divide with its devaluing of human sensuality, and the affirmation of liberatory Dionysian disorder, apparent here when the hero plays the part of a satyr to entertain his fellow soldiers (Serceau 1985a: 41–2).

According to Serceau, Renoir's films of the 1930s undertake an exploration of the social world and the inner self. He identifies a group of films (most notably *La Chienne* and *Toni* but also *Madame Bovary* and *Une Partie de campagne*) in which individuals are prisoners of images that prevent them achieving satisfaction in the real world. He notes too the importance of murder in this period as characters clash with and revolt against a society which oppresses them. As the 1930s progress, the murders are incorporated into conscious collective revolt against a society that prevents human communion, but by the end of the period hope for the transformation of the social frame has been lost. Characters flee reality, becoming their own executioners (*La Bête humaine*) or denying themselves in order to preserve false images (*La Règle du jeu*). Murder reverts to being individual and destructive rather than collective and potentially liberatory (Serceau 1985a: 18–19; 1985b: 16–18).

The main feature of the American period is an exploration of the theme of liberty that considers the unfreedom of waged labour (*The Southerner, Diary of a Chambermaid*) and of lifelong monogamy (*Woman on the Beach*) and asserts the necessity of liberty and equality, not as ends in themselves, but as preconditions to the flow of love (*This Land is Mine*). *Swamp Water* demonstrates that complete freedom from constraint can only be found in isolation from society and thus denies any possibility of pleasurable contact with others (Serceau 1985b: 233–5). *The River* shows the unhappiness both of characters who renounce material satisfaction for chimeric romantic love and of those who seek to deny the flux and disorder of the world. It is seen as Renoir's last pessimistic film. Thereafter, in the fourth and final period identified by Serceau, Renoir turns away from critical realism (Serceau 1985a: 21) and becomes a moralist who seeks to teach us three key notions: the need for self-determination which implies a refusal to be dominated or to dominate; the search for sensual and not imaginary pleasures and the search for love which binds human society together. This final Renoir is a convinced relativist who knows that, in a world of constant flux, it is essential to abandon idealised images of self, others and love and to seek concrete pleasure in the present moment. This is the hard lesson of *Carosse d'or* which opens the way for the radiant affirmation of the same message in *French Cancan*'s hymn to female beauty, sex and love (Serceau 1985a: 23).

Serceau refutes the notion that this final, serene Renoir has abandoned his earlier revolt in favour of a position of benign tolerance. The film-maker is still conscious of the social and economic foundations of liberty and although this consciousness is no longer expressed in the dogmatic language of political ideology, his characters are still prepared, if necessary, to fight for their freedom as evidenced by *Le Caporal épinglé* (Serceau 1985a: 25). Serceau similarly refutes the belief that Renoir can turn his back on the present situation of his fellow man in favour of rose-tinted nostalgia for the *belle époque* or a narrow idealisation of art. Because his Renoir seeks material rather than purely mental satisfactions, he is profoundly conscious of the need to deal with the real conditions of life and concrete obstacles to the achievement of human communion. He sees a society increasingly made up of atomised individuals, which makes the dreams of political fraternity of the 1930s unrealisable and he is aware that the modern world increasingly places alienating images between us and our pleasures while imposing a repressive productivism on us (Serceau 1985b: 426).

Serceau's analysis is original and powerful and opens up promising lines of inquiry, especially for the Renoir of the post-war period. His great strength is his multifaceted analysis of the causes of human unhappiness and the roots of oppression. For conventional critics of the left, oppression and misery must essentially be rooted in class inequality and capitalist exploitation and can thus only be overcome through political revolution. Serceau does not exclude class domination from his model but promotes a more multifaceted model of repression. He is thus able to point out a sharply critical edge to films dismissed by others as conservative because they could not discern conventional left-wing positions. He can also establish connections and points of comparison between films that are generally seen as radically different.

Let us look at one particularly telling example. *On purge bébé* shows how a housewife's obsession with her son's constipation wreaks havoc by shattering the divide between public and private and spilling over into the commercial negotiations of her businessman husband. Instead of seeing its chaos as a standard example of comic disorder, he attributes it to a revolt generated by the domestic oppression of women and can thus link it to the revolution of *La Marseillaise* and the disrupting return of repressed instincts in *Le Déjeuner sur l'herbe* (Serceau 1985b: 421). Apparently unrelated films are tied together as stages in the same philosophical investigation and seemingly disparate revolts are linked as manifestations of subjects' Dionysian struggles against restrictive frameworks.

One could, however, argue that, rather than identifying continuities, Serceau generates them through an all-embracing framework that collapses difference into similarity in an endeavour to produce a coherent and continuous philosophical quest from a profoundly discontinuous career. One could suggest more specifically that, like so many other critics, he reads Renoir backwards using the later films and writings to generate an analytical framework and a set of themes which the earlier films are then forced to fit. Like other *auteurist* critics, he unhesitatingly and repeatedly uses the comments that Renoir made from the 1950s onwards to cast light on the earlier films. Ironically for someone who writes at length about distorting self-images, Serceau involuntarily connives in Renoir's own self-mythologisation. He notably builds on the director's own relativisation and depoliticisation of the notion of revolution to outflank left-wing critics and to present a man whose Dionysian radicalism has outgrown conventional political struggle.

Serceau, in fact, goes further than Renoir himself down the *auteurist* path in his desire to generate a picture of a self-conscious artist single-mindedly pursuing a philosophical quest. Whereas Renoir attaches no specific importance to *On purge bébé*, suggesting that it is merely something that he had to shoot in a hurry to prove his competence with sound film and his ability to work fast and cheaply, Serceau finds in it a critique of domestic oppression of women and of the social repression of the body (Serceau 1981: 183–8). If Renoir were the supremely conscious artist we have been led to believe, we would expect him to have pointed out the presence of these personal thematic constants himself. Serceau needs his Renoir to condemn gender oppression for his critical edifice to stay upright. If oppression is fundamentally inimical to the search for universal communion and if repressed human possibilities must of necessity burst out of repressive social frameworks, then one would expect Renoir's work to constantly denounce the exploitation of woman and their straitjacketing in narrowly defined social roles. If, as I shall suggest, Renoir is not only inconsistent in his attitude to women but at times echoes the most reactionary stereotypes, then there would be at the least a major blind spot in Serceau's analysis. If one were to go on to suggest in a more general way that Renoir unconsciously gives voice to received attitudes and values rather than being the single source of his own consciousness as Serceau assumes then the notion of the films *simply* representing a philosophical quest would become untenable.

Serceau's Renoir is convinced that one has to come to terms with history and society to engage with the real conditions of one's existence and thus to act effectively. But Serceau at no stage explains from what vantage point Renoir can possibly gain an objective knowledge of a socio-historical context which he is always inside of. Not only does he fail to acknowledge the possibility that society may in fact speak through Renoir, but he also fails to deal adequately with the films' historical context and the degree in which the 'truths' voiced by them may be contingent upon a specific historical location. Thus Renoir's American films are seen primarily as meditations upon the conditions and limitations of freedom with no real attempt to deal with the fact that they were wartime films that for that reason might engage in specific ways with American myths of freedom. Ultimately and ironically, Serceau's 'existential' Renoir is a covert essentialist, one who can see through imagined human needs to the pre-social and ahistorical primordial need to grow and to expand and to engage libidinously with others.

Serceau's analysis is both important and original, notably for its refusal to equate Renoir's political disengagement with the conservative quietism of which he is so often accused. He suggests, against many *auteurists* and critics of the left, that the Renoir who moves on from conventional models of social transformation to a broader critique of alienation and oppression maintains a distinct radical edge throughout his career. However, because he cannot acknowledge unconscious and acquired attitudes in Renoir's work, he fails to consider how the films might be traversed by contradictions, how they might be simultaneously reactionary and progressive, critical and conservative.

Essentialist *auteurism*

The analysis of Renoir offered by Maurice Bessy and Claude Beylie in their *Jean Renoir* (1989) is less original than that of Serceau but usefully illustrates the *auteurist* tendency to collapse the diversity of the films into the complexity of the director's character or vision. The authors begin by establishing the apparent disorder of the *œuvre* saying, '(il) paraît progresser sans ligne directrice ni logique interne, en désordre, défiant toute étiquette. Renoir change de registre sans crier gare, se contredit allègrement d'un film à l'autre, quand ce n'est pas à l'intérieur d'un même film' (Bessy and Beylie 1989: 9).[3] Beylie and Bessy reject the oversimple labelling of Renoir as sensualist and lover of humanity, noting that these benign characteristics are counterbalanced by a capacity for abstraction and generalisation as well as for sarcasm, disillusionment and bitterness.

They show their determination to reclaim the 1930s films from the left by tying them firmly into the *œuvre* and by suggesting that the realist label has been foisted on Renoir by a generation blinded by ideology. The search for realism, they assert, is characteristic of 'de médiocres cinéastes soucieux de "coller" à la réalité – psychologique, sociale, politique – de leur temps' (Bessy and Beylie 1989: 14).[4] Reality is only ever a jumping-off point for the creativity of a man interested in fantasy, art and playfulness, someone who always valued the creator more than his creation. From his earliest

---

3 '(he) seems to develop without direction or internal logic, in a disorderly way which defies labelling. Renoir changes register without warning, contradicts himself cheerfully from one film to the next and sometimes within the same film'.

4 'mediocre directors who wish to adhere to the psychological, social or political reality of their time'.

films, Renoir has been looking for the fantastic, for an escape from the real. His characters do likewise. From Mme Bovary's fantasy life and Legrand's desire to flee his miserable existence in *La Chienne*, to the political dreams of the Popular Front period and beyond, they have sought to escape. While the earlier characters may pay for their stubborn quest with their lives, the later ones who have learned the importance of lightness and frivolity, avoid this risk knowing that their happiness resides in the great illusion of the theatre rather than in the miserable seductions of reality (Bessy and Beylie 1989: 17). The theatre is the central pillar of Renoir's work. Realising that human interaction is essentially theatrical, he constantly plays on the impossibility of separating the real from artifice. Throughout his work we see the same *drame gai* unfolding under the ironic but tolerant eyes of a playmaker of genius (Bessy and Beylie 1989: 22).

Bessy and Beylie point the way past apparent contradictions and changes to a 'true' Renoir whose work has always followed essentially the same direction. Renoir emerges as the perfect artist, someone whose blend of irony and *bonhomie* is ideally matched to life's blend of bitterness and charm, someone whose detached but benevolent creativity turns life's theatricality into a rich and pleasurable spectacle. This all too predictable account of an individual of genius who sees the essential truth of life and conveys it in a form that renders its contemplation agreeable echoes a thousand other accounts of the work of 'great artists'. It is easy to pick holes in it, for its flattening out of discontinuities, its ideological and methodological individualism, its wilful denial of Renoir's very real political commitment, and its decontextualisation of the films. Yet it should also be remembered that while such ways of viewing cinema are now unfashionable in British and American academic circles, Bessy and Beylie's vision of Renoir is probably more representative of the wider perception of his work than other more socio-critical forms of analysis. Reception of 'art' cinema is still dominated by *auteurist* readings which privilege the personal style and themes of great individual directors. The requisite mode of viewing for such 'great' works of art is detached contemplation of formal perfection or, as is more frequent in Renoir's case, complicity in the pleasure taken in the process of creation. Reinsertion of the films into their socio-historical context and critical engagement with their politico-ideological stance is unwelcome and undesirable.

Bessy and Beylie make one assertion which is worth returning to because it is echoed by other critics. They suggest that the central unifying theme of Renoir's work is a view of social life as theatre. This 'theatricality' provides one of the best illustrations of how apparent thematic continuity can be used to flatten out variety, deny evolution and produce an individualist account of creativity by downplaying a film-maker's participation in broader cultural patterns. Renoir adapted a number of naturalist and realist novels which already contained within them notions of social life as theatre. He did not need to add the theatricality of society to *Madame Bovary, Nana* or indeed *La Chienne*. It was already there, being a staple of the nineteenth-century novel and its descendants. Rather than being incompatible with realism, it was one of its chosen ways to represent society. Some Renoir films of the early 1930s are, like many other films of the beginning of the sound era, filmed stage plays. Thus *Boudu sauvé des eaux, Chotard et cie* (1933) and *On purge bébé* are manifestations of a general trend in French cinema and not of Renoir's obsessive return to the theatre. Theatricality is clearly present in some of the key Renoir films of the Popular Front era but it is associated with the court and the counter-revolution in *La Marseillaise* and with the devious capitalist in *Crime de Monsieur Lange* and not with the workers or the revolutionaries. In other words, its use is polemical. As Renoir more self-consciously constructed a coherent *œuvre* in the post-war period, the theatre was again a favourite terrain, being linked with pleasurable spectacle and creativity as well as self-deception or deception of others in key films such as *Carosse d'or, Eléna et les hommes* and *French Cancan*. Due to this variety, its use needs to be analysed and not merely noted as proof of consistency and used to link Renoir's films in an unbroken chain while separating them from their broader context.

Pragmatic *auteurism*

Polemical *auteurism* and polemical anti-*auteurism* tend to leave
little room for the exploration of the specificity of cinematic
creation. Raymond Durgnat tries to fill that gap. Rejecting the cult
of artistic self-expression, he begins by subscribing to a pragmatic
auteurism that suggests that each film is a unique interplay of
individual and collective determinations. This leaves room for an
exploration of the specific circumstances surrounding a production (the encounter with script-writers, star actors or Hollywood
studios) as well as broader collective influences. Yet, even as he
sets out on his analysis, there is a suspicion that he may slip
towards more familiar variants of *auteurism*. Comparing Renoir's
reliance on collaborators with a poet's dependence on 'the
accidents of language,' he suggests that, by orchestrating the
multiple, unpredictable factors of a production, the director may
have achieved a higher form of self-awareness (Durgnat 1974: 19–
26). It is thus no surprise when his conclusion locates Renoir
alongside Tolstoy in the pantheon of great individual artists while
collapsing the discontinuity and diversity of the director's work
into a richly complex individual 'vision' (Durgnat 1974: 396–405).

Alternative avenues?

Colin Crisp's impressive overview of the classic French cinema
helps us to go further down some of the avenues that Durgnat
seemed at one stage to be opening up. His overview of French
cinema production and industrial practices from 1930 to 1960
leads him to attack the myth of directorial expressivity. Attributing
the focus on directorial thematic constants to 'slack auteurist
strategies,' he asserts that 'it is easier to correlate thematic aspects
of the classic cinema with the scriptwriter's name or with social
and political determinants' (Crisp 1993: 323). Noting a global
tendency towards 'poeticization' in classic French cinema, he
attributes it to a broad professional culture and not to individual
directors. He acknowledges that the industry's fragmented

structure potentially opened up space for directorial expressivity but suggests that this space was rarely if ever exploited for that end. Turning specifically to Renoir, he writes:

> (N)o thematic or stylistic unity is apparent in the films directed by Renoir: some but not all his films between 1935 and 1939 relate to the Popular Front; most of his post-war films promote a vaguely reactionary pantheism; others from throughout the classic period are totally apolitical, implying support either for an anarchistic amoralism or a romantic glorification of the artist. All of these themes are common to many other directors of the period, where they are sometimes attributed to directorial self-expression and sometimes to social and political determinants. (Crisp 1993: 317)

Crisp overplays a strong hand. His reading of Renoir's films in terms of their typicality is a useful corrective to *auteurist* individualism but his denial of any consistency or expressivity to all of Renoir's films is surely overstated, a polemical reaction against *auteurism* rather than a fully supported position. Renoir's films from the era of the Front are more consistently political than he allows, while there is a clear and demonstrable correlation between Renoir's later films and thoughts he expressed in interviews and other writings. Crisp seems himself to admit this when he refers to the 'vaguely reactionary pantheism' of the post-war films. The fact that something similar can be found in films by other directors is a convincing argument against the uniqueness of Renoir's vision but not against directorial expressivity *per se*.

Burch and Sellier adopt another variant of anti-*auteurism*. In their ground-breaking study of gender in French cinema from 1930 to 1956, they view film as a privileged site for the expression of the social imaginary. They focus on broad recurrent patterns of gender representations that characterise certain periods of French cinema history and to which they attach collective rather than individual authorship. For example, they attribute *La Chienne*'s portrayal of a castrating, unattractive older woman and destructive yet seductive younger one to recurrent, socially generated stereotypes not to the director's individual misogyny (Burch and Sellier 1996: 36). In their consideration of representations of *la garce* (a term somewhere between 'slut' and 'bitch'), they suggest that Renoir inaugurated the lower-class variant with *Nana*, but point out that the stereotype was already well established in other cultural forms (Burch and Sellier 1996: 52). Turning later to the director's post-war work, they cite its reactionary gender representations as evidence that 'great' directors do not escape from the determinations of their era. They note that the light comedy in fashion at the time is a favourable terrain for the expression of misogyny (Burch and Sellier 1996: 264).

Although their main focus is on the broad patterns that show the evolution of the 'social imaginary', they also pick out a group of exceptional films that show a particular awareness of the contradictions of a specific period. There is more than a suspicion of a reintroduction of *auteurism* into the equation when they note that the greatness of certain films by consecrated directors derives from their capacity to engage dialectically with collectively generated representations and even challenge them (Burch and Sellier 1996: 37). They look in detail at two Renoir films, *La Règle du jeu* and *Le Carosse d'or*, noting that both highlight and question the subordination of women while the latter gives its central female character full subject status. Somewhat surprisingly perhaps, their analysis focuses on the relation between the director and his films. They note for example that art becomes the main value in the 'world' of post-war Renoir (Burch and Sellier 1996: 295).

Having abandoned individual authorship, Burch and Sellier struggle to locate the collective alternative. They consider Frenchmen, *petit-bourgeois* men and intellectuals before deciding that the only unchallengeable collective author is the masculine community which makes films (Burch and Sellier 1996: 15). As cinema is not a self-contained universe and as film-makers are a disparate group, this is not a particularly convincing choice. They do not fully explain, in any case, why some films not others should explore tensions in collective representations, while their reintroduction of directorial consciousness is surely a symptom of the difficulties that radical anti-*auterism* has in explaining the specificity of particular films.

Their work is none the less of great importance. Its scope allows them to read Renoir for his typicality and to link him into the broader socio-cultural patterns of his era. Although previous critics (Oms, Poulle) had drawn attention to the regressive portrayal of women in many Renoir films, they had presented it as an aspect of an individual vision and failed to link it to collectively generated representations. Burch and Sellier rectify this failing. Even if their explanation of why certain films are exceptional is not entirely convincing, their recognition that films may challenge as well as reproduce dominant representations is an important one.

Conclusion

Renoir criticism has been dominated by *auteurists* and critics of the left and the quarrel between the two. The former have helped to mythologise Renoir by turning a discontinuous body of work into an *œuvre*, detaching it in the process from the socio-historical contexts which shaped it and to which it responded. The latter have usefully relinked Renoir to these contexts, reading his films as interventions in the political and ideological struggles of their time.

Not all critics of the left have reacted against the methodological individualism of the *auteurists*. Some (Oms, Poulle) have opposed them on ideological grounds, combating their depoliticisation of Renoir's work, while still attributing it to an individual creator whose personal choices and background would account for its shape. Other critics (Faulkner, Burch and Sellier, Crisp) move beyond this individualism to focus on how the films are shaped by and express collectively generated meanings or broad trends in the cinema industry. Their work productively moves us away from the fully conscious individual creator, but its anti-*auteurism* drives it to evacuate a fertile middle ground upon which one might explore how partially conscious individuals and groups engage actively with collectively generated meanings as well as passively echoing them. It is by reoccupying this complex terrain that one can better engage with Renoir's films in all their enormous diversity. One should not deceive oneself as to the scale of the task. It is practically and theoretically impossible to trace and unravel all the potential influences on a film's production. One must simply indicate what seem to have been the major influences while remembering that, in a book devoted to Renoir, one will inevitably be pushed to focus on the director at the expense, not so much of broad ideological and cultural determinants, but of the other individuals and groups involved in the creative process.

Like the other Renoirs we have considered, the Renoir that emerges from this book will inevitably be shaped by a host of factors associated with the time and place of its writing. More specifically it is influenced substantially by earlier critical visions, even when reacting against them. The pages that follow will build on left-wing critics' contextualised engagement with the films' ideological content while drawing on those who recognise the multifaceted nature of oppression and repression (Burch and Sellier and Serceau). Building on the perceptions of Poulle and Burch and Sellier, they will read the films in terms of the tensions and contradictions that traverse them and not see them as simple univocal expressions of ideological positions. Drawing on Crisp, they will read Renoir's work for typicality as well as exceptionality. They will more specifically owe a considerable debt to Serceau's recognition and exploration of the critical edge of the later films, an edge that left-wing critics have failed to explore.

References

Bazin, A. (1989), *Jean Renoir*, ed. F. Truffaut, Paris, Lebovici.

Bessy, M. and Beylie, C. (1989), *Jean Renoir*, Paris, Gérard Watelet.

Burch, N. and Sellier, G. (1996), *La Drôle de guerre des sexes du cinéma français (1930–1956)*, Paris, Nathan.

Chardère, B. *et al.* (1962), *Premier Plan* (special number on Renoir), 22/23/24.

Crisp, C. (1993), *The Classic French Cinema, 1930–1960*, Bloomington, Indiana University Press.

Durgnat, R. (1974), *Jean Renoir*, Berkeley, University of California.

Faulkner, C. (1986), *The Social Cinema of Jean Renoir*, Princeton, Princeton University Press.

Oms, M. (1962), 'Renoir revu et rectifié', in Chardère, B. *et al.* (1962), 22–24, 44–51.

Poulle, F. (1969), *Renoir 1938 ou Jean Renoir pour rien?*, Paris, Editions du Cerf.

Reader, K. and Vincendeau, G. (eds) (1986), *La Vie est à Nous: French Cinema of the*

Popular Front, London, BFI/National Film Theatre.

Renoir, J. (1984), *Renoir on Renoir*, trans. C. Volk, Cambridge, Cambridge University Press.

Schérer, M. (1952), 'Renoir américain', *Cahiers du cinéma*, 2(8): 33–40.

Serceau, D. (1981), *Jean Renoir, l'insurgé*, Paris, Le Sycomore.

Serceau, D. (1985a), *Jean Renoir*, Paris, Edilig.

Serceau, D. (1985b), *La Sagesse du plaisir*, Paris, Editions du Cerf.

3

The early films

This chapter considers the films that Renoir directed during his first decade as a film-maker (1924–34). They will be considered in two groups: the silent films and those that followed the introduction of sound.

The films from the silent period are remarkably diverse in terms of their style, their mode of production and their thematic content. Some (notably *Marquitta* (1924), *Le Bled* (1929) and *Le Tournoi* (1928)) are extremely difficult to see. No attempt will be made to cover them systematically. This has been done very competently by a range of critics (Durgnat (1974), Sesonske (1980), Viry-Babel (1994)). Instead, a selection of the films will be considered from two points of view: first, for their engagement with the tensions and anxieties that marked the France of the 1920s, a time when a country scarred by war went through a period of rapid change; second, for evidence of a consistent social vision. I will begin with two films that engaged with their period, albeit in very different ways, but continue by highlighting the highly conventional nature of the melodrama that dominated Renoir's cinema of this period.

Engaging with the post-war world?

Charleston (1926) is a short and apparently lightweight piece reportedly made on a shoe-string with left-over film-stock. It is most definitely of its era and expresses some of its contradictions, anxieties and prejudices. It shows the arrival of an African explorer in a destroyed Paris. A scantily clad white woman deserts her ape mate to lead the African in an erotic Charleston (a Black American dance which arrived in France in the aftermath of the Great War). The African picks up the dance. The pair climb back into his airship and depart leaving the apeman forlorn in the ruined city.

On the surface, the film celebrates the dance skills of Johnny Huggins, an African-American, and Catherine, Renoir's wife. It captures the atmosphere of the hedonistic *années folles* by foregrounding the active female sexuality and American dance music which came to symbolise the mood of the period. Apparently suggesting complete release from wartime sacrifice, discipline and duty, it taps, at a deeper level, into the disquiet of the post-war period by suggesting a world turned upside down where civilisation and technology have passed to the African. Huggins's character is thus a figure of some complexity, due to his dual 'nationality'. His American origins link him to a New World modernity that threatens to overtake a decadent ruined Europe while his Africanness helps to defuse the threat by making his modernity a joke. Naked primitivism passes to the western woman while the animality, previously thrust on the African by colonialism, passes to her mate who loses his very humanity with the destruction of the civilisation that he as a male had embodied.

The war, to borrow a telling phrase from Mary-Louise Roberts, is everywhere and nowhere (Roberts 1994: 1). The diffuse but pervasive unease it has sown, crystallises around the woman whose foregrounded sexual transgression (betrayal of her mate, involvement with a black man) can be read as an expression of the background ruins. Gender anxiety helped to crystallise a broader post-war sense of disarray (Roberts 1994: 4–12).

If *Charleston*'s evocation of colonial themes is indirect, that found in *Le Bled* (1929), a film commissioned to celebrate the centenary of the colonisation of Algeria, is overt. It can be seen in part as a mobilisation of colonial narratives to respond to the anxieties expressed in the earlier film (although that clearly was not an explicit intention). Its message is encapsulated by the opening text that responds to metropolitan ignorance and exotic stereotypes by celebrating the prodigious economic activity, mechanised agriculture and developed industry of the colony. A later sequence showing conquering soldiers fade into a line of advancing tractors serves to legitimise conquest and to give a heroic dimension to the cultivation of the land while linking past and present in an ongoing project of national expansion. France is invited to recognise itself as a modern nation through this celebration of its subjugation and transformation of Algeria.

This epic frame is given a more human dimension by the melodramatic narrative that forms the main interest of the film, although the characters at its heart do not yet have the stature that the epic requires. The narrative begins when a Frenchman who has squandered his inheritance comes to live with his uncle, a colonial landowner. He arrives in Algeria on the same boat that carries a young woman coming to claim inherited land. Her rather masculine clothes and independent wealth contrast with his poverty-induced dependence to suggest the same post-war sense of a disturbed gender order that we have already evoked. The pair fall in love but neither is committed to the colonial project. Used to a life of ease in Paris, the young man cannot initially adapt to the hard labour required in the colony. It is the villains of the piece, the young woman's cousins, who provoke the drama that allows order to be restored. Their attachment to luxury drives them to covet the inheritance. The female cousin, a classic *femme fatale*, dominates her brother and pushes him to kidnap the heroine. During the ensuing chase, she falls off a galloping horse and is killed while the leading male heroically rescues his beloved, his masculine vigour and dominance now contrasting with her passive vulnerability. They marry, bringing the dangerously independent woman back into the fold. The young man will follow in his uncle's footsteps and farm the land.

The national epic can now continue having found its cast. Punishment or taming of transgressive women and the re-establishment of the broken link between generations of men announces the broader restoration of order that will come when

France turns its back on hedonistic materialism and re-embraces its colonial destiny.

The virgins and whores of melodrama

La Fille de l'eau (1924) combines an entirely conventional melo-dramatic narrative with avant-gardist visual effects (notably in the sequence which shows the heroine's fever-induced delirium). The male characters are split along Manichaean lines: a hero complete with white charger, the heroine's brutish uncle and a vindictive local farmer. The female lead, appropriately named Virginia, is the archetypal helpless orphan of melodrama. A victim of events, her fate is dictated by the character and actions of the men. One episode pits a group of villagers led by the villainous farmer against a gypsy poacher. Their treatment of him could have opened up space for an exploration of how a settled community treats an outsider. The conventional narrative focuses instead on how it affects the helpless waif. Algeria also figures marginally in a film whose happy ending shows the orphan heroine absorbed into a bourgeois family as they depart to take care of their interests in the colony. This purely routine evocation shows how deeply em-bedded the colonial project had become in French culture as well as serving to underline the film's indifference to broader issues.

La Petite Marchande d'allumettes (1928), an adaptation of an Andersen tale, again uses a melodramatic plot as pretext for the creation of a succession of visual effects. The heroine is another frail waif, a match-seller, and thus someone on the margins of society. Her exclusion is figured most clearly when, starving and freezing, she looks in through the window of a restaurant but in a way that produces pathos rather than social criticism. As she lies dying in the snow, she dreams of figures she has seen in a toyshop window. Her dream mirrors the Manichaean narrative of *La Fille de l'eau*. In it, she is protected by a gallant soldier but pursued and captured by death, a dark horseman.

Nana (1926), an adaptation of Zola's naturalist masterpiece, sits oddly alongside the two apparently slighter films we have just considered, yet it too is essentially melodrama. Zola's Nana is a courtesan who destroys and humiliates members of the wealthy élite of the Second Empire against a background of impending war. She is at once the personification of the corruption of a doomed regime and the semi-conscious agent of the revenge of the oppressed and exploited lower classes. Renoir's film decontextualises Zola's story so that the drama is no longer seen as the product of social conditions and the acerbic critique of the ruling class is excluded from the frame. Nana becomes simply a wilful prostitute, a seductress and destroyer of respectable but weak-willed men, in short, a *garce* whose fate is a deserved personal punishment rather than a final unmasking of a society (Burch and Sellier 1996: 52). Her principal victim is rehabilitated. While Zola has him shun his diseased mistress, Renoir brings him courageously to her deathbed to accompany her final minutes when she is haunted by images of her misdeeds. A melodramatic and moralistic story of villainess and victim and of vice duly punished replaces Zola's dissection of the Second Empire.

This collapsing inwards of Zola's story should not necessarily be read as wilful emasculation. It was probably driven by the impossibility of transferring the scope of the original to the cinema screen and by lack of interest in its political force. Renoir's chief interest seems to have been twofold: first, the use of radically contrasting acting styles to convey character; second, the use of décor to create mood (Sesonske 1980: 23–33). As yet, neither character nor décor are placed in the service of a social or political vision. In the absence of such a vision, there is no obstacle to inherited stereotypes, to the whores and virgins, villains and victims of melodrama.

Military vaudeville

Tire-au-flanc (1928), the last silent film that will be touched upon, takes us well away from melodrama but only to deliver us into another popular form, the military vaudeville. The genre's conventionally benign portrayal of military life may have seemed unexceptional before 1914, but, after the horrors of the Great War, it is surprising that it retained its popularity. Surprising also that

Renoir, whose life had been so marked by the war and who went on to make the most celebrated anti-war film of all, *La Grande Illusion*, should have adapted so easily to it. One military training sequence shows the recruits practice their use of the bayonet before plunging down a hillside in disarray as they don gas masks. No attempt is made to give it a sinister dimension, despite the horrific resonance these gestures must have had for so many French people.

The film is a comedy of social disruption that registers the collision of two worlds and in the process the coming to manhood of the hero-poet. The poet, a frivolous young man, is the only male in the female-dominated bourgeois household of his aunt. He is called up for the army, an all-male institution with no respect for his refinement or social status. Learning to express himself through his body and shedding his superior airs, he becomes 'one of the boys', not without first generating considerable disorder, notably at an entertainments evening. Dressed as a satyr, he puts out a fire and tames the regimental villain, thus achieving recognition by the army and winning the hand of his cousin. The final scene brings together masters and servants, men and women, army and bourgeoisie in a broader reconciliation made possible by the hero's social integration. Previously only able to survive in the feminised world of the bourgeois interior, he can now relate to his own gender and through it to other classes.

By far the most notable aspect of the film is its visual inventiveness. Adaptation of a theatrical original for the silent screen called for considerable ingenuity as a dialogue-led form was replaced by one where movement and gesture predominated. Perhaps it was because of the need to create and register the visual chaos of vaudeville that Renoir's camera took on a new mobility (Sesonske 1980: 61).

A silent *auteur*?

Consideration of a range of Renoir's silent films shows a clear lack of a consistent vision or philosophy behind them. Like other filmmakers of the period, and perhaps hoping to reach both a popular and a cultivated audience, Renoir and his collaborators uncritically borrow conventional forms (melodrama and military vaudeville) as vehicles for the exploration of technique and of visual effects. These conventional forms are not innocent. They can act as vehicles for the perpetuation of regressive stereotypes (for example, helpless virgins and destructive *femmes fatales*) and support the status quo (as with *La Fille de l'eau*'s 'normalisation' of the French presence in Algeria or the reaffirmation of gender boundaries in *Tire-au-flanc* and *Le Bled*). Their largely conventional narratives preclude any direct engagement with the France of the 1920s. *Charleston*, apparently one of the most lightweight of the films, is the exception, but as the script was produced by Lestringuez and as it tapped into broadly conventional ways of encapsulating the novelty of the period, there is no reason to root it in an authorial consciousness. The only other film where we have been able to discern a clear and conscious desire to engage with the contemporary world is *Le Bled*, the piece which Renoir was commissioned to film and which can least be seen as his own.

It is easy to identify typically Renoirian motifs in the silent films if that is what one is looking for. Figures such as the poacher or the satyr, themes such as the interaction of different social classes, and set pieces such as the entertainments evening can all be found in later, more celebrated films. But recurring motifs without a clear and consistent underlying vision are only evidence of superficial continuity.

The transition to sound

Renoir's early sound films were literary adaptations. In this, they followed the predominant pattern of French cinema of the period. Three brought hit boulevard comedies to the screen (*On Purge bébé, Boudu sauvé des eaux, Chotard et cie*). Two derived from successful novels (*La Nuit du carrefour* (1932), *La Chienne*). *Madame Bovary* partially broke the pattern by delving back into the nineteenth century and drawing on an established classic, but it was not till *Toni* that Renoir moved away from literary sources.

Because all the adaptations owe an ultimately incalculable amount to the original novel or play, it is impossible to simply treat them as *films d'auteur*. Shared themes may derive from broad cultural patterns inscribed in the source texts rather than from the director.

I will group them as follows. I will consider first the adaptations of boulevard comedies all of which stage the collision between a disruptive character and a constraining social frame. I will then consider *Madame Bovary* and *La Chienne* both of which show the destruction of a self-deluding individual by a corrupt society. I will finish by looking at *La Nuit du carrefour* and *Toni*, two films that stage the collision of tradition and modernity while foregrounding migration and xenophobia.

Disruptive individuals, constricting frames

On purge bébé (1931) was Renoir's first sound film and one he had to make in record time and at low cost to prove that he could be a commercial film-maker. The speed of production and the novelty of sound explain why this was the nearest the director ever came to filmed theatre. He essentially limits himself to recording the performance of a small cast in a décor that never opens onto the exterior world. The film's dialogue faithfully follows Feydeau's original.

The central characters, the Follavoine, are a bourgeois couple with a 7-year-old son they still call baby. M. Follavoine is awaiting the visit of a civil servant through whom he hopes to win the contract to supply the army with chamber pots, objects whose precise function he is reluctant to acknowledge. He is keen to maintain the orderly frame of bourgeois life in order to make the best impression possible. His wife, the agent of disorder, is obsessed by their son's irregular bowel movements to the exclusion of all other considerations – thus the need for the purge of the title. Her obsession wreaks havoc by overturning the barriers and conventions that preserve bourgeois respectability. What should be kept in the private spaces of bathroom and bedroom (slop buckets, vulgar language, references to sexual infidelity, pregnancy and bodily functions) will overflow into the hall, the study and the salon. Refusing the role of self-effacing, decorous wife Madame Follavoine appears throughout in dressing gown and curlers, demanding that her husband take responsibility for their child, thus challenging the conventional exclusion of the domestic from the public domain and the gendered division of roles. Her single-minded concern for her son's regularity causes one marriage to break up, her husband to leave and two challenges to be issued. The purge is eventually taken by the two adult men, with predictably farcical consequences. The boy is the only winner.

The triumph of the child over the adults is symptomatic of a more general overturning of conventional hierarchies that is part of the film's farcical disorder. Bodily functions triumph over the deadly serious business of making money. The domestic overwhelms the public. The wife's concerns overrule those of the husband.

The film stands convention on its head. Should one follow Serceau and construe it as radical? (Serceau 1981: 183–8) Perhaps not. Comedy habitually depends for its effects on temporary disorder and thus tends to normalise the very order it suspends. Madame Follavoine, the chief agent of chaos, is a somewhat absurd monomaniac, a woman obsessed with the control of her son's body. It is hard to justify a reading that takes her revolt seriously.

Chotard et cie (1933) is seen as one of Renoir's minor works. Like *On purge bébé* it depends on a theatrical original for its dialogue. However, it resembles filmed theatre much less. A freely panning and tracking camera and in-depth staging which links interiors and studio shot exteriors give it a distinctly cinematic feel and tie it clearly to Renoir's dominant style of the 1930s. But the depth and mobility are not exploited productively to broaden the social frame. Even when masters' and workers' groups are brought together visually, nothing is made of the contrast. The focus remains limited to internal tensions within the bourgeoisie, tensions that are resolved most amicably by this amusing but conformist piece.

The story is dominated by two characters, Chotard, dynamic

capitalist proprietor of a chain of grocery stores, and Julien, a poet. Chotard's little kingdom is thrown into disarray by the arrival in it of the anarchic artist, his daughter's chosen husband. His initial reaction is to try to assimilate the interloper. This fails. Julien is impervious to the imperatives of the money order and the world of work. Chotard's next instinct is to find another son-in-law but he is stopped in his tracks when Julien wins France's most prestigious literary prize (the Prix Goncourt) and along with it a substantial sum of money. The prize bridges the apparently irreconcilable domains of culture and wealth and paves the way for mutual colonisation. Chotard and his staff become avid readers, neglecting the simple business of making money in the process, while Julien is asked to bring his art within the world of business. He becomes a trademark and must work regular hours and adopt productivist norms with the predictable consequence that he stops writing. When he sees that the business too has ceased to function and that they will all finish on the street, he calls everyone to order. He will write in his own way and turn his hand to commerce while Chotard will concentrate on making money during the week and read on Sundays. Besides, as Julien remarks, business has its own poetry.

The familiar conflict between commercial and cultural bourgeoisies is thus resolved amicably. Each both needs and appreciates the other. They are complementary not irreconcilable. The film had subversive potential. It could have explored how culture's often ferocious critique of the moneyed bourgeoisie masks shared interests and values. But in the end conflict is defused rather than explored in what is a conformist piece.

Boudu sauvé des eaux (1932) can also be accused of conformism but is considerably more interesting and will thus be treated at greater length. It brought Renoir back together with one of the leads of *On purge bébé*, Michel Simon, who played the title role in this, the director's own adaptation of René Fauchois's hit stage comedy. The story is a relatively simple one. M. Lestingois, a freethinking and cultivated bourgeois owns a bookshop by the river in the heart of Paris. He lives with his conformist wife and a pretty young maid, Anne-Marie, with whom he is having an affair.

Boudu, a tramp, having lost his dog in a park, tries to drown himself in the Seine. Lestingois plunges into the river, saves him and takes him under his roof, only to find that he wreaks merry havoc on the household that in turn tries to 'civilise' him. When Mme Lestingois tries to send him packing, he grabs her and, over subsiding protests, has his way with her. Roles are soon reversed as the sexually frustrated woman comes back for more on a second occasion. As Boudu backs away he stumbles through a door to reveal Anne-Marie and Lestingois on a bed. In the meantime, a lottery win (a transparently miraculous solution) gives Boudu a substantial sum of money. Appearances can be saved by marrying him off to Anne-Marie, and she, learning of his new-found fortune is happy to agree. Convention appears to have won through, but as the wedding party rows down the Marne, Boudu overturns the boat, floats away and resumes his previous unfettered existence as a tramp.

It has often been assumed that the original play is mediocre and conformist, but as Richard Boston points out, it has a sharp, critical edge (Boston 1994: 24–9). The film draws on it for the bookshop scenes which make up its main body but also overflows it in several ways. Its adds a prologue showing Boudu in a park and returns him to the 'wild' rather than marrying him off as the play had done. It refuses theatrical flatness by considerable use of composition in depth, linking interior spaces and using doors and windows to frame actions. The Lestingois household opens out onto an interior yard where other life is suggested and, more importantly, it opens onto the teeming streets of 1930s Paris. The addition of the park, the river and the street builds on the play's existing opposition of the 'natural' and the 'civilised' while giving it a dynamic edge as nature is invaded by a conquering city.

The park of the prelude suggests Utopia, a place of play with no constraints, equally accessible to all, and a refuge from the hustle and bustle of the city. However, urban class divisions, laws and restrictions soon make their presence felt in a way that is foreshadowed by the discordant traffic noise that can be heard even while Boudu plays with his dog. First, a woman drags a little boy away from the water where he was playing. Then, as Boudu looks for his dog, he finds that no one will help a tramp. A women has her child give him money, saying that one must always succour the unfortunate even as the impersonality and condescension of the gesture put a safe social distance between them. A policeman responds to Boudu's requests for help by threatening him, but an elegant woman who has lost a poodle receives instant attention. His animal closeness to his dog weighs nothing against the monetary value of the other animal and the social status of its owner. He resists his own categorisation by the urban order as best he can by passing on the money he was given to a bemused wealthy man, but the combat is an unequal one. As the film ends, and even as he seems to have broken free from society, the camera pans round to show a railway bridge and a semi-industrial riverside landscape, clear evidence of the city's tentacular invasion. A goat, an alter ego for Boudu to replace his lost dog, is scared off by the shrill whistle of a train. The urban order is not easily evaded.

Lestingois first observes Boudu among the city's crowds and traffic through a telescope that paradoxically underlines his distance from those he sees even as it seems to bring them closer. No human contact takes place as the passers-by become the objects of his voyeuristic gaze. Boudu is memorably described as a 'perfect specimen' of a tramp, at once a category and an object, but his attempted suicide changes all that, bringing him and his rescuer into close, physical contact and shattering the protective urban anonymity, even as the crowd they draw emphasises the city's use of others for disengaged entertainment.

Boudu's full subversive potential is realised when he is brought into the Lestingois household. His awkward, disruptive and invasive presence is underlined by the audience's constant awareness of his ungainly, lanky body as it sprawls, somersaults, and lounges, dominating the screen and refusing to submit to the discipline of objects and conventions. Even when apparently tamed, it continues to assert itself by its refusal to fit clothes properly. Boudu is a rebel in a society, and particularly in a class, the bourgeoisie, where the body and its functions are repressed, denied or hidden. He spits, floods the floor and smears the kitchen and Madame's bedroom with boot polish. His wetting and dirtying (suggestive of an infant's soiling), highlight the importance of cleanliness, bodily restraint and spatial boundaries in the bourgeoisie's self-definition and sense of its own superiority. Even the generously humanitarian attitudes of M. Lestingois are put under severe strain by Boudu's transgressions, and he comes round to his wife's desire to expel the tramp.

The coming together of husband and wife is deeply significant. They seemed like chalk and cheese. M. Lestingois's cultured generosity and apparent unconventionality suggest a gulf separates him from a conventional, materialistic wife who seems to embody bourgeois meanness of spirit. Boudu's disruptive presence reveals that he is ultimately as convention bound and as bourgeois as she. This is clearly indicated by the first sequence that shows a theatrical stage upon which Lestingois, as Pan, pursues Anne-Marie, as a young nymph. The transparent theatricality of the décor unmasks this as a performance rather than an expression of spontaneous sensuality. Ensuing shots of Lestingois surrounded by books speaking in literary language of pastoral love confirm this first impression. Ultimately, he and his wife are simply conventional in different ways, and neither is capable of dealing with a true 'other', a true outsider without forcing him to conform to their norms.

Christopher Faulkner sees the film as a (rather tame) expression of class conflict (Faulkner 1986: 32–3). His reading, which depends on seeing Boudu as sub-proletarian, might work if the tramp had some social specificity, but he has none. He is rather an anti-bourgeois, a kind of negation of the values and norms of that class, who by colliding with them makes them visible. If one were to seek an oppressed proletarian, one should look no further than Anne-Marie. It is her manual labour which allows Mme Lestingois to produce her respectable bourgeois interior and which frees M. Lestingois to cultivate his mind, as the composition in depth, playing her background labour against their foreground idleness, clearly shows. But, having internalised the values of her masters, she smilingly accepts her exploited status, is dazzled by her master's literary prose and is happy to marry Boudu when he wins the lottery. Of class conflict there is no sign.

Faulkner suggests that the film's radicalism is strictly limited. It highlights petty conventions and undermines myths of humanitarianism and cultural guardianship, but distracts attention from the bourgeoisie's exploitative relationship with other social groups and fails to expose the economic grounds for its claims to superiority (Faulkner 1986: 32–3). This is a convincing reading, given Anne-Marie's smiling compliance with her exploitation, but the film has more to it. Although class is central to it, it is more broadly about modern society's disciplining of the body and repression of instinctual drives and about the multiple mediations (literature, manners, conventions, class values) that prevent direct encounters with the radically other or indeed the other in the self. The spilling out of the sights and sounds of the city into the pastoral spaces of the park and the riverbank suggests that civilisation's mediations and repressions are on the offensive.

The three comedies considered all focus on the clash between disruptive individuals and the bourgeois order. Similarities do not end there. *Boudu sauvé des eaux* and *Chotard et cie* both suggest that a community of interest may exist between the cultured bourgeoisie and other elements of the same class despite their surface disagreements. *Boudu* and *On purge bébé* both focus on the conventionality of the bourgeoisie and its disciplining of the body. Rather than rooting these similarities in Renoir's vision, it seems more sensible to link them to their shared origins in boulevard theatre. All substantially draw on bourgeois stage comedies that represent that class to itself, exploring its internal divisions, liberating it temporarily from its repressions and demonstrating its *largesse d'esprit* by its capacity to laugh at itself. If there is an exception, it is *Boudu* which at times suggests an ability to engage with the contemporary notably lacking in the others. But that is when it moves away from its theatrical source.

Deluded individuals in a corrupt world

La Chienne (1931) is a far cry from the studio-bound, dialogue-dominated theatricality of *On Purge bébé*, its immediate predecessor. Adapted by Renoir and André Girard from the 1930 hit novel of the same title, it took the camera on to the streets of Montmartre for the exterior scenes and relied on direct sound. It brought Renoir together for the second time with the great actor Michel Simon who gives a towering performance as the put-upon, no longer young but still gullible cashier, Maurice Legrand.

We are led into the story through the frame of a little theatre in which puppets claim the story as social drama and then moral comedy before *Guignol* (Punch) says it is neither drama nor comedy and teaches us nothing. He then introduces the three lead characters (him, her and the other man) of what will clearly be a tale of infidelity. We next see a group of men celebrating their boss's decoration in a Montmartre restaurant, as the camera tracks slowly down the table to catch Legrand at its end thus emphasising his exclusion from the jovial crowd. Whispering indicates that a plan is being hatched to prolong the evening (presumably in a brothel), in a way that will afford them great amusement at his expense. But his wife has told him to be home early, a fact that further isolates him, and he leaves alone while, in the background, a gramophone ironically plays a love song. The next sequence places us in a little square. A drunken man (Dédé), located by his slang among the common people of Paris, beats a woman (Lulu) who cannot or will not get him the money he needs from an older man. They are clearly pimp and prostitute, but Legrand, who stumbles on them, and intervenes gallantly to rescue the woman, does not realise this. On arriving home, he stumbles into his apartment and awakens Adèle, his shrewish wife, by falling over an easel. Painting is his only distraction, but she threatens to throw his paintings out before evoking her first husband, Alexis, a 'hero' killed in the war for layabouts like him. He is next briefly seen in his cashier's cage at work before the scene shifts to Lulu's new apartment where she is showing off her new possessions to a friend. She has become his mistress and clearly profited from it.

The deliberately predictable, indeed clichéd drama can now unfold. Dédé extracts money from Lulu who in turn extracts it from Legrand who steals from his wife and later from his workplace. Naïvely, he suspects nothing and even leaves his paintings with Lulu. Dédé sells them, passing them off as the work of an American woman artist, Clara Wood. Lulu poses as Clara, achieving an instant celebrity status that does not prevent Dédé prostituting her to a man who wants his portrait painted. The dead hero returns and demands money to stay dead. He has borrowed another man's name to escape, not from the war, but from his wife.

Legrand briefly seems in command, the puppet turned puppeteer. Luring Alexis into his home, he creates a scene in front of the neighbours and shatters Adèle's reputation by announcing that he has been surprised in her bed by her husband. His exultation vanishes when he surprises Lulu in bed with Dédé. He returns the next day ready to rescue her from Dédé's brutish clutches, but she laughs in his face, and he stabs her to death before leaving unseen. Arriving ostentatiously in a new car, Dédé is seen by everybody, arrested and, due to his lower-class status and dubious past, found guilty and executed. A coda shows Legrand and Alexis, now both tramps, competing for a tip from a rich motorist. They do not notice Legrand's self-portrait as it is packed into the back of the car and speeds away.

The story is a quintessentially urban one of deception, exploitation and social class. It is set in motion by one character's failure to read the urban signs. Lulu and Dédé (and even their names give them away), are instantly recognisable urban types, walking clichés, preening pimp and subservient whore. Yet Legrand insists on inserting Lulu into a narrative of romance and chivalry manifestly unsuited to the fallen urban order. Humiliated at work and at home, he seeks love and recognition from a relationship founded on lies and venality. With inevitable consequences. In a story where the audience's superior knowledge is constantly productive of irony, his blindness is repeatedly hammered home, most notably around the time of the murder. His self-satisfied assembly of the *ménage à trois* scene when he humiliates his wife is an unwitting rehearsal for his own discovery of Dédé in Lulu's bed. And, irony of ironies, as he tramps back in the dark and the rain from Lulu's flat, he is taken across the self-same square where he first met her and Dédé and so disastrously misread the situation. Finally, even as he kills her, street singers tell of troubadours and romantic love, a reminder of the terrible inappropriateness of the story he has tried to tell himself.

A further irony is how Lulu's relationship with Dédé echoes that which Legrand has with her without it bringing them any closer together. Each overreaching their status, he seeks to keep a mistress in the style of a *grand bourgeois*, surrounding her with his artistic creations, while she creates a cosy, *petit bourgeois* interior with all mod cons for herself and Dédé. He loves romantically, she sentimentally, both blindly, failing to see that their beloved merely exploits them. Each request for affection is answered by a request for money.

Money intervenes in all the relationships, turning interactions to transactions and people into mere instruments of other people. The fate of Maurice's paintings illustrates this perfectly. Initially, the only self-expression he was allowed, they are turned into a commodity by Dédé and thereafter cease to belong to their creator. The substitution of the name Clara Bow for his merely emphasises the alienation of the artist from his work. This alienation is complete when Legrand fails to recognise his own self-portrait. Again, ironically, there is a clear parallel between Lulu and Legrand, as she too is turned into a commodity by Dédé. Her alienation is complete when she plays the part of Clara, a character invented and promoted by others for their own ends. When the wealthy man settles for sex with her instead of a portrait, it merely indicates the ultimate blurring of one commodity into another in a world governed by money. Possession of her body or Legrand's art allows the wealthy to affirm their own identity even as that of others is erased through commodification.

Legrand struggles from the start to create a positive image for himself, only to find that society in each cases projects a negative one on to him. This first happens at the celebratory dinner when he is cast as the butt of the joke, the unmanly man who instead of using women is dominated by his wife. On his return home, he finds that he is merely the negative of his wife's 'heroic' first husband whose portrait has pride of place even though there is no room for him to hang his paintings and thus inscribe his identity upon his surroundings. His relationship with Lulu at last seems to offer him a positive self-image as reflected in the eyes of a loving woman and a home where his paintings hang. But here his erasure is even more complete. The paintings disappear and, worse still, Lulu imagines Dédé even as she makes love to Legrand. When at last the truth is out, she invites him to look at himself in a mirror, implicitly suggesting that he see himself through her eyes, thus effacing his own self-image with an externally generated one. It is little wonder he does not recognise his self-portrait at the end. It is a picture of an artist, a positive identity that society will not let him have. A film that began with the celebration of the public recognition of Legrand's wealthy bourgeois boss ends with the humble cashier's effacement from the urban order. Tramps are non-individuals with no status.

The drama is clearly one of class from start to finish, yet class alone cannot explain it. Legrand's lowly, caged status at work means that he must seek his satisfactions in a private domain where gender intervenes. While the other men can affirm a positive identity, whatever their status, by their shared exploitation or domination of women, Legrand is dominated by his wife and manipulated and exploited by Lulu. Instead of compensating for his lowly status, his relationships with women exacerbate it. But, as they come to concentrate and embody his more general alienation, he can avenge himself on society by his treatment of them, his character assassination of his wife neatly paving the way for his murder of Lulu. The film's concentration of humiliation and vengeance around the figures of women gives it a powerful misogynist charge (Burch and Sellier 1996: 36).

Lulu is a key urban figure. As a prostitute, she embodies the debased social relationships in the city, encapsulating both the commodification of the self and, through her chameleon-like changes of role, the deceptiveness of the urban landscape. Legrand's absurd idealism is a perfect foil to her corruption. The collision that they enact between artistic sensibility and a fallen world is a deeply and deliberately clichéd one which relies on predictability for its comic effects. The film invites us to view urban corruption through blasé, cynical eyes.

Madame Bovary (1934), an adaptation of Flaubert's dauntingly celebrated novel, plunges us back into the mid-nineteenth century, its action being set at the time of the bourgeois monarchy of Louis-Philippe. Yet Emma Bovary is a prototypical modern heroine, a victim of the objects and narratives that she consumes, and a woman who struggles against bourgeois domestic confinement. As in *La Nuit du Carrefour* (below), Paris is a key off-screen space, a site of danger and debauchery but also freedom and fashion, a longed-for centre that constitutes Emma's provincial town as a peripheral backwater. Rouen serves as an intermediate space, a substitute for the capital that the heroine never reaches.

A farmer's daughter, Emma has attended a convent where she has imbibed much poetry and learned a preference for romantic dream over solid rustic realities. She mistakenly sees Charles Bovary, a prosaic local doctor, as her passport to a more noble existence. Realising his true nature, she seeks romantic love with two men, Rodolphe, a local landowner, and Léon, a notary's clerk. Fleeing real commitment, Rodolphe abandons her. Léon reappears and the pair act out an affair in a hired apartment in Rouen. But Emma's extravagance has caught up with her. Faced with the humiliation of a public sale of her property, she desperately seeks to raise money only to find that neither the wealthy Rodolphe nor Léon is willing to make sacrifices for her. She kills herself.

Her refusal of the confines of her existence is evident from the first sequence. The camera tracks forward into a pastoral scene of fruit trees and farm animals as sunny music is heard but Emma is inside the farmhouse and has turned her back on the simple scene outside. She prefers to contemplate engravings of Mary Queen of Scots, in whose time life was seemingly less narrow, sentiments nobler and men more chivalrous. She tries to drag Charles into her fantasy world by attaching romantic connotations to his horse-riding but he prosaically points out that a horse is ideal for bad roads. The sympathetic Charles is a stolid, hesitant and unambitious character, one manifestly unable to fulfil her expectations.

Emma's pretensions inevitably collide with the prosaic pragmatism of other simpler characters. She wishes to marry by candlelight at midnight. Her father wants to kill some pigs and invite all the neighbours to a feast. When she goes to the priest in search of spiritual succour, he suggests she may be suffering from the heat, advises she drink some tea and suggests that if one is well fed and warm enough, one has little to complain about.

Emma's lovers seem more likely to fulfil her desire for a heightened existence. Rodolphe scorns the mediocrity of everyday life and pronounces himself above convention. When he takes her riding in the woods, he seems to have taken her from the mundane, enclosed life of the village to an open and natural space. But the ride through the woods is itself a cliché. Léon seems to exist on a similarly elevated plane, talking of his desire to devote himself to some 'noble' career and suggesting that he is a slave to Emma. But this apparently heightened emotion is hollow, a performance of a pre-existing romantic script. Léon reveals this inadvertently when he tells Emma that the opera they have just seen can speak for him. Melodramatic theatricality mediates between character and feeling. When the chips are down, when Emma needs money quickly, Rodolphe and Léon show their true colours. Financial self-interest reveals romantic rhetoric to be a hollow sham.

Bourgeois self-interest is at its most transparently visible in the shape of Charles's mother. She selected her son's first wife for her fortune, only to find that (in her brutal terms), the harness was worth more than the horse. People are reduced to what they are worth. Lheureux, the shopkeeper, has similarly mercantile motives. He seduces Mme Bovary with the fashionable clothes that are a route to social mobility in this age of nascent consumerism, only to reveal his true motives when he calls in her debt. At this stage, he suggests that beautiful women can always achieve salvation through men, his thinly disguised invitation to prostitution revealing that Mme Bovary herself risks becoming a commodity.

Ultimately, the character is hemmed in between the brute materialism of some, the acquisitiveness of others and the hollow romanticism of those who appear to offer a way out. The film's *mise-en-scène* makes her suffocation tangible. Time and again interior shots use a frame within the frame, usually a doorway, to suggest the restricted framework of the characters' lives, the narrowness and claustrophobia of their little bourgeois world.

When Emma has first made love to Rodolphe, the next shot pins her back into the narrow space of her room, framing her within less than a third of available screen space. Charles appears and blocks the narrow doorway, clearly suggesting that he now traps her and shuts out her light. Even at the moment of one of her greatest triumphs when a local lord invites her and Charles to a ball and she is swept up in the movement and elegance of the waltz, a series of heavy pillars cut across and contain the movement. There is no escape from the social frame.

The use of frames also reinforces the theatricality of the overblown acting style of Emma, Rodolphe and Léon. Their inflated dialogues, drawn substantially from Flaubert's text, undermine Emma's most dramatic moments. When Léon makes his initial declaration of love in the opera house at Rouen, the scene is shot in a curtained box that becomes a reflection of the stage. Later, when a despairing Emma castigates a mean-spirited Rodolphe, curtains on both sides of the scene combine with her melodramatic gesture to suggest performance rather than authentic feeling. Clothes, objects and spaces are sucked into the bourgeoisie's *mise-en-scène* of elegance, sensibility and social superiority. Emma's mistake is to fail to recognise that this décor only comes at a cost and that if bills aren't paid, it can be taken away.

Interior frames constrict but they also link. Shots through doors and windows repeatedly attach individuals and small groups to a broader setting, reminding us that actions always take place in a social context. Servants, a gardener, rural labourers and even a blind beggar suggest a broader world beyond the claustrophobic little bourgeois clan that occupies centre stage, but the film's focus throughout is on that class and not on the labour of those who make its privileged lifestyle possible. Like *Boudu sauvé des eaux*, it is an assault on the bourgeoisie's pretensions and self-interestedness rather than a broader analysis of exploitation or oppression.

Yet despite this, it would not take much to see Emma as a proto-feminist heroine and a victim of the narrow domestic confinement that the bourgeoisie imposed on its women. She struggles fiercely to broaden the frame of her life and the range of her actions, only to be let down by the lack of commitment of her lovers. Faced with woman's status as a financial minor, she revolts and takes command of her husband's affairs. Having been Rodolphe's pupil, she takes control of her affair with Léon, the cigarette smoked by Rodolphe in the first love scene symbolically passing to her in the second with the younger man. Although at times she faints and languishes in stereotypical fashion, there is also a great vigour to her as she rushes to her lover's house or castigates the men who have let her down. Ultimately, however, her revolt is contained and turned against her. She is destructive, neglects her daughter and fails to respond to her husband's simple kindness. Most of all, she is inauthentic. Her revolt is born of romantic cliché and bourgeois snobbery. It is thus impossible to sympathise with her predicament.

If the film has a moral, it is that one should accept one's lot. One key episode pushes us to this interpretation. Homais the pharmacist pushes Charles to operate on Hippolyte, a man with a clubfoot. Hippolyte is happy with his current state, feeling that the deformed leg is stronger than the other, but the operation goes ahead, and the leg goes septic and is amputated. Taught, in the name of progress, to want something better, Hippolyte ends with something worse. Similarly, a hierarchical society and romantic literature combine to teach Emma to turn her back on the concrete satisfactions of what she has and to see her husband's simplicity as coarseness. The film's critique of the bourgeoisie would seem, if anything, to be driven by nostalgia for a lost simplicity, but there is so little that is positive in it that it is far easier to be clear about what it is attacking: a class and its pretensions.

La Chienne and *Madame Bovary* converge on several points. Both invite a knowing audience to contemplate the tragi-comic spectacle of an individual who misapplies second-hand chivalrous and romantic values to a fallen world, unmasking its corruption and their own delusions in the process. This similarity is unsurprising as both are based on realist novels, works which typically focus on the power of money and class and ground their realism at least partly in distanciation from more romantic or heroic literary forms. There are, however, key differences between the two texts. *Madame Bovary* focuses mercilessly on the provincial bourgeoisie and petty nobility while *La Chienne* latches onto the mercenary values of the urban order. Moreover, while *La Chienne* casts its male lead in the role of artist, Emma Bovary, as a woman, only has access to the role of cultural consumer. A closer parallel to her might indeed be Lulu whose blind love for Dédé and attempts to create a cosy but utterly conventional interior for them to share has clear echoes of her celebrated predecessor.

Modernity and tradition

Renoir's film *La Nuit du Carrefour* (1932) provided the first cinematic appearance of Simenon's celebrated fictional detective, Maigret. It shows a distinctly modern vision of France where motor transport and the telephone have created a rootless and opaque world that sits uneasily alongside the traces of a more traditional society. The film's prime location is a crossroads about 30 kilometres from Paris. Around it are three buildings: a garage, the house of a travelling insurance agent, and that of a Danish 'brother and sister'. Following the discovery of the body of another foreigner, a Dutch jewel dealer called Goldberg, Maigret is called in. Suspicion initially falls on the upper-class Dane, Carl Andersen, but is then implicitly broadened as Maigret observes the characters at the crossroads. His investigations are interrupted when the murdered man's wife arrives and is shot in turn. None the less he pieces the mystery together, discovering that the garage is a front for a fencing operation, that the insurance agent uses his travels to move stolen property around, and that Andersen's 'sister' Else is his mistress and her first husband, Guido, the murderer. Maigret's unhurried movements and slow dismantling of subterfuge places a reassuring stillness at the very heart of the film's rootless movement.

The film is notable for its creation of what Sesonske calls 'an atmosphere of the bizarre, the unpredictable' around the crossroads (Sesonske 1980: 105). The Danes' house is characterised by a jumble of objects and a shadowy and uneasy mix of respectability, decay and sleaziness presided over by Else's combination of girlish innocence and calculating seductiveness. Misty, night-time sequences punctuated by car lights and half-glimpsed actions add to the mystery which is deepened rather than lessened by the contrasting clarity of the daytime sequences and the apparently transparent ordinariness of the garage where brightly lit spaces and characteristic in-depth composition suggest that there is nothing to hide. The film creates its atmosphere without any recourse to extra-diegetic music. What music it has comes in the form of a languorous dance tune which both Else and the garage owner mendaciously link to an innocent past and which contrasts sharply with the mechanical noises coming from the road and the workshop.

One fundamental contrast, that between the modern and the traditional, underlies all the others. It is announced in the opening shots of a telephone-cable-lined road cutting through a field where heavy horses pull a plough. The staccato noise of a motorbike shatters the rural calm. Later, more horses are seen plodding slowly down the road. Nearby, there is a village we never see. The village, the horses and the plough all belong to a traditional rural France of local spaces, slow rhythms and predictable activities. The road, the cars and the telephone usher in a world of fleeting contacts, rapid movement and uprooted people. The crossroads itself is a non-place, by definition a space of flux. All the major characters in the film circulate in an anonymous national and international space. As a result, the police cannot initially pin down the exact nature of who they are dealing with. Identities may be invented rather than real, while material objects may lose their solidity to become a theatrical backdrop to the characters' performances.

The performances are dishonest ones, meant to deflect attention. The garage owner and the insurance agent, Michonnet, enact class-marked variants of indigenous respectability even as they shift the blame to the foreign 'intruders'. Michonnet puts on a show of self-righteous middle-class indignation at events around him while the garage owner performs a sentimentalised Parisian Frenchness. Admitting childhood peccadilloes, he vaunts his status as self-made *petit patron*, offers Maigret an aperitif, plays an accordion, goes to dine in Paris with his companions and talks nostalgically of his youth. This deceptive enactment of a stereo-typical popular identity functions to ground identity in a world of flux and to exclude cosmopolitan elements that the same flux has brought.

The film's unmasking of the sort of xenophobia that was so prevalent in the 1930s might suggest that it has a progressive political edge, but, just to prove that its heart is not necessarily in the right place, it turns the foreign jewel dealer, with the Jewish-sounding name, into a thief and centres the enigma on the foreign woman. By seeing the prostitute from Hamburg beneath her veneer of respectability, by linking her sexually to the men in the drama, and by resisting her seductiveness, Maigret gets to the heart of the mystery. His reading of female appearances and dis-placed urban signs contrasts with Maurice Legrand's disastrous misreading in *La Chienne*.

The contrast between the crossroads and the tranquillity of the rural might have been used to generate nostalgia for a vanishing past, but the film refrains from moving in this direction. It is interesting above all for its atmospheric capturing of a double-edged modernity. The modern brings with it a rootless, elusive world but it also provides the tools (the car, the telephone, the telegraph) that help the hero to tame that world. The final chase sequence emphasises its poetic qualities, when a camera mounted in a sports car picks up a stunning, sinuous interplay of car lights and half-seen shadowy objects as it plunges us down the curving road.

Toni (1934) is Renoir's last film from the period in question. Faulkner usefully draws our attention to its novelty. Entirely location shot using direct sound, it has no literary source unlike its predecessors. More importantly, it is overtly of its time and broadens the social scope of Renoir's output. Whereas the earlier films had essentially represented the middle classes to themselves, this one centres immigrant workers (Faulkner, 1986: 43–50). Placing his focus on class conflict, Faulkner pays inadequate attention to ethnicity in a film that is a radical intervention in bitter 1930s struggles to define nation. A decade marked by rampant xenophobia saw parties of left and right converge on essentialised accounts of Frenchness (see Lebovics 1992).

The film begins with the arrival of Toni, the hero, in the southeast of France alongside other Italian immigrants. He finds work in a local quarry, and accommodation and love with Marie, a Frenchwoman who lets out rooms. With the arrival of Josefa, a young Spanish woman, his affection shifts. Marriage to her promises sensual pleasure and access to her uncle Sebastian's vineyard. But Albert, the quarry foreman, takes a more direct route to her favours, riding roughshod over her protests. Two years later, he is tired of Josefa who by now has a young child. The dying Sebastian makes Toni promise to watch over his niece. Unable to force Toni to commit himself to her alone, Marie attempts suicide only to be pulled from the water before she can drown. Beaten by Albert, Josefa takes his gun and shoots him. Toni steps in to remove Albert's body and fake a suicide but is detected and takes flight. Josefa confesses to save him, but Dominique, a local landowner shoots him as he flees. The film closes as another group of Italians arrive.

Based on an authentic *fait divers* communicated to Renoir by a policeman friend, the story is given tragic form and thus conforms to certain recognisable conventions. The *fait divers* conventionally disrupts the fabric of the ordinary and, true to type, *Toni* is embedded in the daily life of a small semi-rural community. It shows characters who prepare meals, hang out the washing and go about their work even as key events occur. This everydayness exists in tension with the powerful structuring force of tragedy. Events are announced in advance, not least at the level of the recurrent metaphors that structure the film. Animals are frequently evoked. Domestic animals (for which read daughters) are likely to be stolen, even while their impotent owners (for which read fathers) patrol with guns. Animals become flesh to satisfy hungers. Wild animals (suggestive of untrammelled instinct) excite desire and fight to hold on to their mate. Primitive desire and violence thus subtend the everyday and suggest the inevitability of transgression and retribution. The undertaker is an ominous guest at the film's double wedding of Marie and Toni, Alberta and Josefa. Successive shots take the couples out of the festivities and surround them with deathly black.

The film's form is circular, giving a sense of inevitable repetition. Toni dies on the bridge he crossed when he arrived even as other immigrants arrive for the cycle to recommence. Singing groups of men (performing mainly in Italian or Corsican) recreate the chorus of classical tragedy – on the edges of the action, and witness to a drama that could have touched them too. Their songs of cuckolded husbands, emigration and the stirrings of nature link events to a pattern of recurrence. Ironically they also sing of romantic love.

The film's tragedy, as Faulkner points out, is generated by a specific social context (Faulkner 1986: 52). It is rooted in the clash of two value systems, one patriarchal and traditional, the other individualist, cynical and modern, both exploitative and attached to property. The former is associated with two immigrant farmers: Sebastian, a rather pathetic figure, and Dominique, a ridiculous one. The latter is embodied by the selfish Parisian, Albert, a man associated with the industrialised world of the quarry. Toni's tragedy comes from his blind commitment to a patriarchal order that has lost control in a new environment. While he consults the patriarch, Albert deflowers the niece and mocks the innocence of his rustic rival. But Albert and Toni both seek to acquire property through Josefa, even if the former is purely selfish in his attitude while the latter respects the codes of honour that accompany patriarchal possession.

The film's apparent circularity is undermined by the rooting of its tragedy in an inherently unstable collision between rural tradition and urban industrial modernity. It is further challenged by reference to a specific historical conjuncture. Early in the film, characters discuss the enormous industrial progress made in the region, a phenomenon which spills over into a push to rural mechanisation driven by Albert, the agent of modernity. But Albert overstretches and runs up debts. This evocation of a rapid modernisation that turns sour seems a clear if underdeveloped reference to the broader situation of a France where rapid 1920s growth gave way to prolonged slump in the 1930s. The film seems torn between a desire to be of its time and an aesthetic aspiration towards the timelessness of tragedy.

History is further inscribed within it by its treatment of immigration and xenophobia. Its engagement with these themes is complex and contradictory. It opens by situating itself in the Latin south of France where nature destroys the 'spirit of Babel' and 'fuses' different races. A traditionally conservative reference to the way the land shapes national character is here mobilised to more progressive ends to suggest that variety can be assimilated. Mention of Latinicity complicates things by suggesting that the capacity of Italians, Spaniards and French to merge together may be rooted in a shared cultural heritage. Toni's ability to establish an understanding with Sebastian through mutual commitment to the land and to the codes of patriarchy endorses both models of integration. Yet Toni fails to integrate, as his loss of Josefa and his death most eloquently testify, and, anyway, the world he joins is crumbling. The film overflows its own overt discourse on immigration.

It overflows it in more than one way. First, negatively. Toni resembles the stereotype of the quick-tempered, honour-obsessed Latin. Moreover, the film's use of a *fait divers* could be seen to be coming perilously close to the way popular-press reports linking immigrants to crime fed into racist discourse and indeed made it more effective by giving it a concrete, lived dimension (see Noiriel 1988: 278–81). However, its refusal of xenophobia and essentialist nationalism ultimately overwrites its negative aspects. Its first sequence shows a discussion between two characters who complain of outsiders stealing their jobs. Despite their broad southern-French accents, both turn out to be recent immigrants who came in search of work. One says that his country is the one that feeds him. Thus, immigration is grounded in necessity, nationality acquired and loyalty to a country material and contingent. The discourse of racism is adopted only to be radically undermined from within. Moreover, and even more remarkably, the film constitutes Albert, the Parisian, as the disruptive outsider, the man whose disrespect for the rural order sets the tragedy in motion and whose violence and acquisitiveness pushes it towards a conclusion. A man, moreover, who is not suited to the land, even to the point of spurning its products. He complains bitterly when Josefa serves him a ratatouille made from products of their own garden and one which Mediterraneans can share. He wants the northern *Châteaubriant aux pommes*. Transnational regionalism is stronger than national affiliation.

But this broader regional unity is itself overwritten by a solidarity born of shared labour which spreads beyond Latinicity and Frenchness to include those of non-European origin. The most durable relationships are those that bind Toni, Fernand and a black worker at the quarry. When Dominique suggests Toni has tried to drown Marie, the black worker springs to his defence and consoles him. Fernand stays profoundly loyal throughout. Albert is also excluded from the workers' solidarity, but this time because of his role as foreman and not because of his northern, urban roots. Community and exclusion are shown to be complex multi-layered and contextual. Buchsbaum, whose analysis to a degree parallels my own, writes that the film, 'proffers a vision of *community* with no national identity *per se* ... the community of *Toni* not only repudiates any myth of an essentialist True France, but also resists any assertion of the world in the film as belonging to a national entity' (1996: 34).

While I would substantially endorse this reading, I would suggest that it is insufficiently aware of the film's failure to recognise its own complexity, as most obviously evidenced by the contradiction between an overt discourse of shared Latinicity and an implicit message of transnational workers' solidarity.

The complex and contradictory treatment of gender parallels that of nation. The women are made subhuman by the film's dominant metaphor of animality which figures them as disruptively and primitively instinctual or as domestic animals to be guarded or consumed. Patriarchy excludes them from decision-taking, treating them as labour and property, but no better alternative seems available. Josefa must labour at Sebastian's behest. When he marries her off to save face, she is not consulted. She protests at the mercantile nature of the transaction but Gabi cynically tells her that she is part of the livestock. Marriage to the moderniser Albert leads to no greater liberty. The exploitation of her physical labour continues unabated and she is completely marginalised when her husband and Gabi argue over Sebastian's legacy. However, faced with physical violence, she fights back and shoots her husband. Initially an unconscious agent of disorder, she becomes a lucid victim and one who in the end rebels and has the courage to admit to her crime when another is accused. Marie is her own mistress from the start. Owning her house, she takes in whom she chooses. Driven to despair by Toni, it is she who makes the decisive break, a break that does not prevent her sending him food. Jealously possessive, she is also generous, tolerant and independent, and indeed one of the most positive female characters in all of Renoir.

Whereas the destructiveness of Emma Bovary and of Lulu (in *La Chienne*) had overwritten their social subordination or exploitation, making them apparently deserving victims of themselves or others, in *Toni* the reverse occurs. We are allowed to sympathise with female characters who become aware of their oppression and ultimately revolt against it.

Toni would seem to mark a decisive turning point in Renoir's cinema. It moves workers and immigrants to centre stage, challenges xenophobia and essentialist constructions of nation, reveals women's subordination, and engages directly with the contemporary. It can clearly be seen as a decisive move towards political commitment, one that lays the ground for the progressive cinema of the Popular Front period. But this is at best a simplification. As we have suggested, it overflows its own overt discourse on key issues, mixing the regressive with the progressive and lacking a language to express the latter overtly. And even if the workers' solidarity here can be seen as a prelude to their assertive intervention in the later films, *Toni* can easily be seen as more progressive in its representations of gender and nation than some of the Frontist films that fall back on essentialism and stereotype.

Conclusion

There is no easy way to pull together Renoir's first ten years of film-making into some neat conclusion, but some key patterns and turning points can certainly be noted. The originality of the silent films must generally be sought in how they are filmed and not in their explicit content, which is largely conventional melodrama. Sound moves Renoir away from melodrama and into adaptation of boulevard comedies and novels which give his cinema a social dimension it had lacked. One could suggest that its critique of modern society in general and the bourgeoisie in particular is evidence of a clear and consistent authorial stance that is a clear advance on their conventional, silent predecessors. It would be more realistic to see this consistency as a product of bourgeois culture's longstanding critique of the bourgeoisie and its values. The film's heavy reliance on their sources is clear evidence of their rootedness in a tradition. The same sources also demonstrate how supposedly Renoirian themes merge inextricably into broader cultural patterns. The collision between the Dionysian and the Apollonian, an oft-cited authorial theme, feeds off the traditional comic collision between disruptive forces and constraining conventions while the unmasking of the bourgeoisie's theatre of respectability and self-deception is a recurrent theme of the modern novel.

A further indication of the films' substantial dependence on their sources is their general failure to engage with the contemporary world. The late 1920s and early 1930s saw profound changes and momentous events. Fast growth, rapid modernisation and substantial immigration were brought to a halt by the arrival of economic crisis, stagnation and rising xenophobia. It is remarkable how little this turmoil breaks into the sound films' re-enactment of familiar quarrels or the clichéd predictability of silent melodrama. When it does break through it is in an uneven way. *Charleston* brilliantly suggests the deep cultural anxiety beneath 1920s hedonism. *Boudu* at times overflows its stage-bound origins to show the spread of the urban order. *La Nuit du carrefour* engages more consistently with the contemporary by staging the poetry and the threat of the increasingly rootless modern. It is not until *Toni*, however, that Renoir's cinema combines contemporary relevance with a political edge. Its ambivalent mix of progressive anti-essentialism and stereotype, its hesitation between historical openness and tragic closure suggests a film-maker struggling to find a voice, a voice that no sooner had it emerged would merge into a Popular Front choir.

References

Boston, R. (1994), *Boudu Saved from Drowning*, London, BFI.

Buchsbaum, J. (1996), '"My nationality is cinematography"': Renoir and the National Question', *Persistence of Vision*, 12/13, 29–48.

Burch, N. and Sellier, G. (1996), *La drôle de guerre des sexes du cinéma français (1930–1956)*, Paris, Nathan.

Durgnat, R. (1974), *Jean Renoir*, Berkeley, University of California.

Faulkner, C. (1986), *The Social Cinema of Jean Renoir*, Princeton, Princeton University Press.

Lebovics, H. (1992), *True France. The Wars over Cultural Identity, 1900–1945*, Ithaca, Cornell University Press.

Noiriel, G. (1988), *Le Creuset français. Histoire de l'immigration, XIXᵉ–XXᵉ siècles*, Paris, Seuil.

Roberts, M. L. (1994) *Civilization without Sexes. Reconstructing Gender in Post-war France, 1917–1927*, Chicago, University of Chicago.

Serceau, D. (1981), *Jean Renoir, l'insurgé*, Paris, Le Sycomore.

Sesonske, A. (1980), *Jean Renoir. The French Films, 1924–1939*, Cambridge, MA, Harvard University Press.

Viry-Babel, R. (1994), *Jean Renoir. Le jeu et la règle*, Paris, Denoël.

1 *La Chienne*, 1931. Note the typical composition in depth that brings together contrasting spaces and moods. In the foreground, Maurice Legrand tries to insert a positive image of self into a hostile space. His wife's first husband looks mockingly down in soldier's uniform while she controls the household finances

2 *Boudu sauvé des eaux*, 1932. Boudu's indisciplined body challenges and reveals the disciplining frame of bourgeois domesticity

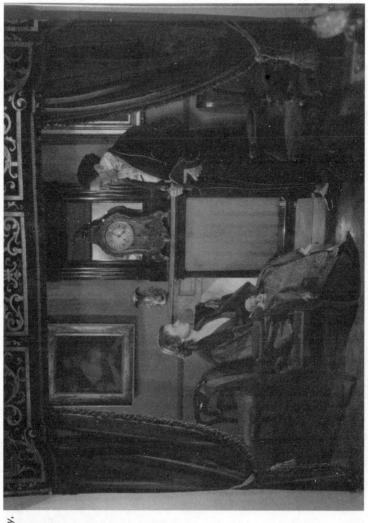

3 *Madame Bovary,* 1933. Even at the height of her despair, Madame Bovary's drama is still contained by the theatrical falseness of bourgeois convention (note the framing curtains)

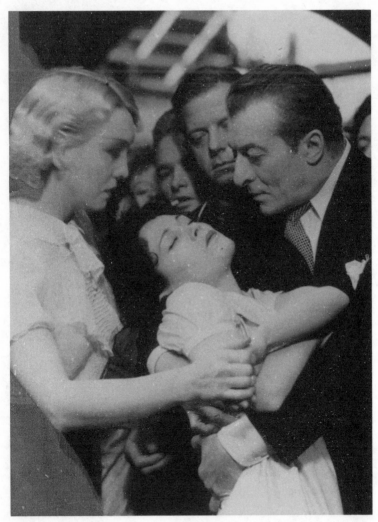

4 *Le Crime de Monsieur Lange*, 1935. The film engages with popular culture while challenging its limitations. The melodramatic foreground is complicated by the emergent workers' solidarity of the background. Two different types of story compete for narrative space

5 *La Grande Illusion*, 1937. Elusive community: the love of good food seems to draw the French together. Differences of class push them apart. Note the stiff formality of de Boieldieu on the far right

6 *La Bête humaine*, 1938. Renoir meets poetic realism. The lonely and marginal rail-way yard locale and the shadows emphasise the social isolation and hopelessness of the lovers

7 *La Règle du jeu*, 1939. A judgement on a society: the frivolity of game-playing collides with the murderous intent of the jealous husband. Note the typical complexity of the image, its bringing together of different groups, its composition in depth

8 *The River*, 1950. An image symptomatic of Renoir's failure to engage with contemporary Indian society. The Indian characters all play supporting and stereotypical roles: the servant, the exotic snake-charmer, the anonymous crowd

9 *Eléna et les hommes*, 1956. The surface lightness of farce is given a sinister undercurrent by the weapons that line the room

4

The Popular Front years

Sometime between the completion of *Toni* and *Le Crime de Monsieur Lange* (1935), Renoir made a decisive move towards the political left, a move which took him, like many intellectuals of the period, towards the French Communist Party (PCF). Although his commitment unravelled as the Front itself disintegrated, his films from this period can only be understood in the context of its struggles, contradictions and evolution.

The Popular Front

The Front responded specifically to the extreme-right-wing demonstrations in Paris on 6 February 1934 that had been seen as an attempt to overthrow the Republic. It was, more generally, a reaction to the rise of European Fascism, which was enough of a threat to force the fragmented French left to put its differences temporarily aside. Impetus for unity came from below as well as from above, from rank and file as well as party and union leaders. However, a key change was a shift in policy by the PCF. Abandoning its virulent critique of the socialist party (SFIO), and forsaking its policy of 'classe contre classe,' the Party reached out its hand to French Catholics, peasants and shopkeepers in an attempt to build an inclusive social base for a broad coalition against Fascism. Overcoming their misgivings, the other parties of the left hesitantly came together with the Communists to establish a common programme (signed in January 1936), that was reformist rather than radical, defensive rather than revolutionary, and which papered over some of the inevitable ideological differences that existed between the different parties. Despite the underlying fragility of the alliance, the Front triumphed in the elections of 1936.

Between the two rounds of the election, and in anticipation of victory, French workers launched a massive strike wave accompanied by factory occupations which, in the eyes of some commentators, constituted a pre-revolutionary situation that the political leadership failed to exploit or actively worked to defuse. When the Front assumed power under the leadership of the socialist Léon Blum, negotiations between government, unions and employers brought dramatic concessions to the left and, in the heady weeks that followed, the forty-hour week and paid holidays were introduced, extra-parliamentary right-wing leagues were banned and the Bank of France (previously dominated by the major shareholders of the notorious *deux cent familles*) democratised. Membership of the reunited CGT (the trade union confederation) soared, while that of the parties of the left, particularly the PCF, climbed sharply.

These heady days of collective strength and political triumph were not to last. The Front was soon divided by internal and external difficulties. The outbreak of the Spanish Civil War in July 1936 set the Communists, who favoured intervention, against the Socialists who reluctantly blocked it. A massive flight of capital and mounting budgetary deficits set the Front an immediate challenge. Was it to press on with a radical programme, taking on the challenge from capital, or was it to retreat and thus seek to accommodate those who opposed it? Against strong PCF opposition, Blum chose the latter path, announcing a pause in the Front's programme in February 1937. Denied special powers with which to face the economic crisis by the right-wing Senate, he resigned in June 1937, although the Socialists still participated in the new Radical-led government till January 1938, even returning to lead another short-lived Blum government in March 1938. However, by now, the original coalition was irremediably split.

The Radicals assumed power under Daladier in April, moved sharply to the right, and set out to reverse the gains of 1936, enthusiastically abetted by the employers. An abortive national strike at the end of November brought decisive defeat for the workers and provided a sad echo to the festive occupations of the spring of 1936. In the meantime, in September, France had signed the humiliating Munich agreement which abandoned its ally Czechoslovakia to Hitler's territorial demands. Munich was the death-knell of the Front. The Communists opposed it bitterly. The Socialists, torn between anti-fascism and integral pacifism, were split down the middle.

The Front had represented a dramatic about-turn for the PCF which had escaped from its isolation by exchanging revolutionary internationalism for prudent reformism, nationalism and a commitment to national defence. August 1939 saw another bewildering shift as the Party endorsed the notorious Germano-Soviet non-aggression pact. Its embrace of nationalism was now seen as a cynical manoeuvre that had temporarily obscured its subservience to the Moscow line. Renoir and the Party had already parted company by this stage.

It is very tempting to see Renoir's films of this period as a transparent expression of Frontist values, mirroring their ideological contradictions even as they sought to conceal them. It is also tempting to follow the Front's fortunes through the mood of the films: the radical upcurve before and immediately after electoral triumph (*Le Crime de Monsieur Lange, La Vie est à nous* (1936) and *Les Bas-fonds*), a tame downcurve as the Front fragmented and lost all momentum (*La Marseillaise*), post-Frontist despondency as gains were clawed back (*La Bête humaine*) culminating after Munich in an embittered assault on a society unwilling to renew or defend itself (*La Règle du jeu*). Some variant of this pattern lies behind the powerful readings generated by the most prominent left-wing critics of the Renoir of this period – Buchsbaum (1988), Faulkner (1986; 1996) and Fofi (1973) – our guides for much of this chapter. But all three tend to underplay the complexity of the films' engagement with a tormented period. They do not transparently reflect Frontist ideology or a specific conjuncture. They need to be considered as active interventions in a contested and evolving terrain, interventions which pursue ideological struggle in the arena of representation and have to find their own way to politicise cinema while reaching out to a popular audience (see Chapter 2 in this volume). We will consider the films in chronological order, grouping them in pairs that allow patterns to emerge and key similarities and contrasts to be brought out.

The radical upcurve?

Le Crime de Monsieur Lange (1935) was made during the heady early days of the Front. It brought Renoir together with the radical left-wing theatre company, Le Groupe Octobre, and more specifically with Jacques Prévert, the socialist–anarchist poet–playwright. More than one commentator has suggested that the film's blend of anticlericalism, antimilitarism and radical politics should be credited to Prévert and the Groupe rather than the director. Key changes occurred after Prévert became involved. Antimilitarism and anticlericalism were introduced. The focus of the action moved considerably away from the individual to the group and its collective needs while the reformist gesture of profit-sharing was replaced by a workers' cooperative. This undoubted radicalisation should not obscure the fact that the original treatment, which absolved the murder of a corrupt capitalist, was hardly a conservative endorsement of the status quo (Bazin 1989: 154–68).

Prévert is credited with tying all the action into one Paris courtyard which houses not only the printshop where the men work, but a laundry run and staffed by women and the sleeping quarters of some of the protagonists including the hero, Lange. The effect of this change is to intermingle the personal and the political and considerably broaden the thrust of the original treatment. The final film suggests that the replacement of a corrupt capitalist with a workers' cooperative can go hand in hand with the emergence of non-oppressive relations between the sexes and a transformation of the living conditions of ordinary workers.

The film begins when a group of simple (male) workers in an

inn on the Belgian border recognise Lange as a murderer described to them. Valentine, his female companion, emerges from the room where he is asleep and begins to explain his crime. Her voice is quickly replaced by the flashback that will constitute the main body of the film, but not before it has invited the improvised popular jury (and the film audience) to see Lange through her loving eyes.

The main story establishes a set of contrasting individuals and groups. Lange is an adolescent dreamer at heart. The decisiveness of his fictional creation, Arizona Jim, contrasts sharply with the diffidence he demonstrates in his dealings with women. Batala, the printshop owner, is a flamboyant rogue. His theatrical persuasiveness allows him to escape from the consequences of his shady dealings and to seduce those around him, be it Lange, who is persuaded to sign away the rights to his western story, or Estelle, a frail young woman whom he gets pregnant. The printworkers and laundrywomen demonstrate a simple *bonhomie* and spontaneous solidarity that highlights the duplicitous, exploitative individualism of the capitalist. Valentine, a model of self-confident autonomy, shows that exploitative relations are not set in stone by her ability to resist Batala's seduction despite having been his mistress in the past. The courtyard, although a site of oppression, also contains in dispersed form the social forms and attitudes needed to create a Utopia.

Batala's apparent death allows the courtyard to realise this Utopian potential. The workers find self-confident voice and deal as familiar equals with creditors, contemptuously dismissing the notion that the machines should be sold. Living conditions are immediately improved for all those on the yard. An advertising board is removed from Charles's window, flooding his once dark room with light and bringing him back into contact with his beloved Estelle as the space between his room and the laundry is unblocked. The baby that Batala had fathered is stillborn, a piece of news greeted with general amusement, and so a fresh start is possible for the couple. *Arizona Jim* is a smash hit. A celebratory banquet gathers the courtyard's occupants together in egalitarian community.

But the past is not shaken off so easily. At the moment of

triumph, and to focus our attention on precisely what constitutes the fundamental barrier to Utopian social transformation, Batala returns to lay claim to what the cooperative has built, attempting to seduce Valentine for good measure. This threatened return to the social and sexual status quo stings Lange into action. In one of the most celebrated sequences in French cinema, the camera tracks him along the upper floor of the building and down the stairs, leaving him to carry out a 270-degree pan round the courtyard before catching up with him again as he shoots Batala.

Bazin was the first to note that this pan sums up the whole *mise-en-scène* of the film which is organised in circular form round the courtyard. Although he has been accused of formalism, a close reading of his analysis shows that he is quite aware of how the circling camera encapsulates the sense of tight community associated with the yard (Bazin 1989: 40–3). It would be fairer to accuse him of depoliticising a movement whose political significance is fully restored when Faulkner shows how it collectivises the murder by detaching it from the individual and invoking the community for whose benefit it is carried out. Faulkner suggests that its extravagant virtuosity draws attention to the film's signifying practice thus breaking with the illusionist practice of conventional realist cinema, and pushing the spectator into an active political reading of the drama (Faulkner 1986: 67–70). His insightful reading tends to fetishise camera positioning, surely not the only thing that determines active or passive consumption of spectacle.[1]

One should add that the movement is not only spatial but chronological. Taking in the key spaces in which the drama has occurred, it effectively provides a summing-up just as we are about to return to the popular jury of the start. A summing-up completed when the camera follows the drunken caretaker as he staggers round the yard seeking help before finally returning to the body. He brings the festive throng to the window and then a somewhat dishevelled Charles and Estelle thus reminding us sharply what happiness Batala's disappearance made possible.

1 As part of his very informative overview of critical responses to the Renoir of the Popular Front, Keith Reader has produced an illuminating account of how the pan has been read over time (Vincendeau and Reader, eds, 1986: 43–8).

Overconcentration on the famous pan has tended to distract attention from the virtuosity of the rest of this climactic sequence which is a rehearsal for the lunatic brilliance of *La Règle du jeu*. The comic nature of the whole gives Batala's murder a distinctly carnavalesque feel. Its tone is set by the initial drunken banquet scene wherein the caretaker, an inadvertent jester, launches into an entirely out-of-place Christmas song. Batala unknowingly prolongs the comedy when, dressed in clothes stolen from a priest killed in the train crash, he says he is on his way to visit a dying man even as his own death draws near. His attempts to seduce Valentine hardly befit his usurped costume. The murder itself is accompanied by hoots of laughter from the banquet.

The overflow of sound from one space into another again shows how the film ties each individual action into a collective frame. Bazin notes that the film has two key types of shot, each of which locks events into a context: first, the pan, which provides a lateral extension of the frame; second, the shot composed in depth which links two or more spaces and the actions which occur within them (Bazin 1989: 40–3). Faulkner (1986) again complements Bazin by showing how the Renoir of the later 1930s 'socialises' space, placing individuals and their actions in a context shaped by class relationships. A perfect illustration of this is provided by shots which link Batala's office to the printshop and set his individualism and cynical manoeuvring off against the group solidarity of labour.

The film not only makes social relationships of solidarity and exploitation visible, it also makes different versions of historical time palpable through an interplay of circularity and linearity. The circularity of the courtyard is mirrored by the temporal circle of the plot which brings the viewer back to the moment it started. The circle is broken when the popular jury acquit Lange and official justice's maintenance of the status quo is thwarted. The regressive temporality of fate is doubly refused when Lange prevents Batala's repossession of his company and Batala's child dies, freeing Charles and Estelle from the past. Valentine of course had led the way by refusing to let her past relationship with Batala determine her future. Edith, Batala's secretary belongs to a different temporal order. Even as Batala abandons her, she allows herself to be picked up by another bourgeois, learning nothing from her dependence and condemning herself to repeat the past.

Located between progressive and regressive time, the court-yard shows the possibility of radical social change and its limits. Despite all that happens inside, Lange has to flee because an unjust order still reigns in the broader world. His headlong plunge towards the border is in this sense an escape from an oppressive present. An earlier breakout from the courtyard is more hopeful – Charles's triumphant cycle ride down the Champs Elysées, using Arizona Jim to deliver the message, suggests that the values of the cooperative have a receptive audience in the heart of the capital. If a change in consciousness is a precondition for more concrete social change, then the film is optimistic. Its ending can, however, easily be seen as pessimistic. As Valentine and Lange escape along the beach, two small and vulnerable figures, the fatalistic song that Valentine had sung on their first evening as lovers is heard in instrumental form. Its title, Au jour le jour ('From day to day') and its conclusion 'quelle triste vie' ('what a sad life'), suggest regressive repetition. Yet it also evokes liberatory love and Valentine's refusal of fatality. It is perhaps both an indication of the unacceptable nature of the present and a reminder that it can be changed, given the will.

Faulkner and others have suggested that the film is fatally marked by the contradictions of the Popular Front, seeming to call for radical social change but suggesting that there is room for almost everyone in the new social order (Faulkner 1986: 71). Just as one capitalist disappears, the cooperative accommodates another in the shape of the son of the principal creditor, Monsieur Meunier. This inclusiveness would seem to parallel the Front's attack on the 200 most powerful capitalist dynasties rather than capitalism itself. One should not however underestimate the radical nature of this exceptional film. Meunier plays distinctly second fiddle to the workers and his incorporation hardly erases the apologia for political assassination.

The film's radicalism goes beyond the conventionally political and calls for a transformation of popular culture, which it first constitutes as a contested domain. It opens by inviting a popular audience to endorse its radical politics by identifying with the ordinary men who 'acquit' Lange. It shows that popular culture in the hands of Batala and his ilk can be a vehicle for alienation, miserabilism and conservatism but overwrites these negative aspects with its emancipatory message, Valentine's song being one example of this. Employing highly conventional melodramatic motifs – the innocent girl seduced, the fugitive from justice – it transforms them by locating them firmly in a political context, refusing to cast the little people either as criminals or passive victims. The Arizona Jim stories are thus a prototype for the film itself and what it hopes to achieve. They suggest clearly that a suitably transformed popular culture can take a radical message to a receptive public.

One might suggest too that *Lange* marks a radical if ambivalent break with the regressive and often misogynistic portrayal of women that typifies the French cinema of this period (Burch and Sellier 1996: 23–37). Valentine is a revolutionary figure. She actively chooses and wins her man, refusing to be defined by her sexual past. She has achieved economic independence through the ownership of her laundry which becomes a model of female solidarity to parallel the male printshop. She also plays a key role in the film's narration, framing the main story with her plea for Lange. Significantly, when we are asked to move beyond a simple factual determination of guilt, a woman's viewpoint is introduced, suggesting that a more passionate and compassionate vision of justice necessitates the return of the repressed 'female' voice.

However, and to emphasise the ambivalence of the film's gender politics, we should note that the popular jury that the audience is called to side with and the co-operative which transforms the courtyard are male groups. The Utopian imagination which inspires the venture is doubly male, originating with Lange and focusing on Arizona Jim, a hero imported from the arche-typally 'manly' world of the western. When women's oppression is foregrounded it seems to be subsumed under a more general class oppression (Burch and Sellier 1996: 45). Estelle's frail build and sexual innocence feed off the very stereotypes of feminine fragility that Valentine had so resolutely challenged which suggests that her autonomy and liberated sexuality may have their roots as much in a casting off of fatalism and bourgeois morality as in a specifically gendered challenge to the social order. She is none the less a revolutionary and enormously refreshing figure in the cinema of this period.

Lange and *Toni* shot Renoir to the forefront of left-wing film-making. Unsurprisingly, it was to him that the Parti Communiste turned to supervise a team making *La Vie est à nous* (1936), a propaganda film to be shown in the run-up to the elections of 1936. Its reputation as a *film maudit* has been enhanced by its initial non-release on commercial circuits, its subsequent disappearance from view, and the desire of *auteurist* critics to make it 'disappear' again by playing down Renoir's part in it or by focusing on its style at the expense of its politics. Re-released in 1969, it was seized upon by the generation of 1968 as a beacon of radical film-making.

Faulkner usefully summarises its exceptional nature when compared to the standard product of commercial cinema. Financed collectively, it was distributed through union and party meetings. Cast and crew gave their services for free, while direction was shared by a group of film-makers (with the result that it is very difficult to determine Renoir's exact role in the project) (Faulkner 1986: 74). Both Faulkner and Buchsbaum present it as the most radical of Renoir's films of this period. Buchsbaum sees it as the most important political film of the brief flowering of Popular Front films made outside conventional cinema (Buchsbaum 1988: 283–4). Faulkner goes as far as presenting it as formally and stylistically Renoir's most remarkable contribution to the cinema because its radical form makes it impossible for it to be depoliticised by dominant modes of film criticism (Faulkner 1986: 78). Fofi's analysis recognises its powerful and original eclecticism. Identifying the influence in it of Russian montage, proletarian theatre (with its spoken chorus and its sketches) and Renoir's past fictional work, he sees it as a model for a difficult genre. However, he is scathing about its lack of serious analysis and use of schematic slogans and even more severe on its politics, finding that 'it illustrates perfectly the Communist Party's meagre revolutionary outlook at that time (and since)' (Fofi 1973: 22–3).

The film begins with a rather dull documentary exposition of the natural resources and wealth of France accompanied by a voice-of-god narration which simply lists France's output and world ranking for different products. The initial impression that we are watching an official documentary is quickly undermined when the film cuts to a schoolteacher who is revealed to be the source of the commentary. Placed within a fiction and attached to a particular source, the voice-over is stripped of its omniscience. We watch the next documentary images very differently once the seamless linking of voice and image has been broken. The productive capacity of France's modern economic sectors is emphasised but we also see the richness of the nation's cultural heritage, a richness that includes its cathedrals and palaces (which are shown with no reference to the unequal power relations and the labour that their existence implied). As the documentary turns to the glories of Paris, and more specifically the output of the capital's celebrated *haute couture* industry, the image cuts back to the classroom, this time showing young boys whose shabby clothes tell a very different story.

The film then introduces its third mode of communication, the chorus which draws out the initially implicit message by explaining that France does not belong to the French but to the 200 families which rob her. A photo-montage follows, further adding to the film's eclectic form and showing us leading capitalist families, before giving way to another fictional scene. We see a boardroom with a sign that says 'achetez français' ('buy French') and where a company chairman speaks of inevitable sacrifices that must be borne by the workers and of the need to destroy unsold production. These latter comments are spoken across images of the destruction of various food products as fiction is superimposed on document. The film cuts again to show wealthy ladies expressing their preference for foreign cars while the chairman from the preceding sequence is shown losing heavily at gambling.

The film has now added another key stage to its implicit argument. Effects of the Depression are born by the workers while a capitalist class with no real loyalty to France behaves hypocritically and selfishly. Associating this class with just 200 families paves the way for a broad, inclusive appeal which builds on the French revolutionary mobilisation of the nation against a privileged minority.

The workers, silent presences during the documentary sequences, now find their voice as they mass outside a factory gate calling for work and bread. They give way to images of the upper classes and then of French Fascists as they shoot at targets wearing workers' flat caps. This clear indication that Fascism works in the interest of the wealthy orientates our interpretation of ensuing shots of the riots by the extreme right that sparked the formation of the Popular Front. Another texture is added to the film by high-contrast, chaotic night-time newsreel footage. Shots of the Croix-de-feu, the largest of the extreme-right-wing leagues, marching through Paris in paramilitary style give way to images of Hitler, thus associating indigenous and foreign Fascism. Sound montage makes Hitler bark like a dog. Mussolini appears and as he speaks the film repeatedly cuts to images of war, reminding the audience of Italy's military conquest of Ethiopia.

This intimidating array of threats and injustices calls for a solution; the Communist Party is there. Shots follow of Communist counter-demonstrations and the funeral cortège of demonstrators killed by the police. The lesson that the Communists lead anti-Fascist opposition and have paid for it with their dead precedes newsreel footage of properly Frontist demonstrations which the film subordinates to its own didactic intent by demonstrating the Party's leading role. The newsreel is punctuated with shots of the front page of *l'Humanité*, the party's main paper, which serve to fix the meaning of the images and to promote *l'Humanité's* position as an authoritative and unchallenged source of information. 'La Marseillaise' is tied into the anti-Fascist struggle and subordinated to the 'Internationale'. The Party remains true to its internationalism even as it embraces the nation.

Pictures and footage of Soviet and French Communist leaders

lead the way into a new phase of the film. Marcel Cachin is seen reading several letters at *l'Humanité*'s office. The letters introduce three fictional episodes in which the Party springs to the defence of different groups starting with its 'natural' constituency, the industrial proletariat, but also embracing the peasantry and the middle classes, groups which had to be won over if the Front was to be a success. At the same time, the Party is seen to defend the vulnerable (women, older workers, the unemployed) and the family (a key institution that the party had previously criticised but which it moved to defend as it came out of its political isolation).

The third episode, the most developed, and the one directly attributed to Renoir, focuses on an unemployed engineer. Tired and hungry, he is about to give in to despair when Party members gather him up, feed him and welcome him into their midst. His previous aimless loneliness accentuates the warm solidarity and purpose of the group. The previously detached chorus is integrated into events to hammer home the message of solidarity. The engineer returns next as a member of an audience at a fictional meeting addressed by real party leaders and which bring out key themes in the Party's election campaign. The speeches sum up problems raised by the film and show that the party is the solution for them.

The participants in the various fictions are then swept up in the final singing of the 'Internationale' which shows marching groups coming together in a show of purpose and collective strength. Epic shots of the marchers are softened and personalised by intercut close-ups of happy faces or adults holding children. The 'Internationale' continues over the opening images of France but the film has pulled the different sections of society together, reclaimed the nation in their name and substituted Party 'truth' for the false objectivity of documentary.

La Vie est à nous has been credited with finally giving a voice to an industrial working class notoriously absent from the cinema screens of the 1930s. Having re-enacted their silencing in the opening sequences where references to production ignore the producers themselves, the film ends by centring them. However, their reinstatement comes at the price of their subjugation to PCF propaganda. This is perhaps most in evidence in the episode when their undisciplined spontaneous reactions (smash the machines, kill the time and motion man) have to give way to Party discipline for success to be achieved. The film is remarkably different from *Le Crime de Monsieur Lange* where the workers' cooperative is seen to be a spontaneous expression of popular solidarity and egalitarianism. If both films show the Front's initial upsurge, they do so in very different ways.

Another key difference between the two films should also be noted. Whereas *Lange* challenges conventional morality and shows a heroine capable of assuming control of her own life, *La Vie est à nous* is entirely conventional in its gender politics. Buchsbaum cites the presence of Martha Desrumeaux among the speakers at the end as proof of the film's progressive politics (Buchsbaum 1988: 136–7). He neglects to say that her appeal is couched entirely in terms of women's domestic role, even when she addresses working women. The final of the three dramatic episodes also re-enacts and reinforces women's domestic confinement. A celebrated shot, usually analysed in formal terms, and cited as evidence of Renoir's hand due to its composition in depth, shows the unemployed engineer leave silently in the background while his wife, oblivious to his departure, cooks him an egg in the foreground. Enclosed in domestic space, the woman cannot participate in the husband's political journey through despair to collective strength. Unemployment is presented in stereotypical fashion as a male trauma (see Reynolds 1996: 109–18).

The film is a disconcerting blend of simplicity and complexity. Its message is simple and builds, as Fofi noted, on familiar slogans. Its dialectical mixing of fiction, chorus, newsreel, documentary, speech and newspaper is complex and original. It is its formal diversity which has led a succession of left-wing analysts to see the film as a landmark in French radical cinema. Bonitzer *et al.* set the tone writing for *Cahiers du cinéma* after it had taken its post-1968 leftist turn. They show that the dialectical interaction of fiction and document unmasks how apparently objective documentaries serve the dominant ideology by masking inequality. They remain however fully aware that the film must produce a univocal, propagandist message while not appearing to do so (Bonitzer *et al.* 1970: 48–50). Expanding their initial perception, Faulkner suggests that the film uses documentary and fiction to denaturalise each other. Taken in by neither, spectators can enjoy a 'continuous interrogative relationship with the text so that they can analyse the conditions of their own social existence at this historical moment' (Faulkner 1986: 77). Buchsbaum's analysis essentially agrees with Faulkner's, but he has more space to develop it. Noting the left's continued attacks on newsreels for their biased reporting, he shows how the film mobilises fiction to undermine their apparent objectivity. He sees the doctored newsreel shots of de la Rocque, the Croix-de-feu leader, as evidence of the film's refusal to accept the inviolability or objectivity of images (Buchsbaum 1988: 111–12).

Although Buchsbaum and Faulkner are both conscious that the film is a piece of propaganda, neither questions how a spectator's 'interrogative' relation with it can be reconciled with its clear aim to control their response. Both seem to fail to recognise that it destroys the apparent objectivity of documentary and newsreel to create space for an alternative 'truth' propounded by the PCF. A more rounded analysis of its signifying practice would consider how it works to shut down meaning even as it seemingly opens it up. The film's form, as Bonitzer *et al.* (1970) note, is akin to that of a speech (or an essay). Beginning with an exposition of a set of problems, it proceeds to a diagnosis before proposing a solution and showing how that solution can achieve demonstrable results in practice. This tight, overall structure effectively controls (or seeks to control) our interpretation. Its culmination in political speeches delivered by Party leaders to a receptive audience may help to remind us that its ideological core and many of its details were derived from Thorez's famous Villeurbaine speech of January 1936. However fresh and spontaneous it may be creatively, however eclectic its collective production allowed it to be formally, we cannot forget that on the ideological plane it is highly monolithic, as suits a piece of propaganda for that most hierarchical and monolithic of parties, the PCF.

The message that there is one single truth and one reliable

source of information is hammered home by the chorus, by the shots of *l'Humanité*, and by the letters which fix the meaning of the fictional episodes. The film may destabilise fiction, documentary and newsreel, but it also turns each to its advantage. Documentary provides a general picture. Newsreel evokes a specific historical moment. Fiction addresses the concerns and experience of the everyday while providing entertainment and emotional involvement. Used in combination, they constitute a powerful ideological tool, one that can relate a general diagnosis of social injustice to a specific historical conjuncture while involving the spectator. Any overall assessment of the film needs to balance its formal innovation and its radical break with conventional production practices against its subjugation to the ideology of the PCF.

The imprisoning social frame

The contrast between *La Vie est à nous* and Renoir's next film, *Une Partie de campagne* (1936) is enormous. The first is a polemical intervention in a specific historical conjuncture, the second a literary adaptation set in 1860 which turns its back on the problems of its day and takes us on a tragi-comic trip into the country. Its detachment is all the more surprising when we consider that it was made during the first heady weeks of the Front's triumph with many of those Renoir had worked with on his two previous highly political films. This detachment is accentuated by the fact that Renoir abandoned it unfinished to turn his attention to *Les Bas-fonds*. It was only completed after the war thanks to the determination of its producer, Renoir's friend, Pierre Braunberger. Unlike its PCF-sponsored predecessor, it seems a very personal project. Renoir himself adapted the short story by Maupassant, a writer he much admired and a friend of his father. The film's choice of locale and motifs (the river bank, the picnic on the grass, the boating party) are all Impressionist staples while the celebrated swing sequence inevitably evokes Auguste Renoir's famous painting, *La Balançoire*.

Ironically, however, what seems a deeply personal film can

only be attributed to Renoir with one or two caveats. The montage of the film was not his own, although the editors tried to respect their perception of his wishes, while the music, which holds the film together and dictates its tone, was added after the war. Renoir later claimed that he had always intended it to be about forty minutes long, and that it was complete as it stood, but there is clear evidence that there were extra scenes he never shot and that he was happy for Braunberger to commission Brunius and Prévert to round out the story (Viry-Babel 1994: 84–5). Who exactly should be given credit for the version that was released to critical acclaim in 1946 is unclear.

The plot is deceptively simple. A Parisian hardware merchant (M. Dufour) borrows a cart and drives his family and his clerk, Anatole, into the countryside. They stop at an inn and are observed by two young bourgeois (Henri and Rodolphe) who decide to seduce the fleshy Mme Dufour and her slim and beautiful daughter Henriette. Henriette is troubled and excited by the unaccustomed proximity to nature. The Parisians eat on the grass and while M. Dufour and Anatole fish, Henri and Rodolphe row Mme Dufour down the river on their fast boats (*yoles*). Both women are seduced, the mother willingly and comically, the daughter, reluctantly and tragically. An intertitle moves us forward several years and tells us that Henriette has been married off to the ridiculous Anatole. The closing coda shows a chance meeting of Henri and Henriette at the site of the original seduction. Their fleeting moment together has marked both their lives indelibly. Henriette leaves with Anatole.

An early sequence brings out the complexity of this apparently simple film. The two young bourgeois throw open the shutters of the inn to reveal Henriette and her mother on the swings, a shot which is typical of the Renoir of this period, bringing together as it does two social groups and two different spaces. The two women are doubly dissected by male eyes and bourgeois scorn for the *petite bourgeoisie*. But the same sequence also invites us to share Henriette's subjective sensations as a swaying camera looks to the treetops with her, capturing the dizzy excitement and exhilaration she feels as she strains to escape from those around her. Escape is impossible. She is pinned from all sides. By the prying eyes of Rodolphe as he tries to see up her dress. By the eyes of a young seminarist as he looks at forbidden fruit before being brought back to order by his superior. By a group of young boys hidden behind a wall. As she seeks to touch nature, her own and that around her, society hems her in, in the shape of men's attitudes to women, a repressive Christian morality and the judgement of another class. Opening the window, a liberatory act that had brought the young lovers together in *Le Crime de Monsieur Lange*, is now a gesture of capture. However high she can swing, the window frame will always be there to contain her motion.

The swing sequence encapsulates Henriette's broader story. Whatever her desires dictate, her path is laid out by society. Although everything pushes us to link her with Henri (not least the similarity of their names), she is destined for Anatole, her father's ridiculous assistant. Henri too is marked forever by the moment they share on the island but is still a free agent as the film ends. Henriette is tied to Anatole. She has to help him into his jacket and then row him back to the inn, parodying and undoing the original romantic boat-trip to the island, underlining her unfreedom. When she was rowed, she was the victim of a seduction. When she is rowing, she is at the service of her husband. Rowing or rowed, there seems little space for her to decide her own fate.

The remarkable (and exceptional) close-up of her tear-filled eye as she struggles before giving in to Henri places her feelings at the centre of our viewing of the film. Although the women in the film are pawns in male games, they are also subjects endowed with feelings and desires. By bringing out their dual status as subject and object, the film highlights their objectification and social subjection.

Society is inescapable despite the natural setting. The classes relate to nature and to their bodies in radically different ways. The two bourgeois are lean, fit and at ease with body and senses, their thin clothes suggesting an unrepressed sexuality. The *petits bourgeois* are constrained by clothes which restrict their bodies and which are unsuitable for the country pursuits they attempt to engage in, although stays inevitably loosen as the day proceeds. Dufour's portly frame, Anatole's frail body and both men's stiff clothes look suitably absurd when they try to engage in physical activity. The Dufours are intruders in another class's domain and nothing they can do will change that. They bear their class with them in their clothes and their bodies.

The film seems to show the bourgeois in a flattering light as people whose casual dress, bodily ease and pleasure in nature contrast with the stiffly repressed class beneath them. This impression is undermined when we realise that their apparent naturalness is born of a desire to differentiate themselves from social inferiors. Rodolphe's preening shows that his apparently natural attitude to his body is an affectation while Henri's remark that they will have to go further away from Paris to escape the likes of the Dufours reveals that their 'spontaneous' enjoyment of nature is partly driven by the need to be different from a lower class. Even an act as apparently simple as eating is mediated by class – Rodolphe and Henri turn up their noses at fried fish precisely because this is what the Parisians ask for.

Gender too intervenes in the characters' perceptions of nature. While Mme Dufour and her daughter are moved by a sentimental pantheism and drawn to cherry trees and caterpillars that turn into butterflies, their menfolk see a river full of predators and prey. The darker view triumphs when the sentimental attitudes of Henriette leave her open to the predatory behaviour of Henri, something that is brought out with cruel force when the nightingale, that symbol of romantic love, precipitates her undoing.

As Henriette and Henri return from the island, a long and beautiful tracking shot seems to confirm the implicit message that our view of nature is always mediated by the social. The camera points resolutely back down the rain-dimpled river to the place and moment that has marked two lives and shut off their futures. The full pathos of the shot emerges from the tension between the visual pleasure it offers and the social forces that intervene to prevent its enjoyment, a tension that was present in the scene of the swing but which had not yet been worked through to its logical conclusion.

The film draws productively on its double lineage of Impressionism and literary naturalism, bringing together the ironic social
dissection of Maupassant with the sensual surfaces of Auguste
Renoir and his artistic contemporaries to explore brilliantly the
social repression of the senses and the mediation of all appre-
hension of nature. It sits uneasily alongside the other films of the
period. It approaches some key Frontist themes, notably the lower
classes' right of access to the countryside, to leisure and to sport
and prefigures the horrified reaction of the upper classes to
popular invasion of their leisure space as the forty-hour week and
paid holidays made themselves felt. Yet, it does so in a decidedly
non-radical way, showing as it does the triumph of the repressive
social frame over attempts to break out of it. It seems closer to
films like *Boudu* which explore similar tensions between the
natural and the social, than to the committed films, which
perhaps explains why *auteurist* critics show considerably more
interest in it than those of the left.

Les Bas-fonds (1936) is a creative reworking of Maxim Gorki's
celebrated play *The Lower Depths*. It sits more easily alongside the
rest of Renoir's Frontist output than its immediate predecessor
although its politics are somewhat ambiguous. The Communist
Party was apparently pleased that Renoir had agreed to adapt a
work by one of the Soviet Union's most celebrated writers, then in
his last years of life. While noting his pleasure at Gorki's approval
of the screen adaptation, Renoir shows no sign of awareness of the
writer's virtual imprisonment at the hands of the Soviet author-
ities (Renoir 1989: 27–8).

The film revolves around two characters, a baron who has
gambled all of his and some of the state's money away and a
housebreaker, Pépel, who lives in a multiply occupied slum in the
'lower depths.' The former is played by Louis Jouvet, the great
theatrical actor, and the latter by Jean Gabin, France's most
celebrated screen actor and the archetypal ordinary man of the
cinema of this period. Chance brings them together. After one last
fling at the tables, the baron leaves to commit suicide and
surprises Pépel in his home. The two settle down to talk together
and when Pépel is arrested the baron clears him. They are soon

reunited in the basement whose tenants are exploited by Kostilev, a grasping hypocrite who talks of religion but deals in stolen goods. Pépel is having an affair with Kostilev's wife Vassilissa but loves her virginal younger sister, Natacha. The couple conspire to marry Natacha off to a policeman to buy his complicity, but Pépel intervenes, and when Kostilev beats her, kills the petty tyrant, abetted by the other tenants. After a short sentence, he is released and last seen with Natacha on a country road away from the imprisoning frame of the lower depths.

The film delegitimises a social order built on corruption and exploitation by unmasking pretensions to aristocratic superiority and *petit bourgeois* respectability. The process begins in the famous first scene that shows the baron pinned in the centre of an imposing room as a circling camera imitates the motion of the unseen superior who is rebuking him for the misappropriation of state funds. The great arc of the circle highlights the grandeur of the setting and the apparent distance that separates the virtuous state servant from the errant one. Yet the next shot, catching the pair in close and amiable conversation, shows that what went before was pure theatre, and that class solidarity prevails over any pretence of disinterested service to the state. The unmasking is complete when the baron uses the embezzled money to pay off gambling debts to his complicitous superior.

A song sung at the casino where they meet further develops the film's underlying thesis. Recounting how bandits steal, murder and are loved before ending on the guillotine, it provides a sound bridge to Pépel as he sets off to rob the baron's house, catching him as he passes before the watchful eye of two policemen. Pulling together the dark street, a stereotypical locale for criminality, and the luminous, elegant world of the upper classes, the song undercuts the social system that separates them by emphasising the underlying similarity between the baron and Pépel who are both thieves despite their different status. It also emphasises their differences. The police patrol the street not the haunts of the élite and, when the baron has Pépel released from prison, his presence produces fawning civility. As in *Lange*, the law maintains the status quo.

The song programmes Pépel's life for him but its pessimism is overwritten as the cyclical time of social fate is breached by his redemptive love for Natacha and the narrow frame of the *crime passionnel* is rent by group involvement. There are clear echoes of *Lange*, but this time the group plays an active role in the murder, a fact which might suggest that this film was more radical. But, while the workers in *Lange* are joined by a clear class solidarity that provides the core values on which the cooperative is built, the oppressed in *Les Bas-fonds* are social flotsam and jetsam with no shared labour to weld them together. The flimsy cloths which partition their domain suggest a space of shared misery and social fragmentation. No shared project can take them beyond the collective murder of Kostilev. The film simply abandons them, but not before one, an actor, has hanged himself.

Yet Pépel and Natacha have shown a way out through their refusal of fatalism. While the other occupants flee the reality of their situation through drink, religion, romantic illusion or impossible dreams of escape, they simply leave it, suggesting that the lower depths are as much a fatalistic mind-set as an inescapable social prison. One virtuoso shot bolsters this interpretation. Natacha is eating in a river-bank restaurant with her unattractive policeman suitor. An exceptionally long lateral tracking shot takes in festive diners in the fresh air, before finding the couple ensconced at an indoor table at which Natacha is getting drunk and steeling herself to accept her fate. Two stereotypically different attitudes to life are juxtaposed, one marked by Russian fatalism, the other by a French zest for life. Pépel walks in and leads Natacha out into the open air where she is able to express her true feelings. Nature seems to constitute a Utopian space, a haven of freedom beyond the miserabilism of the lower depths and the theatrical hypocrisy of aristocratic luxury.

This happiness found outside society only emphasises the lack of a transformatory project at the heart of the film, something for which Faulkner, for example, lambastes it (Faulkner 1986: 82–3). Yet it is Frontist in its mood. It refuses fatalism, unmasks a corrupt order, and shows the oppressed move from passivity to revolt. Some, such as Poulle, have seen in it a regressive move away from social realism and towards the poetic realist aesthetic that so marked French cinema in the later 1930s (Poulle 1969: 103). In support of such a comparison, one might cite the sombre atmosphere of the lower depths, the frustrated dreams of escape, the glow of redemptive love and, not least, the presence of Gabin in the role of the social outsider. Yet, unlike in the poetic realist films of Carné and Duvivier, Gabin does not die, love prevails and social fate can be challenged. Renoir's Frontist inflection of Gabin's persona (the archetypal ordinary Frenchman) is decidedly more upbeat than many of his roles of the 1930s, and can be seen as part of an ongoing intervention in the popular culture of the period, an intervention begun with *Lange*.

Although *Une Partie de campagne* and *Les Bas-fonds* were shot back to back in the summer and autumn of 1936, there is a gulf between them. The former suggests the impossibility of escape from an imprisoning social frame even in the heart of nature. The latter shows the frame totter and depicts nature as a Utopian space where characters can reinvent their social role. Paradoxically, however, the more broadly progressive of the two films is the more regressive in gender terms, abandoning the awareness of a specifically gendered oppression of the first film and reverting to a Manichaean stereotyping that opposes Natacha's virtuous virgin to Vasilissa's destructive *femme fatale*.

Progressive and regressive nationalisms

La Grande Illusion (1937) represents Renoir's contribution to the cluster of celebrated anti-war films that appeared in the 1930s. Yet the film, scripted with Spaak, breaks with convention by showing nothing of the horror of the trenches that so dominates other representations. Some of its characters, notably the aristocrats, view war as somewhere between a duty and a sport. Although its anti-war credentials are now widely accepted, it has also been accused by such as Poulle and Oms of jingoistic nationalism and worse (Poulle 1969: 104–6; Oms 1962: 46–7). It has been eulogised and damned at different moments in its career and no one has ever really agreed what the great illusion in the title refers to, although everyone has their own preferred version. The film is profoundly ambiguous.

Some of its ambiguity can be traced to the time separating the period when it was made from the period it refers to. It had to be seen as an 'authentic' expression of the mentality of the combatants of World War One. Yet it also had to be an adequate response to its own period, particularly the threat of Fascism. Without putting anachronistic sentiments into the minds of the characters, it had to negotiate a path between the antimilitarist pacifism that the war had generated among so many and the anti-Fascism and left-wing nationalism that were such prominent features of the Popular Front. It was far from treading a lone path in this. The tension between anti-Fascism and pacifism tormented the left at this time.

The film is an ensemble piece, but one figure, Maréchal (Gabin), stands out above the rest. Other key players are the German and French aristocratic career officers, von Rauffenstein and de Boieldieu, and Rosenthal, an enormously wealthy Jewish officer. These are supported most notably by Cartier (Carette), a theatrical performer, and a key component in the creation of the almost festive atmosphere in the first prison camp, and Elsa, the German woman who shelters the escapees. The characters collectively embody a range of class positions and nationalities so that their interplay constitutes a meditation on what divides or unites men (women, with the notable exception of Elsa, being almost entirely absent from events).

The film is structured in three main sections bracketed by a prelude and coda. The prelude is a short scene at a French airbase where Maréchal's plans for his free time are brusquely interrupted by the arrival of de Boieldieu who wishes to verify the nature of a smudge on an aerial photograph. The two are shot down and invited to lunch by von Rauffenstein, a German squadron leader. The first section shows the two Frenchmen in a prisoner-of-war camp where they are absorbed into a tightly knit group of French captives whose time is divided between preparation for a concert party and an abortive escape attempt. They make the vital acquaintance of Rosenthal who effectively nourishes the group. The next section, much darker in tone, takes Maréchal and de Boieldieu to a medieval fortress where persistent escapees are housed. In it, they link up again with Rosenthal and von Rauffenstein, now too badly injured to fight actively and reduced reluctantly to the role of gaoler. De Boieldieu sacrifices himself to facilitate the escape of Maréchal and Rosenthal, who are unable initially to reach the Swiss border due to an injury to the latter's foot. Elsa takes them in, thus introducing the third major section of the film. They live harmoniously with her and her daughter in a rural enclave where, after a modest Christmas celebration, it emerges that Maréchal and Elsa are in love. The coda takes the two Frenchmen over the Swiss border and back towards the war.

The prelude contrasts the French and German messes. The former is a model of informality. Groups of men sit playing cards while Maréchal, the hero, listens to a popular song and looks forward to visiting Joséphine, a woman he is perfectly happy to share with his comrades. A banner spread across the bar suggests affectionate disrespect for the squadron leader. The visual similarity of the German mess emphasises the different behaviour patterns. Von Rauffenstein, played with theatrical panache by Erich von Stroheim, dominates the scene with his stiff formality and military bearing. His men gather round him respectfully with much heel clicking. A portrait of the Kaiser presides. This hierarchical militarism contrasts with the relaxed fraternity of the French mess which Maréchal, the common Frenchman, will carry forward into the main body of the film.

The first major section of the film explores differences of class, most noticeably when the French prisoners eat together at the invitation of the wealthy Rosenthal. The meal unites the French in a stereotypically shared appreciation of good food, but also shows how different their peacetime experience has been. A schoolteacher remarks that he has never eaten so well. Discussion of Paris entertainment reveals that Maréchal prefers the simplicity of the bistrot and a good *pinard* (ordinary red wine), to the élite haunts and expensive tastes shared by the noble de Boieldieu and the wealthy Rosenthal. The fact that the Russian prisoners and the

German soldiers alike are condemned to eat cabbage suggests that the French have yet to face up to the harsh realities of war, a fact which is emphasised by the way their theatrical preparations for escape blur with their preparation of an escapist spectacle. The wood they use to prop their tunnel is significantly taken from the theatre.

The men's playfulness is punctured when a dead escapee is carried back into camp and when one of their number nearly suffocates while digging. More importantly perhaps, war's theatricality is put at a critical distance when they watch a group of German soldiers parade to music and the seductiveness of the spectacle, especially the sound of marching feet, is brought home to them. They fail to learn the lesson and their own very different spectacle of music-hall songs and comic transvestism is drawn into the struggle in a way that will again emphasise the power of nationalist spectacle. Preparation for their show is interrupted by news of Verdun, the battle which came to encapsulate the horror, slaughter and ultimate pointlessness of the war.

Renoir drew knowingly on the meanings that had accreted retrospectively round Verdun. His film makes specific reference to the struggle over the key fort of Douaumont. When it falls to the Germans, the camp guards sing triumphantly together, sharing in victory without paying its cost, savouring a togetherness sealed by music but dependent on subjugation of another group. Cemented together in opposition, and transcending their class differences, the French vow to counter the singing by going ahead with their show. As they perform, news breaks of the recapture of Douaumont by the French. An Englishman in drag pulls of his wig and calls for 'La Marseillaise' which Maréchal uses to draw performers and audience together in an act (an action, but also a show) of bellicose defiance of their captors. We learn immediately that Douaumont has fallen to the Germans again. Punished by solitary confinement, Maréchal goes hungry and a little mad but is saved by the compassion of a German guard.

The episode illustrates the vanity of bellicose nationalism but also its power to seduce and to cement unity in a group with a clearly identified enemy. As Serceau has suggested, the ebb and flow around Verdun is used to evoke the more general lesson that defeat and the ensuing desire for revenge can lock two foes into an unending cycle of war (Serceau 1981: 214–15). More specifically, it suggests the succession of wars between France and Germany, begun in 1870, continuing in 1914 and threatening to go into a new phase as the film was being made. The 'Marseillaise' is fraught with ambiguity. Sung by prisoners to their gaolers, it reminds us of its revolutionary roots. Sung theatrically by vicarious participants in a bloody and pointless struggle, it is a reminder of its appropriation by jingoistic nationalism during the war. Its very ambiguity is illustrative of the Popular Front's need to reorientate symbols of nation even as it sought to claim them.

The inheritance of the French Revolution floats over the episode in the bleak final prison where the reluctant prisoners are reunited with von Rauffenstein who reserves a warm welcome for his fellow aristocrat, de Boieldieu. Critics have tended to focus on the values and tastes which unite the two career soldiers. Of at least equal importance is what separates them. The German is attached to the old hierarchical order and places de Boieldieu above the common Frenchman and the bourgeois Jew. His bracketing of ethnic outsider and social inferior encourages us to see his words as a reference to both aristocratic élitism and the exclusions of Nazism. He clings to his military role even when all pretence that war is a chivalrous game has been swept away and he has become nothing more than the administrator of a prison regime. De Boieldieu's solution is radically different. Denying that Rosenthal and Maréchal are in any way inferior, he decides to sacrifice himself to procure their freedom, an act that proclaims his loyalty to the values of the French Revolution and to an egalitarian and non-exclusionary social order. The future belongs to the alliance of the bourgeoisie and the popular that originally overthrew the *ancien régime*.

The medieval castle is a much bleaker place than the original camp as its name, *Wintersborn*, and the wintry weather associated with it suggest. The earlier, playful activities give way to a single-minded focus on escape. Social relationships lose their former density. Two couples emerge, one aristocratic, the other democratic, as the sterile competition of nationalisms gives way to a lucid choice between political reaction and progress. Theatre and game-playing, previously distractions from escape and obstacles to lucidity, are now put in the service of the breakout as de Boieldieu's musical performance buys his two comrades precious time.

The escape further plunges Maréchal and Rosenthal into the harsh reality of war, exposing them to a physical adversity that the latter's food parcels had hitherto kept at bay. At this stage, cold and hungry, Maréchal gives in to another regressive sentiment, anti-Semitism, momentarily abandoning a limping Rosenthal before returning penitently to his side. Having traversed jingoistic nationalism and atavistic anti-Semitism, he is now ready for inter-national fraternity at Elsa's farm, a setting whose open, natural surroundings contrast strongly with the two prison camps. The farm sequence takes up several key themes and motifs and brings them to a conclusion in a way that highlights the tight structuring of this apparently loosely constructed film.

Language differences are a cause and a symbol of non-communication from the start. Although Rosenthal speaks German and de Boieldieu English, Maréchal has been locked within a single language, French. In the company of Elsa, he now learns German, the language he had failed to acquire from the guards in the camps. Freed from relations of domination and subjugation, international communication can develop.

Christianity also plays a key role. Its iconography was already in evidence in the castle episode, most specifically in the shape of the crucifix, with its connotations of suffering. An enormous cross presided over von Rauffenstein's chamber, a chapel, one assumes, whose role is overwritten by its occupation by a prison governor. An Iron Cross adorns the chest of the chaplain, alongside a crucifix and a red cross, indicating the hopeless entanglement of Christianity's spiritual and comforting roles with war and nationalism. A purified Christianity returns at the farm when Elsa washes the feet of the suffering Rosenthal (a gesture of Christian succour and humility), and when the crib brings all the group together to celebrate Christmas, a time of new hope. Rosenthal, whose Jewishness makes him Jesus's 'brother', is at the core of the celebrations. This purified and inclusive Christianity offers a model of European fraternity.

Verdun, linked previously to theatrical nationalism, comes back in a very different form when we learn that Elsa's husband died there, leaving her daughter Lotte without a father. The battle which had previously been used for vicarious, short-lived triumphalism is now overwritten with profounder private sentiments as Elsa points to photographs of the family dead, linking each loss to a German victory and showing that private loss outweighs national triumph.

The film works its way round the war, never showing it, but showing different attitudes to it, what makes people fight it and how it affects lives. At the start, Maréchal lived in a state of unconscious innocence. Like Rosenthal, an artillery officer, or de Boieldieu, the staff officer, for whom the war was an irritating smudge on an aerial photograph, he had no immediate acquaintance with the suffering involved. The aristocrats in particular represent a chivalrous vision of war that both occludes and helps to justify the mass slaughter of the trenches. The German's role as a fighter pilot is significant. Pilots, seen as knights of the sky, were used to perpetuate images of war based on individual heroism and acts of daring. Rather than focus on the horror of the trenches, as other films of the 1930s had done, *La Grande Illusion* explores the myths that legitimise and romanticise war before slowly and surely puncturing them.

Yet Maréchal retains one enormous illusion even as he returns to the struggle. He believes they can make this war the last, a remark that rings hollow in 1937. The film's characters must continue to speak with the voices of 1914–18, even as the film itself makes coded references to the mid-1930s and enunciates a Frontist position. Fascism, for example, cannot be overtly evoked, yet, when the prisoners observe the marching men beneath their window, it evokes the threatened situation of France in 1937 and the power of Fascism to hypnotise masses through military spectacle. It is in this context that we should view the portrayal of Rosenthal that deliberately invokes the potential appeal of anti-Semitism before reaffirming an open, inclusive vision of Frenchness.

Rosenthal's foreign origins are clearly signalled, yet his immigrant parents have several châteaux with 'authenticated' ancestral portraits while he himself is in the fashion trade, that most French of industries. He embodies a stereotypical Jewish rootlessness and ability to usurp wealth and penetrate social structures. But he is placed right at the heart of the French community in the film and escapes alongside the archetypal Frenchman, Maréchal, whose own display of visceral anti-Semitism is a challenge to the French to examine their own prejudices. Rosenthal's ability to become culturally French within one generation refutes the essentialist view of nation and paves the way for the political definition that the film puts in its stead.

The film is an enormously sophisticated intervention in the ideological struggles of its period, which balances the need to represent wartime mentalities against the imperatives of its day, purging French Republican traditions of militaristic nationalism and xenophobia, while still exploring their appeal. Because it was condemned to communicate its politics implicitly for fear of anachronism, it opened itself to an enormous potential range of interpretation during its own time and later. Lindeperg notes its profound ambiguity and capacity to appeal for very different reasons to critics of both the left and the nationalist right in 1937. She goes on to explore why it aroused such hostility on re-release in 1946, noting that its sympathetic portrayal of ordinary Germans, its plea for Franco-German reconciliation and its evocation of anti-Semitism were unacceptable for some after the experience of the Second World War (Lindeperg 1997: 209–20). The historian Marc Ferro likewise explored the film's ambiguity, a quality which did not prevent him accentuating what he saw as its latent reactionary tendencies. Accusing it of anti-Semitism, Anglophobia, Germanophilia and an élitist preference for the chivalrous airman over the ordinary soldier, Ferro suggested that it gave a foretaste of the ideology of the collaborationist Vichy regime. Gender, an element almost entirely ignored by other analysts, is used to support his argument. Noting the film's reference to female infidelity, he links it to Vichy's defence of family values. Typically of his somewhat reductionist reading of the film, he does not consider the complexity of its gender politics (Ferro 1993: 184–90).

The film is haunted by the destabilisation of gender boundaries associated with the war (Roberts 1994: 1–9). Almost entirely absent from the film, women are the constant object of men's thoughts, as the initial stability suggested by Maréchal's happiness to share the prostitute with his fellow soldier gives way to repeated anxiety. Evocation of their newly short hair and dresses suggests a blurring of roles, while their unaccustomed sexual freedom is emphasised by reports of infidelity and discussions of venereal disease linked to female promiscuity. Rosenthal's misrecognition of a man as a woman during the escape underlines the gender anxieties and uncertainties.

Gender is further destabilised by the situation in the camp which takes the soldiers out of the manly theatre of war and plunges them into a world of domesticity and private feelings. They bond with such intensity that clear couples emerge. Latent homo-eroticism comes to its peak when they gather to unpack the women's clothes that have come for their performance. A young Frenchman puts on a dress and a bemused silence falls as the camera tracks slowly back to pin the eroticised male in the centre of the room and highlight the ambivalence of the gaze cast upon him. Cross-dressing continues into the show itself and is only brought to an end when the Englishman pulls off his wig and calls for the defiant 'Marseillaise' that draws all the men into a virile stance. It is as if the film cannot find a middle path between complete unmanning and a bellicose masculinity.

The final section provides a way out by building the desired compassionate international order within the private world of the family where men can be tender and still be men. With the arrival of Maréchal, the previously self-reliant Elsa retreats indoors, reclaims nurturing from the men and relinquishes the heavy tasks. Their relationship restores a family structure and gender order thrown out of kilter by the war. Despite its remarkable exploration of gender, the film ultimately retreats to a conservative position. Its two Utopian moments are symptomatic of this. Both the initial egalitarian harmony of the French mess and the closing rural idyll reinforce highly traditional and polarised views of women, in the first case a prostitute that all men could share, in the second a wife and mother.

Renoir's next film, *La Marseillaise* (1937), was already in gestation when *La Grande Illusion* was being shot and can be seen as part of the same reorientation of nation and reaffirmation of republican values as its predecessor. Both have to negotiate the tension between the prevailing pacifism of the period and the need to resist Fascism. For *La Marseillaise* this negotiation implies the establishment of a sugar-coated, peace loving Revolution. Having to engage with the very present memory of a savage war, *La Grande Illusion* had a much harder task on its hands. This goes some way to explaining its much greater complexity.

La Marseillaise begins by showing how an out-of-touch Louis XVI, ensconced in the sterile ritual of the court, misreads the revolutionary assault on the Bastille as a revolt. Its focus then shifts to the southern French countryside, where Cabri, a peasant is arrested simply for killing a pigeon that was eating his crop and faces the galleys at the hand of the local lord. Defended by the mayor, a small property owner who distances himself from the interests of the wealthy aristocracy, and aided and abetted by the common folk, he escapes through a window and makes for the hills. There he joins Bomier, a stone mason, and Arnaud, a customs clerk, both fleeing persecution. The film unmasks the repressive social relationships that shelter behind an illusion of legality, retrospectively explaining and justifying the assault on the Bastille, while neatly sidestepping the cliché of the violent Parisian crowd. Cabri's leap through the window is ultimately a leap in historical time. It signals a move from the frozen state of the *ancien régime* to the progressive time of the Revolution.

Cabri, Bomier and Arnaud return to Marseilles when they see smoke from burning châteaux. They participate in the non-violent capture of the royal fort that threatens Marseilles and liberate victims of aristocratic persecution. The film's on-screen Revolution is good-natured and peaceful even while it acknowledges the existence of violence off-screen. We will only see violence when we are firmly on the side of the revolutionaries and convinced that their actions are those of a peace-loving, democratic and inclusive group driven to action by internal repression or foreign invasion. Thus the first appearance of the 'Marseillaise', that most blood-thirsty of anthems, is associated with the fraternal gathering of the Marseillais as they prepare to march north to Paris.

Their march, cementing their fraternal bond, takes them through the heart of France as they discover and symbolically unite the nation. Their arrival in Paris, along with a group of Bretons, joins the capital to the extremities of the nation although their celebratory banquet is aborted by aristocratic provocations and a skirmish. This violence is a prelude for the assault on the Royal palace which signals the abolition of the monarchy and the introduction of universal male suffrage. The closing shots of the film show the Marseillais as they march towards Valmy, and the historic victory of the army of newly enfranchised citizens over invading counter-revolutionary forces.

La Marseillaise is an intervention in the long-running struggle to define the Revolution, the founding event of French political modernity, a struggle which established the principal faultlines that would dominate the country's politics well into the twentieth century. Support of or opposition to the values of the Revolution marked out left and right respectively while the left could be further subdivided by its allegiance to different phases and factions of the Revolution. Renoir's film makes clear its manifest preference for the radical Revolution of 1792 over the moderate one of 1789, while its characters state their allegiance to Robespierre, the iconic figure of the radical left. It sets out to oppose the right's counter-versions of events, giving a human and sympathetic face to the revolutionary crowd, customarily depicted as an irrational, destructive and faceless mob in right-wing accounts. More specifically, it invites our close identification with the Marseillais who were played by actors associated with Pagnol's films, and thus with an image of meridional directness and sociability. It counters accounts – notably that of the celebrated historian Taine – which suggests that they were a band of stateless thugs, by giving them all resolutely French names and clearly demonstrating their respectability (Grindon 1994: 43–4). It refuses to portray the aristocrats or the royal family as innocent victims, instead showing them to be weak or willing accomplices to oppression and foreign invasion. More generally, the Revolution, so often associated with savage violence, is depicted as fraternal and peace-loving.

Such a representation is inevitably selective. Isolating the time when the Revolution was on the strong upward curve, which saw the establishment of universal male suffrage and the first great victory of the citizens' army, it eliminates awkward facets of the ensuing period, notably the bloody repression of internal dissent and the murderous in-fighting among factions which paved the way for Napoleonic dictatorship. Even within its own time span, the film erases and sanitises episodes. The slaughter of the Swiss guard that had defended the royal palace is only hinted at and presented as swiftly controlled retaliatory violence. The massacre of the populations of the Paris prisons which occurred between the fall of the palace and the battle of Valmy is also forgotten. The film simplifies its Revolution in order to clarify its political message.

La Marseillaise contains a Frontist message that barely seeks to hide behind the historical period it purports to represent. It reclaims the national anthem from the right while reviving the left-wing definition of nationalism as the fraternal union of the people against a privileged few. It stretches out its hand in true Frontist manner to the peasantry and to the church, promoting the broadest possible alliance of the nation against its enemies. The nobles who take refuge in Coblenz while waiting to march with Germans on Paris can clearly be assimilated to those right-wingers who expressed their admiration for Hitler.

Frontist it clearly was from its inception. Launched in pomp at a meeting which gathered representatives of all those involved in the Front, and intended to celebrate its unity, it ironically highlighted its disintegration. Only the CGT, the trade union confederation, which provided extras for the crowd scenes, and the Communists, who advised Renoir on the political orientation of the film, remained as active participants. The desire to fund the film by popular subscription having also foundered on the rocks, it is tempting to read it as symptomatic of ideological short-comings and political failure.

This is certainly how Fofi sees it. He comments scathingly that the film 'castrates' the Revolution and epitomises 'the weaknesses and equivocations of the Popular Front and the PCF's policy during those years' (Fofi 1973: 37). Faulkner barely finds a place for it in his book. He suggests a clear parallel between the film's production history and its politics, writing; 'just as the original production initiatives collapsed, resulting in conventional methods of financing, distribution and exhibition, so the treatment turned out to be conciliatory rather than revolutionary' (Faulkner 1986: 100). Buchsbaum is even harsher, remarking, 'left political film-making in France ended with the production of La Marseillaise'. Seeing the film as a retreat from the formal and political experiments of La Vie est à nous, he comments damningly that it 'failed to distinguish itself from the familiar costume dramas of the commercial industry' (Buchsbaum 1988: 279). The substance of his criticism is that the workers could not recognise themselves in the pre-industrial artisans of an anachronistic film which targeted the aristocracy instead of capitalism, the true enemy.

Other critics diverge dramatically from these dismissive positions and develop analyses that can guide us more productively through the film. Grindon usefully locates the film in terms of the internal political divisions of the Front. Rather than seeing it as tamely symptomatic of the Front's disintegration, he links it to a Communist Party still committed to the Front and desperately trying to persuade its flagging partners to maintain their original commitment to an anti-Fascist, left-of-centre alliance. Somewhat surprisingly, perhaps, he equates Louis XVI with Léon Blum, maintaining that Louis's failure to side with the common people against foreign invasion and internal counter-revolution parallels Blum's failure to intervene in Spain and timid legalism in the face of internal opposition (Grindon 1994: 37–45). While the specific link of Blum to Louis might not necessarily convince us, Grindon usefully shows how the film is an attempt to stir the French into action rather than simply a symptom of the Front's failure.

Grindon analyses the film's mobilisatory strategies, suggesting that all historical fictions rely on two sub-genres, the romance and the spectacle, the former focusing on individuals, the latter depicting a broader social frame. Noting how dominant representations had depicted a Revolution that threatened the romantic couple, he shows how *La Marseillaise* breaks with convention when its Revolution unites rather than separates the lovers. Blending the political and the romantic, the film shows a competition for the heart of the nation which the king loses. In a shadow play put on in a Paris theatre, 'Madame la Nation' symbolically turns away from the monarch while Bomier successfully courts Louison, the Parisienne, bringing north and south together and uniting the nation around left-wing ideals (Grindon 1994: 48–55).

Grindon's analysis of the film's spectacular dimension focuses on three key areas: the collective hero, the food motif, and the opposition between nature and artifice. He first shows how Renoir generates a sense of unity by repeatedly showing huge crowds in extended takes and by using panoramic crane shots to frame groups. The unity of the collective hero is reinforced by the Marseilles accent that the main characters share and by the collective singing of the 'Marseillaise', which draws all voices into one (Grindon 1994: 56–7). He then turns to food and its mobilisation to explore how power relations shape everyday experience. The film explores unequal access to resources when the aristocratic pursuit of hunting for pleasure is contrasted to the populace's need to kill animals to survive. Food can also show unity as when Bomier and his friends cement their union by hunting and eating together. Grindon, sums up by saying, 'Food infuses the film with the politics of everyday life ... The food motif reminds the audience that the Revolution was not based simply on political principles but, like the struggles of the modern era, arose from common hardship, economic exploitation, and political injustice'. He notes finally how spatial compositions and the representation of landscape 'elaborate an opposition between nature and artifice, freedom and constraint, the Revolution and the old regime'. The first, positive term is in each case associated with the democrats while the aristocrats and royalty are associated with interiors that are 'artificially constructed, rigidly defined and thoroughly enclosed' (Grindon 1994: 62).

Grindon's analysis again illustrates how Renoir's Frontist films engage with and transform the popular, reaching out for it by incorporating romance while embedding their political message in everyday life. Regina Janes usefully extends this analysis by showing the lengths Renoir's film goes to distinguish popular nationalism from the national populism of Fascism. It achieves this by individualising a group of common people rather than celebrating discipline, the military or the charismatic leader. Avoiding the Fascistic connotations of rigid ranks of marching men, Renoir has his marchers 'amble and straggle until a real, desperately necessary battle confronts them' (Janes 1995: 302). The 'Marseillaise' is not initially sung *en masse* but passes from person to person and from group to group, its adoption signalling conscious adhesion to its values and not surrender of self. Janes concludes that Renoir's film successfully adopts a strongly nationalist position while distancing itself from the nationalism of the far right.

Because Janes and Grindon do not simply dismiss the film's politics, they are able to explore its force and originality in a way that Fofi, Buchsbaum and Faulkner fail to. However, like their predecessors, they largely neglect gender in their accounts, a failure that is more than a little surprising in both cases. Having rightly noted the centrality of the romance to the film, Grindon fails to extend his insight by analysing the very different roles it gives to men and women. Janes is very aware of the prominence of women in Renoir's film but seems content to note their presence without considering what specific form it takes.

Close analysis reveals an astonishing contradiction at the heart of a film, which can be seen as the welding together of two conflicting gendered stories. In one, women are seen to play an assertive, powerful and violent role, claiming the right to a voice and an active role in the public domain. In the other story, a male narrative of coming of age, bonding and nation-building, gender hierarchies and male occupation of the public arena are strongly affirmed.

In its early stages the film reproduces the founding myth of the (gendered) social contract.[2] When the two Marseillais unite in the hills with Cabri, they return to a 'state of nature' (a pre-social existence), which allows them to form an egalitarian proto-community of men whose heterosexuality is affirmed by their desire for a woman to do the cooking and, it is implied, cater for sexual needs. Cabri, the older man, warns that a woman would cause jealousy and disrupt the communitarian ideal. The rest of the film can be seen in part as an attempt to deal with this disruption.

Bomier, perhaps the most important character, is initially dominated by women. He is prevented from joining the male band that will march on Paris by his attachment to his mother and the debts he has contracted to give money to a duplicitous woman who has exploited his attraction to her. Accused of imitating the King's subordination to a woman and of sacrificing his honour and dignity, he is temporarily threatened with exclusion from the fraternal band. A famous scene shows him in the kitchen as his mother prepares a meal. He invites her to sit, the new-found equality outside seemingly penetrating into the domestic world, but, unable to adapt to new ways and seemingly resigned to subservience, she refuses. However, it is only with her consent that he can become head of the family, clear his debts and thus be allowed to leave with the other men. She is both subservient and dominant. The absence of her dead husband and thus of patriarchal authority suggests that the Revolution has unsettled the status quo and uncertainty will reign until firm boundaries can be re-established between gender roles.

The process starts when the singing Bomier departs to enlist. Left behind with their emotions, the women shut the window to enforce their own confinement within domestic space and repetitive time, even as the composition in depth allows us to see Bomier disappear down the street to break the constricting frame

2 Carol Pateman argues that the conventional account of a move from a patriarchal view of society to a contractual one occludes the continuity between the two, whereby contractually free males maintain patriarchy's exclusion and subordination of women (Pateman 1988).

of his world. He will participate in a gendered building of nation, linking its territory through the all-male march on Paris, endowing it with a virile and warlike anthem, and defending its frontiers and the freedom of male citizens at Valmy.

This narrative shows the passage from the patriarchal system of the monarchy to the fratriarchal system of the Revolution. To become autonomous men, the brothers have to kill the 'father,' an act whose horror is diminished when their guilt is transferred to Marie-Antoinette, the foreign woman and primary source of the disorder within the state. Straying into the public domain and subverting the king's authority, she manipulates his emotions to make him betray his people and accept the notorious Brunswick declaration. Her private ties to her Germanic family take unacceptable precedence over her public loyalty to France. Her usurpation of power means that the monarchy must be overthrown to replace an 'unmanly' father with more virile sons who can better defend France.

This narrative of domestication and scapegoating comes most openly into conflict with the story of active female participation when an outspoken woman uses her right to speak at a public meeting for a violent attack on Marie-Antoinette which is an astonishing blend of xenophobic misogyny and female assertiveness. She says, 'Madame Veto trahit parce qu'elle est autrichienne! Parce qu'elle est orgueilleuse! Parce qu'elle déteste la France ... Elle oublie qu'un peuple, ça ne se mène pas comme un mari et que nous les femmes, nous sommes là'.[3]

Bomier, the generous 'heart' of the Revolution, will never quite free himself from female influence. Even as he marches to depose the king, his thoughts are with Louison, the woman he has met in Paris and his 'reward' for breaking out of the protective maternal space. After his death, it is left to Arnaud, the 'head' of the Revolution, the man who is always in control of his emotions, to complete the male monopoly of public space and historical time by attributing to women a purely symbolic role in a gendered

3 'Madame Veto betrays because she is Austrian! Because she is proud! Because she hates France ... She forgets that a people cannot be controlled like a husband, and that we women are there'.

narrative of liberation and coming of age. In the film's final speech he compares the people's romance with liberty to the situation of a man who has at last spoken to his mistress but has yet to possess her.

It is no accident that it is Arnaud's voice that closes the film. Although it seems to allow the interaction of multiple voices, including those of women, aristocrats and different revolutionaries, his ultimately controls its interpretation. The reactions of Bomier, the spontaneous voice of popular consciousness, have to be reined in by him more than once. At one key moment, Arnaud reminds him that he must obey those he has elected, a comment that suggests both the PCF's Frontist commitment to parliamentary democracy, and its disciplined and hierarchical structure. Arnaud's alignment with Robespierre, the most prominent of the Jacobins, is significant, for the Russian Revolution was routinely justified by reference to its French predecessor and the Bolsheviks equated with the Jacobins. Renoir was conscious that his sympathetic portrayal of the Marseillais was also a defence of the Russian revolutionaries of 1917 (Renoir 1974: 248–53).

Like *Le Crime de Monsieur Lange*, this film is both conciliatory and radical. In line with PCF policy, it holds out its hand to a broad section of French society, seeking to reassure them with images of a peace-loving Revolution. But it also strives to reanimate a failing Front and to persuade the French of the need to stand up to Fascism in the name of democracy. It presents a Revolution that is profoundly orderly, yet at the same time it vindicates the overthrow of an unjust legality. Rehabilitating the revolutionary crowd, it places the common people at the centre of the national story. Capturing the mass popular participation and the festive mood of the demonstrations and factory occupations that marked the Front in its early days, it also unwittingly reveals, like *La Vie est à nous*, the subjugation of the popular to a single organising voice. It inevitably suffers by comparison to *La Grande illusion*. Its clear political intent and propagandist presentation of the Revolution contrasts markedly with the other film's long, implicit struggle to disengage an anti-Fascist progressive nationalism from its bellicose and regressive variant.

Disengagement from the Front

Renoir's next film, *La Bête humaine* (1938), was a conventionally produced star vehicle for Gabin and Simone Simon. An adaptation of Zola's great novel of the same name, it diverged considerably from the original by concentrating and simplifying the novel's multi-stranded and episodic plot and relocating the story in the present day.

The novel uses the railway to explore the notion of progress, using a mighty locomotive as a symbol both of the transformatory power of technology and of the regressive, 'bestial' nature of passion. The wealthy and corrupt class that controls the railway has created oppressive social conditions which exacerbate base human drives and render progress impossible. The ending illustrates this clearly by recounting a murderous struggle between a train driver (Jacques Lantier) and his engineer (Pêcqueux) on a train ferrying troops to the Franco-Prussian war. Both plunge to their deaths leaving the driverless train to plunge on.

Renoir's film is built around the plot of incest and murderous jealousy that forms the heart of the novel. Roubaud, a stationmaster, is married to the beautiful Séverine (Simone Simon) who is probably the daughter and certainly the mistress of Grand-Morin, one of the railway company directors. Roubaud makes her help him to murder Grand-Morin. Lantier (Gabin) is a witness but faced with the silent pleas of Séverine, tells the police nothing, even though this silence may incriminate the poacher Cabuche. Séverine deliberately seeks out Lantier's company and inevitably the two become lovers. She pushes him to kill Roubaud but he cannot and becomes estranged from her. When she encourages the attentions of another man, he again determines to murder Roubaud but loses control and murders her instead. Coming from a line of alcoholics, Lantier is subject to blind rages that are directed towards women who excite desire in him. The film's ending is very different to that of the novel. The tortured Jacques jumps from the locomotive to his death, leaving a grieving Pêcqueux to halt what is an ordinary passenger train. Despite the looming European conflagration, war is not a feature of the film.

Faulkner has provided some of the most interesting comment-
aries on this film. His first reading of it is largely critical and
echoes to a degree that of Poulle (1969: 24–64). He states
categorically that it is not a Frontist film and represents a move
from the social determination of character to 'individualist
psychological fatality'. It abandons social realism for the atmospheric romantic fatalism so typical of the 'poetic realist' films of
Carné and Duvivier. He concludes that it is none the less an
impressive film whose value lies in its (inadvertent) indication
that the desired moment of revolution or significant social change
had passed for good (Faulkner 1986: 101–3).

He has recently produced a more complex reading which
highlights a clash in the film between naturalism (the portrayal of
exterior social reality) and expressionism (the projection of inner
states and passions onto the exterior world). Naturalism allows for
the optimistic celebration of technology in evidence in the celebrated opening sequence of a high-speed train journey. Expressionism focuses on the sordid private intrigues which are a sign of
the inevitable return of that which western modernity subjugates.
In raising up reason, technology and capital, Europe devalues and
represses the irrational, the body and the working class. The
working-class body (bestial, sexual and subversive) came to
concentrate these repressed and unassimilable elements in the
eyes of dominant groups. Even as the film suggests the possibility
of technology driven progress, it implies its impossibility by
foregrounding the primitive bodies of Lantier and his engineer.
Trapped by this inherited portrayal of the worker as simply the
negation of bourgeois values, Renoir cannot move to a truly
progressive representation of the social situation (Faulkner 1996:
82–101).

This challenging reading is flawed in one key respect. While
one might accept that there was no alternative progressive representation of the worker at Zola's time, it is hardly a convincing
notion once the Popular Front had lionised the working class as
the vanguard of progressive social change. If Renoir had no
alternative but to recycle bourgeois stereotypes of an atavistic
proletariat, it is hard to see how he could have produced the

extremely positive vision of the common people of his earlier Popular Front films, a vision that is still in evidence in this film. Proletarian solidarity is indeed present from the first sequence when Pêcqueux and Lantier work in close harmony to drive the mighty locomotive without needing to speak. It continues through the depot scenes where they share their food and sleeping quarters and remains solid even when Lantier confesses the murder to his friend. Their unshakeable camaraderie (which is not present in the novel) is in stark contrast to the destructive and oppressive class and gender relationships that otherwise make up the film. It is as if Renoir knowingly played off an inherited regressive image of the workers and a Frontist outlook in order to express both the pessimism of 1938 and a commitment he refused to relinquish (see page 19). The proletarian hero is torn between two worlds, one progressive, the other destructive, with the latter inexorably claiming him.

The two worlds are presented at the start of the film. The epic opening shows the united workers in control of the powerful engine but the next static sequence in the railway station places them on the margins of an oppressive society. As they walk away in dirty overalls, Roubaud, the stationmaster, reproaches a wealthy capitalist for smoking in a railway compartment. As a result, his position is threatened. Only Séverine's connections with Grand-Morin save him from the repercussions of his principled action. Society is dominated by a corrupt and wealthy elite. The locomotive cab is a cocoon rather than a site of mastery. Lantier is drawn out of its protected space when Séverine involves him in the cover-up of the murder, an involvement that is at once a broadening out and a narrowing down. He is drawn into the broader drama of unequal classes yet simultaneously lured into the claustrophobic world of the couple and away from the potential solidarity of his own class. This becomes most evident on the night of Séverine's murder. At the railwaymen's New Year's ball, her presence obsesses him and precludes any shared enjoyment. The choice of date is extremely ironic. Rather than signalling a new start, it shows characters whose future is shut off by their past.

From the start of the film, Jacques and Séverine are victims rather than makers of their fate. While he is tainted by the vices of preceding generations, she owes her very existence to Grand-Morin's sexual exploitation of his servants. Renoir's earlier Frontist films had shown characters drawing on popular virtues to shape a better future. This film shows them engulfed by a corrupt order and an oppressive past from which they cannot escape for they bear its marks within them.

The entire spatio-temporal economy of the earlier Frontist films is stood on its head as the stifling interiors reach out to shut off open space. The railway's ever presence – windows look onto it, key events happen by it – accentuates the claustrophobia of the film and underlines the impossibility of escape from the social relations of modern industrial capitalism. The natural world, linked in *La Marseillaise* to freedom and social renewal, is now associated with the lost, pre-sexual innocence of a past to which there can be no return. When Lantier finds the virginal Flore in a pastoral riverside scene, his inherited insanity drives him to try to murder her. Cabuche, the poacher, who had previously killed a man in a fight, seems to have rediscovered his innocence in his woodland walks with Louisette, Flore's sister, but Grand-Morin's predatory sexual behaviour brings about the girl's death and despoils the idyll. Another pastoral space, a park, is linked to Lantier and Séverine's early unconsummated relationship, but the move to sexual love takes them into the dark, enclosed space of a hut in the freightyard

The tying together of sexuality and oppression gives all sexual relations a destructive charge, a charge that is born by the women who become scapegoated for regressive social relationships when the proletarian hero's anger is channelled towards them rather than the oppressor. As in Zola's novel, a misogynist subtext overflows an overt focus on class oppression. Séverine, social victim and *femme fatale*, lies at the heart of things. As the daughter–mistress of a wealthy man who sexually exploited the women in his employ, she seems to embody the fate of the lower orders at the hands of the élite. Yet she is also deceitful and destructive, playing the dutiful wife, inciting Jacques to murder, abandoning him when he fails. Her death is accompanied by an off-screen song which tells of the fickleness of women in a way that renders it less tragic and indeed adds an implicit justification for it. In the end, her apparent vulnerability and respectability increase her deceptiveness. The film's real victim, the one that Pêcqueux's sad farewell invites us to mourn, is Lantier.

The contrast between the adulterous, duplicitous, dark-haired Séverine and the blond, innocent and virginal Flore takes us back into the Manichaean stereotypes of women that have for so long structured 'high' and 'low' culture alike. While the interplay of progressive and regressive representations of the workers had suggested a very conscious attempt to capture the mood of a particular historical moment, the portrayal of the women is simply regressive.

Renoir's next film, *La Règle du jeu* (1939) completely turns its back on the dark intensity of *La Bête humaine*. Having established a production company (the NEF) with friends, he was able to chart his own path and move decisively away from the doom-laden atmospherics of the poetic realist mode that dominated prestige French cinema of that period. Breaking with naturalism, he turned for inspiration to the traditions of French classical theatre, lightening his palette even as France lurched into its darkest moments. Three influences stand out, those of Marivaux and Beaumarchais from the eighteenth century and Musset from the nineteenth. Although it is impossible to identify the exact contribution of each, one might approximate thus: from Marivaux, Renoir drew an elegant cynicism and characters whose lives revolve around love; from Musset, essential elements of his plot and an uneasy tragi-comic tone; from Beaumarchais, the implicit critique of a smug ruling class on the edge of a catastrophe and parallel love affairs between masters and servants. By blending elements from his predecessors and adding and swapping roles, Renoir produced a plot that was more complex and confused than anything he had inherited. The wife, husband, lover and lover's friend, for example, are borrowed from Musset, but an extra lover is added, while the husband is given a mistress and the lover an admirer.

Events are triggered by the transgressive behaviour of André Jurieux, an aviator and national hero who is in love with a married woman, Christine. When he touches down after a long-distance solo flight, she fails to greet him. He broadcasts his disappointment through the radio, making public what should have remained private. Christine's husband, the Marquis Robert de La Chesnaye, who has had a mistress throughout their marriage, now decides he loves his wife and will fight for her. Geneviève, his mistress, will not release him easily. Jurieux attempts suicide by crashing his car. His friend, Octave, a passenger at the time, decides to intervene and persuades Robert to invite Jurieux to his country château (*La Colinière*) along with a broader group of the upper bourgeoisie. When his gamekeeper, Schumacher, catches a poacher, Marceau, Robert hires him as a servant. Marceau will try to seduce Schumacher's wife, Lisette.

Robert has now inadvertently assembled all the actors of the drama. While the early parts of the film alternately focuses on groups or pairs located in different places, its main body is able to look at the behaviour of a large group in a single locale. Events in the château are built around two dazzling set pieces. The first is the hunt, a mass slaughter of animals, after which Christine sees Robert give Geneviève a farewell embrace through a spyglass. Mistaking this for the continuation of an affair, she decides she will imitate his infidelity. The second, the *fête de La Colinière*, sees the main characters create chaos by pursuing private ends after uniting briefly for a stage performance. Christine passes between three aspiring lovers chased by her husband as Schumacher hunts Marceau and his wife with a revolver. Peace is temporarily restored. After changes of costume and partners, Schumacher, abetted by Marceau, shoots and kills Jurieux, mistakenly thinking it is Octave running to meet Lisette. All that remains is for Octave to depart with Marceau and for Robert to gloss over the murder by suggesting Schumacher had mistaken Jurieux for a poacher.

Aware of the film's debt to classical theatre, and aided by Renoir's predilection for extended and partially autonomous scenes, critics have sought to identify a three- or five-act structure in it. Such an analysis is of dubious value, and tends to underplay a modernist virtuosity expressed in repeated clashes of genres and disorientating stylistic diversity. Early sequences offer stark contrasts between brilliantly lit, luxurious interiors, swirling night-time crowd scenes at the airport and daytime shooting of Jurieux's high-speed car accident. The hunting sequence generates its ferocity through an accelerating spate of rapid cutting that is completely unlike the rest of the film. In interior scenes at the château, a panning and tracking camera exploits long corridors and capacious spaces to follow the bewildering interaction of large and small groups. Composition in depth and long takes allow several actions to be developed simultaneously, generating an overwhelming impression of disorder. The film's final part picks up the initial alternation of well-lit indoor and dark outdoor shots, now isolating the main characters as they take the momentous decisions which will send Jurieux to his death.

Sesonske is surely right when he suggests that it is more fruitful to examine the film in terms of an alternation between order and disorder, which accentuates the repeated failure of social cohesion (Sesonske 1980: 427–37). The film assembles several groups which fail to come together in any positive manner. André denies the airport crowd the image of public heroism they had sought. The radio audience is bound up in private concerns while the group at the château repeatedly dissolves as individuals pursue selfish aims. Even couples of friends or lovers are unable to stabilise the constant flux as everyone betrays or abandons someone else. The hunt and the film's conclusion are exceptions. The first brings together masters and servants in a coordinated orgy of killing while the second unites the characters in a lie about Jurieux's 'accidental' death. This is a society which has no shared project and can only unite in deceit and destruction.

Deceit runs through the film and is constantly emphasised by the theatrical motif. The film's title, translated as 'The Rules of the Game', could also be rendered as the rules of acting. Classical theatre, as we have noted, provides the cast and the plot of the drama. At various key moments characters refer to what they are doing as 'theatre' or 'comedy,' while the *maître d'hôtel*, Corneille, is named after one of France's most celebrated playwrights. An entire class performs polite respectability as the world falls apart. Robert's final mendacious speech, delivered from a stage-like platform to an audience, consecrates the final triumph of theatre over truth. Jurieux, the character who broke the rules by broadcasting the truth, has been eliminated. He had long since ceased to pose any threat to the established order.

Deceit is accompanied by frivolity, by the constant game-playing that the title also implies. From the start, Robert is seen playing with clockwork figures while Geneviève's assembled guests play cards. The hunt, a ritualised, rule-governed social game gives way to yet more card-playing during the eventful evening at *La Colinière*, where the chequer-board floors, below and above stairs, suggest the characters themselves are like pawns in some absurd game.

What gives the film its edge, what makes the theatrical frivolity so culpable, is the lurking presence of death and war that is present from the moment the film takes us to *La Colinière*. Gunshots are heard from the neighbouring estate where a cull of rabbits is underway, a cull with sinister echoes for a France bounded by Nazi Germany and a Spain in the final stages of civil war. The gamekeeper, Schumacher, has a Germanic name, and a distinct willingness to use guns against people as well as animals, a fact that is initially hinted at when he executes a four-legged poacher, a cat, just before he captures Marceau, the two-legged one. The posture of the dead Jurieux, executed in full flight, visually echoes the slaughter of the fleeing animals and further serves to equate the hunt's savagery with the human slaughter of war. Finally, and most transparently, the *fête* includes a *danse macabre* during which skeletons descend from the stage and move among the audience.

The *fête* takes the film to a paroxysm of chaos and brings together the major motifs of death, theatre and game-playing. Stuffed animals, a reminder of the hunt, are scattered as the main characters pursue each other around the house while death dances behind them. Jolly music accompanies their fighting, stripping it of all dignity. Even as Schumacher fires live bullets at Marceau, card games and dancing continue, murderous intent being taken for part of the show by an audience that can no longer distinguish theatre from reality. Showing a reflected public within the film itself, the film holds up a highly unflattering mirror to French society in 1939.

The other turns in the *fête* are at once disconcerting and highly suggestive. The first piece, 'En rev'nant de la revue', is a Boulangist song and thus part of a French anti-republican tradition. However, the singers' Tyrolean costumes are a sharp reminder to the contemporary audience that Hitler has taken control of Austria. General Boulanger's nationalist defiance of Germany in the 1880s is thus implicitly contrasted with the French right's appeasement of Hitler around the time of the Munich agreement. The second song, 'Nous lèverons le pied', a light-hearted piece, is sung by characters in wigs and costumes that suggest they are Orthodox Jews. Frivolity collides with deadly seriousness as an indigenous tradition of anti-Semitism is evoked even while Jews face intensifying persecution in Germany. Taken as a whole, the *fête* ties the ruling classes into an anti-republican tradition while castigating their egotistical irresponsibility in the face of the rising external threat.

Instead of restoring order to his chaotic domain, La Chesnaye, their leader designate, takes a ludicrous pride in presenting a *limonaire* (a kind of barrel organ) to the audience. His fascination with the clockwork toys, which were enormously popular during the eighteenth century is indicative of a broader, collective flight into the past. Turning their back on the modern – present at the start in the shape of the aeroplane, the sports car and the radio – the characters travel back in time to the château, a microcosm which comes to stand for the nation itself, its upstairs–downstairs division and patrolled estate embodying an unequal society and a threatened territory. With tremendous irony, the land of revolution is now represented by a symbol of counter-revolutionary ideology and pre-revolutionary time.

The common people have lost all capacity for history-making or political change. Marceau, the poacher, is only too happy to take on the uniform of subservience. When he is dismissed he even thanks the Marquis for having bettered him by making him a servant! Lisette is happy to sacrifice her marriage to stay in the service of 'Madame'. When they dine together, the servants display all the prejudice and pretension of those above stairs. Forsaking the attempt to marry progressive politics and popular culture that marked the Popular Front films, Renoir's film locks the common people within the subordinate and self-repeating roles that classical theatre reserves for them. There is no one who can renew this sterile society as it heads for war.

The Frontist films figured the possibility of renewal in their *mise-en-scène* by showing characters breaking out of closed spaces and by opposing the natural world's freedom and vitality to the rule-governed theatricality of a decadent social order. In *La Règle du jeu* the reverse happens. Those characters who existed outside the theatre (Jurieux, Christine, Marceau) are engulfed and corrupted by it. The natural world, present through the estate, is now a site for the ritualised destruction of the hunt. More specifically, the film both echoes and reverses the spatial economy and narrative of *La Marseillaise*. In the earlier film, an episode of poaching leads to arrest, escape to nature and the burning of châteaux. In the later one, the arrested poacher turns his back on nature to work inside the château. *La Marseillaise* shows a weak leader who has an Austrian wife and likes to hunt. A noble named La Chesnaye is prominent in the defence of his palace. In *La Règle du jeu*, La Chesnaye, now the leader himself, has an Austrian wife and hunts but shows no capacity to defend his territory from disorder or intruders. This time, no virile band of brothers is there to do his job.

Renoir's undoing of his own version of the progressive national myth of origins signals the end of his political commitment, a fact indicated in coded form when we are told that La Chesnaye and Christine have been living a lie for three years, the same span of time that separates *La Régle du jeu* from the victory of the Front. The end of his love affair with the common people and with popular culture leaves him with nowhere to turn, for his alternative audience, the wealthy bourgeoisie, is the main target of his savage assault on French society. At one moment in the film, Octave, the character that he himself played, evokes a great concert given by Christine's conductor father to an appreciative public. As he raises an imaginary baton, he halts. There is no public, only the sound of the futile and selfish behaviour in the château.

Despite or perhaps because of its acerbic critique of a whole society, Burch and Sellier suggest that the film provides a progressive analysis of gender relationships. They note the confinement of Christine in a gilded cage that they contrast with Jurieux's conquest of the sky. They suggest that Robert treats Geneviève as simply another object to collect. Only Lisette is able to assert her liberty by keeping her husband at a distance and leading the men on a merry chase, but, ironically, having defied patriarchy, she puts herself entirely at her mistress's service swapping one alienation for another. The finale sees a closing of male ranks in any case as the errant women are brought under control. Burch and Sellier partially undermine their own argument when they note that the disordered gender relations in the film are overdetermined by a broader social disintegration (1996: 74–9). In any case, Christine is so lacking in self-awareness and Lisette so destructively frivolous that it is hard to believe that the film is asking us to sympathise with their state.

Conclusion

The Popular Front period radically transformed Renoir's film-making, drawing it into contemporary political struggles, and endowing it with a sense of nation and history that it had previously lacked. The sense of history was double edged. If the surge of enthusiasm that took the Popular Front to power suggested that radical social transformation was possible, the internal and external forces ranged against the Front meant that this change could be for the worse. Before *La Bête humaine*, the films repeatedly convey both hope and its fragility. Whether it be Lange and Valentine fleeing into exile, Pépel and Natacha on the open road, Maréchal and Rosenthal running through the snow, or Arnaud and the citizen soldiers marching towards war, the films end by showing characters heading into an uncertain future, aware that their world can be shaped, aware too that it may be shaped in ways they cannot control. With this sense of historical becoming, the social frame of the films of the early 1930s loses its solidity. Characters are now no longer simply held and constrained by spaces. They can shape them and escape from them and by so doing change the contours of the stories we see them through, breaking the unending circularity of popular song or the restricted narrative frame of melodrama, reshaping the popular even as they reach out for it. But as the Front crumbles and the hope for progressive change is lost, constraining spaces reclaim their solidity, and the past reaches out to shut off the future, tragically in *La Bête humaine*, grotesquely in *La Règle du jeu*. At the same time, Renoir's cinema signals its abandonment of the attempt to politicise the popular by locking the common people into forms inherited from the naturalist novel and classical theatre.

Frontist commitment and the sense of history and nation give the films of this period a coherence that those of the early 1930s signally lacked. This coherence also embraces *La Bête humaine* and *La Règle du jeu*, films which are expressions of the Front's failure. But coherence does not mean uniformity and the fact that the films are indelibly marked by the Front's evolution does not mean that their meanings are simply determined by it. *Le Crime de Monsieur Lange* and *La Vie est à nous* both date from the radical early phase of the Front and reflect its combativeness but as much separates them as unites them, not least because the latter was made for the PCF. *La Grande Illusion* was being shot while *La Marseillaise* was in gestation and both are part of a Frontist project to reassert a progressive nationalism, but having to deal with the horrors of the Great War, the former has a complexity that the latter, a more propagandist piece, lacks. *La Marseillaise*, conventionally seen as a sign that the Front had run out of steam, is a call for renewed radicalism and thus a reaction to the Front's curve not a product of it. Its politics can only be understood if we recognise that the Front was split by ideological struggle. Those critics who read it in terms of some mythically homogenous Frontist ideology blind themselves to its radical edge.

Readings in terms of a conventionally defined politics flatten out other discontinuities. *Lange* and *Une Partie de campagne* bring gender to the fore, the former giving women a key role in its Utopian reinvention of social relations, the latter inviting us to identify with a woman trapped by oppressive social forms. *La Vie est à nous* and *La Marseillaise* both camouflage their marginal-isation and domestication of women by paying lip-service to their involvement in political struggle in a way that is perhaps indicative of the gender conservatism of the PCF at the time. Inflected by their literary sources, *La Bête humaine* and *Les Bas-fonds* revert to Manichaean stereotyping. No smooth curve can be detected and those films usually seen as the most radical are not necessarily radical in gender terms.

The Front undoubtedly transformed Renoir's cinema. But it did not 'author' it. Each film needs to be seen in the context of the Front and its evolution but seen also as a separate 'event', the coming together of a particular group of people in specific circumstances to deal with a specific theme or text.

References

Bazin, A. (1989), *Jean Renoir*, ed. F. Truffaut, Paris, Lebovici.

Bonitzer *et al.* (1970), 'La Vie est à nous, film militant', *Cahiers du cinéma*, 218, March, 44–51.

Buchsbaum, J. (1988), *Cinéma Engagé. Film in the Popular Front*, Urbana, University of Illinois Press.

Burch, N. and Sellier, G. (1996), *La Drôle de guerre des sexes du cinéma français (1930–1956)*, Paris, Nathan.

Durgnat, R. (1974), *Jean Renoir*, Berkeley, University of California.

Faulkner, C. (1986), *The Social Cinema of Jean Renoir*, Princeton, Princeton University Press.

Faulkner, C. (1996), 'Renoir, technology and affect in *La Bête Humaine*', *Persistence of Vision*, 12/13, 82–101.

Ferro, M. (1993), *Cinéma et histoire*, Paris, Gallimard.

Fofi, G. (1973), 'The Cinema of the Popular Front in France (1934–1938)', *Screen*, 13(4): 5–57.

Grindon, L. (1994), *Shadows of the Past: Studies in the Historical Fiction Film*, Philadelphia, Temple University Press.

Hunt, L. (1996), 'The many bodies of Marie-Antoinette', in Jones, P. ed., *The French Revolution in Social and Historical Perspective*, London, Arnold, 268–84.

Janes, R. (1995), '*Danton* does not sing 'La Marseillaise': Andrzej Wajda, Jean Renoir, and their French revolutions', *Studies in Eighteenth Century Culture*, 25, 293–307.

Lindeperg, S. (1997) *Les Ecrans de l'ombre. La seconde guerre mondiale dans le cinéma français (1944–1969)*, Paris, CNRS.

Oms, M. (1962), 'Renoir revu et rectifié', in Chardère, B. (1962), *Premier Plan* (special number on Renoir), 22/23/24, 44–51.

Pateman, C. (1988), *The Sexual Contract*, London, Polity.

Poulle, F. (1969), *Renoir 1938 ou Jean Renoir pour rien?*, Paris, Editions du Cerf.

Reader, K. and Vincendeau, G., eds, (1986), *La Vie est à Nous: French Cinema of the Popular Front*, London, BFI / National Film Theatre.

Renoir, J. (1974), *Ecrits, 1927–1971*, (Gauteur, ed.), Paris, Belfont.

Renoir, J. (1989), *Le Passé vivant*, (Gauteur, ed.), Paris, *Cahiers du cinéma*.

Reynolds, S. (1996), *France between the Wars. Gender and Politics*, London, Routledge.

Roberts, M. L. (1994), *Civilization without Sexes. Reconstructing Gender in Post-war France, 1917–1927*, Chicago, University of Chicago Press.

Schérer, M. (1952), 'Renoir américain', *Cahiers du cinéma*, 2(8): 33–40.

Serceau, D. (1981), *Jean Renoir, l'insurgé*, Paris, Le Sycomore.

Sesonske, A. (1980), *Jean Renoir. The French Films, 1924–1939*, Cambridge, MA, Harvard.

Viry-Babel, R. (1994), *Le Jeu et la règle*, Paris, Ramsay.

'Renoir américain'

André Bazin's initial response to the American films of Jean Renoir is an instructive one. Suggesting that the only positive features of the films are like surviving fragments of a shipwreck, he finds evidence of the struggle of Renoir's French genius with the standardised American production system (Bazin 1952: 10). His reaction is typical of the *Cahiers* critics' search for authorial creativity beneath the veneer of the standardised Hollywood product. Typical too of the view of French intellectuals of different political persuasions that American economic power in general and Hollywood in particular represented a major threat of massification and homogenisation to French culture in the post-war period. But Bazin then reconsiders and suggests that the films show evidence of an inner struggle during which Renoir distils and purifies his style in the course of a transformation that is more spiritual than aesthetic. He does not reject entirely his early analysis of a struggle between Renoir and Hollywood, but he now frames this struggle positively by locating it in a narrative of personal growth. Renoir, he suggests, faced his own negation in America. Having been totally rooted in the France of his day, he only escaped complete destruction by transcendence of the conjunctural and the national through the search for a human essence. Rather than absorbing him, Hollywood makes him become international (Bazin 1952: 12–13).

Maurice Schérer (aka Eric Rohmer) a fellow *Cahiers* critic, denies categorically that Renoir had in any way been hamstrung by the Hollywood system. He supports this assertion by detecting a complete freedom to improvise on the set in the two films that most obviously feed off American myths, *The Southerner* and *Swamp Water*. Great artists do not decline. Renoir has simply sought the more denuded style that is characteristic of the late period of creative geniuses, so that while an early American film like *Swamp Water* still echoes the virtuosity of *La Règle du jeu*, a later one such as *The Woman on the Beach* has a generally static camera. Renoir has, at the same time, moved beyond the surface realism of the 1930s to an exploration of inner truth and spiritual life (Schérer 1952: 33–40).

Although different in detail, these readings share a belief that the films remain the expression of a great individual artist and show an essential continuity beneath surface changes while taking Renoir to a new level of spiritual exploration. Writing thirty years later, Serceau still shares many of the same assumptions. He locates Renoir's Hollywood production in an ongoing existential quest and suggests that it is thematically tied together by an exploration of freedom and its limitations (Serceau 1985: 231–7).

In contrast, Christopher Faulkner considers this period to be one of uncertainty and transition for Renoir when the director has no clear sense of direction and no coherent or consistent message to communicate. He has a generally low opinion of 'Renoir américain' and rejects the *auteurist* notion that the works form a coherent part of a cohesive *œuvre*, commenting that the films have little in common even with each other (Faulkner 1986: 126–7). He only analyses two of the American films, *This Land is Mine* and *The Southerner*. The former is considered to be a prolongation of Renoir's work of the 1930s, one that echoes the expression of disarray of the bourgeois artist–intellectual first manifested through Octave in *La Règle du jeu*, while the latter gives the first indications of the new conservative ideological directions that will come to mature expression in the films of the 1950s. Faulkner suggests that *The Southerner* is 'his most American film, fitting neatly into determinedly (and determined) American ideological–generic structures' (Faulkner 1986: 145). He agrees to a degree with Bazin and Rohmer in his reading of it, seeing it as seeking an 'essentialist "inner" reality that transcends historical conditions of time and place', but for him this is evidence of the desocialisation of Renoir's cinema, its loss of the capacity to represent the concrete realities of the class struggle at a particular historical moment (Faulkner 1986: 156). Faulkner also shares with Rohmer and Bazin the belief that the 1940s are a transition period for Renoir, but for him this transition is not a broadening and a deepening of an essentially unchanging personal outlook, but an ideological rupture due to spatial and historical separation from the Popular Front.

Durgnat very helpfully suggests some of the complexity of analysing this phase of Renoir's production, distancing himself from the two extreme assumptions that Renoir was swamped by Hollywood or that he remained entirely unaltered and self-consistent. He suggests that Renoir may have made a 'pre-compromise' with Hollywood which allowed him latitude but still forced him to develop in certain directions (Durgnat 1974: 270). This distinction between a Renoir overwritten by American codes and ideologies and one capable of negotiating his interaction with them is a useful one. However, in somewhat characteristic manner, Durgnat ultimately adopts a distinctly *auterist* position. Jettisoning the complexities he himself had unveiled, he sums up the films in terms of the director's 'developing social thought', writing that Renoir 'seems to be pursuing a series of reflections on the nature of society, the intricacy of relationships, and the need for an effort of sacrifice, before the individual can acquire, not what he thinks he wants, but what he really wants' (Durgnat 1974: 296).

Renoir's letters throw relatively little light on his artistic evolution in the United States although they do highlight the difficulty he had adapting to the studio system while acknow-ledging the considerable latitude he enjoyed for some of the films (Renoir 1994). More sustained and concentrated comment on the American years can be found in the same issue of *Cahiers du cinéma* in which the key Bazin and Rohmer articles appeared. He compares himself during this period to someone lost in a jungle, but determined to move on despite not knowing where he is going. He none the less reads this disarray positively as a sign that he has not lost touch with an unstable world (Renoir 1952a). In another piece in the same number of *Cahiers*, he talks of the war as a turning point in his life after which he is 'reborn'. Although he does not separate out the relative importance of the conflict from the exile it imposed upon him, it is clear that he believes that he must radically reinvent his art, seeking a style to express a new personality, and a tone suited to different times (Renoir 1952b). Interestingly, Faulkner and the *auteurist* critics tend to coincide in giving less importance than Renoir himself to the war. Interested above all in conflicts within society, Faulkner does not seem able to incorporate war between nations into his analytical frame, while Bazin, Rohmer and Durgnat seem incapable of engaging with the complexities of a specific historical conjuncture because of methodological individualism or a humanist belief in an unchanging human essence.

One key problem is that critics seem to assume a dehistoricised and homogenised America that is somehow the antithesis of France. Perhaps this is because 'Renoir américain' was seen on European screens when the cold war was raging and the world seemed polarised between two monolithic blocs. It is assumed that the Renoir of the Popular Front could not possibly have survived into the American period. However, the picture becomes more complex if one accepts that the 1930s and 1940s were a time of ideological struggle when ideas of the left had a much greater audience in America than they would have in the 1950s. Even if Roosevelt's New Deal should be seen as an attempt to shore up capitalism rather than to fundamentally challenge it, the Great Depression of the 1930s had served to radicalise sectors of American society and create an audience for more genuinely socialist values. Some of Renoir's key associates at this time, people like Dudley Nichols and Clifford Odets, were known to be active on the liberal or radical left. Moreover, once the Soviet Union had become involved in the fight against Nazism and the USA had entered the war at the end of 1941, official government policy was recognisably Frontist, supporting an international alliance between liberal democracy and Communism to defeat Fascism. With an official Communist line that prioritised national unity and left the class struggle on the back burner, the apparent ideological gap between the liberal reformist democracy of New Deal America and the policies of the Communist left was narrower than ever. There is thus no reason to assume that Renoir, even if somehow swallowed up by America, could not have remained loyal to Popular Front values, and indeed to the left, much longer than is generally assumed.

The dramatic ideological and political turnabouts of this period (which critics almost entirely neglect) could help throw light on Renoir's own disarray. He had been deeply disillusioned by the collapse of the Popular Front and, disgusted, one must assume, by the non-aggression pact that Stalin signed with Hitler. But soon after he arrived in the United States, the Soviet Union was actively engaged in the war against Fascism, while Frontist values would again come to the fore in the left-wing dominated French Resistance. In the light of these dizzying reversals it might be better to see Renoir as pulled this way and that, rather than as following any clear progression.

Some consideration of Renoir's own personal relationship to France and the United States is also necessary. His direct knowledge of France was from the 1930s. His two Hollywood portrayals of his country need to be considered in the light of that. Although it is inevitable that they were inflected by Hollywood, the United States and the wartime context, it would be surprising if his 1930s vision did not also play a major part. On the other hand, Renoir experienced the United States as a refuge, a haven of freedom in a world where freedom was increasingly in short supply. Hollywood was also the film capital of the world. It would be unrealistic to expect a newly arrived exile director who was desperate to prove himself to immediately engage in a critique of American capitalism and institutions or indeed of a society with which he was generally unfamiliar. There was far less reason for political restraint when speaking of France, a country seen to be collaborating with the enemy.

There were other reasons less connected to personal circumstances for which Renoir would have found it difficult to criticise the USA. Although the country was officially at peace when his first American film was shot, it was soon engaged in the fighting and film-makers were under great pressure to provide essentially positive images of the country. Koppes and Black describe how the Office of War Information (OWI) did not wish to present America as perfect but wished to generate national unity and show how diminishing inequality meant that everyone had a stake in the war's outcome. Hollywood often resisted the OWI line, but this was because it was considered too political and not because the studios objected to delivering positive images (Koppes and Black 1988: 67–9). After December 1942, the Office of Censorship issued a new code banning the showing of labour, class or other disturbances (Koppes and Black 1988: 125). A further relevant consideration is that the two films wherein Renoir depicts American society (as opposed to the isolated individuals of *Woman on the Beach*), are set in a south whose film censors were notoriously touchy about how their states were depicted. Koppes and Black suggest that Hollywood had to avoid negative portrayals of the south and kowtow to the censors' racist attitudes (Koppes and Black 1988: 85).

My own reading of 'Renoir américain' will draw on some of the analyses considered above while remedying, I hope, their shared failure to relate the films sufficiently to the conjuncture. What I will retain from Faulkner's argument is his notion of the ideological shift in Renoir, but where he implies a linear transformation, I will suggest, inspired partly by Renoir's own comments, a more complex toing and froing before Frontist values are finally abandoned. Durgnat's undeveloped suggestion that Renoir was able to some extent to negotiate his encounter with Hollywood is a necessary corrective to the ideological determinism of Faulkner. Bazin's notion that Renoir transcended the narrowly national is a useful one, but he pays far too little attention to the degree to which the war itself, rather than exile alone, may have led Renoir to question what he saw as the key values of the West.

I will suggest that the films can be usefully grouped along the following lines. *Swamp Water* and *The Southerner* can be seen as an outsider's engagement with myths of America. *This Land is*

Mine and *Diary of a Chambermaid*, while noticeably inflected by Hollywood, have clear links to Renoir's Popular Front films. *The Woman on the Beach* and *The River* deal in their very different ways with the profoundly destabilising effects of the war and attempt to come to terms with it. Both show men psychologically or physically maimed by the fighting.

Myths of America

Swamp Water (1941), Renoir's first American film, is set in Georgia, in and on the edges of Okefenokee, an enormous swamp. Its engagement with American myth is immediately apparent when it restages the encounter of man and wilderness in a narrative structured around a family and a self-contained rural community. The treacherous swamp is unpeopled except for the presence of one man, Tom Keefer, who has fled after apparently committing a murder. The main character of the film, Ben, will affirm his right to independent manhood by braving the swamp against the express orders of his stern father, becoming a successful trapper and trader with Keefer's help.

Yet the real Okefenokee had not been unpeopled. It had been hunted by Native Americans who had been 'displaced' by settlers. These settlers had in turn had their activities limited by federal government which had made Okefenokee into a nature reserve as attitudes to nature shifted and wilderness became something to preserve and contemplate rather than something to tame and exploit. Renoir thus connived wittingly or unwittingly in the mythic erasure of two conflicts: the genocide of Native Americans and the struggle between the state and private interests.[1] By way of contrast, it is worth recalling his radical appropriation of American mythology in *Le Crime de M. Lange*, a film whose fictional western hero had been seen to side with the American Indians against the men in uniform and with the little men against the powerful.

1 Renoir's letters show that he was fully conscious that Native Americans had lived in the swamp and that there was also a substantial black population (Renoir 1984: 66).

Although *Swamp Water* occludes the dark sides of American history, it does explore tensions in national mythology that were particularly relevant to a fast-changing country poised between economic crisis and war. By the time the film was made, the United States was a predominantly urban country dominated by large-scale capitalism and where, following the Great Depression, the central state played a strong role. The frontier had been closed before the end of the nineteenth century, consigning the encounter with the wilderness to the past. However, the mythical healing powers of the rural had regularly featured in 1930s Hollywood production (Shindler 1996: 146). In times of tension or large-scale social change, as John Rennie Short has pointed out, rural myths become more prevalent (Short 1991: 30). For a country increasingly dominated by big business and with large-scale unemployment, evocation of the rural allowed a return to simpler, more innocent times and the reaffirmation of foundational values. A focus on the tight-knit social bonds of the rural helped Americans to reimagine a sense of community and interdependence in a modern world increasingly characterised by anonymous or impersonal interaction. The staging and resolution of the tension between rugged individualism and community had particular relevance to a society whose capitalism needed to be tempered in the light of the Depression.

Renoir's film begins its exploration and containment of tensions within key American myths by focusing on the family. Durgnat has pointed out the Oedipal nature of the initial situation, remarking 'incest hovers over Ben's family' and adding 'psycho-analytically, the film is structured about Ben's efforts to come to terms with, and take his true place in, society against two equally disquieting father-figures' (Durgnat 1974: 232). As the film begins, Ben's father, Thursday, is told by his younger second wife that she gets lonely when he is away hunting. Behind her apparently maternal affection for Ben, there lurks the hint of the possibility of a more illicit attachment. Moreover, Thursday is clearly a barrier to his son's achievement of manhood, ruling his household with a rod of iron, keeping his son perpetually in the place of the child, and denying him access to the forbidden territory of the swamp.

Banishment from the family follows the breaking of the father's law.

As the film progresses, the initial fraught tensions are displaced onto outsiders. The murder which would have removed the all-powerful father is now born by Keefer, and later, as the film resolves into a happy ending, by the villainous Dawson brothers. Illicit passion devolves to Jesse Wick who comes to visit Thursday's bored wife in the absence of the patriarch and becomes the potential target for his violent rage. The Oedipal crime of stealing the father's wife is further and rather comically displaced onto the Dawsons whom we learn are pig thieves who abscond with other men's livestock. Finally, female betrayal passes to Mabel, Ben's beautiful but fickle girlfriend who goes to the dance with another man and reveals Keefer's presence in the swamp.

The displacement of Oedipal crimes onto scapegoats allows the family to be rehabilitated and a broader social bond to be simultaneously re-established. Ben initially sees his father only as a vengeful law giver but later discovers that he is a loving protector. Thursday wrongly doubts his wife's fidelity. Keefer misrecognises Ben, seeing him initially as a threat that may have to be destroyed and later as a traitor. In a more general way, he wrongly learns to mistrust an entire community, later to be reassured by Ben that many of them are 'good men'. The swamp encapsulates this drama of ambivalence and misleading appearances. A labyrinthine place of danger for the community, it shelters and nourishes Keefer. Its quicksand proves fatal to the Dawson brother who fails to detect it, even as it saves Ben and Keefer from his murderous intent. Like the swamp, women must be read properly. Mabel's studied control of her appearance allows her to win the undeserved affections and attentions of the men and to set them against each other. Learning his lesson, Ben sees beyond the wild appearances of Julie, Keefer's daughter, to a hidden beauty that he uncovers and can thus control.

The society in *Swamp Water* is one dominated by men but there is clear tension between their characteristics and the maintenance of community. This tension echoes one expressed in that key American genre, the western, where rugged, violent manhood cannot be integrated into the tame and civilised world that it had apparently fought to establish. The western hero typically has to move on.[2] *Swamp Water* interestingly shows us men who learn to live in both wilderness and community by negotiating a compromise between rugged individualism and interdependence. Thursday is initially an inflexible, strong and violent man. Similarly, Keefer seems unable to deal with others except through violence. As the film progresses, however, both he and Thursday discover a softer side to themselves, which tempers their more 'masculine' qualities without replacing them. Keefer learns to work with Ben while both men reveal their paternal protectiveness. The film is one of absent mothers – both Ben's and Julie's mothers being dead – but it would seem that the softened fathers can find sufficient 'maternal' qualities in themselves to hold families and community together. Ironically, their softening enables them to take centre stage in both home and wilderness, increasing the male-centredness of the narrative rather than lessening it.

Their softening also helps to legitimise the key foundational myth of the self-made man, an individual entrepreneur, who carries the rugged individualism of the frontier into the business world. Ben is such a figure. He achieves independent adult status through survival in Okefenokee and exploitation of its natural resources but economic individualism is tempered by his partnership with Keefer, his soon to be father-in-law. Keefer himself seeks profit mainly for his daughter. Male bonding and bonds of kinship thus serve to domesticate and legitimise the more savage side of the pursuit of wealth and the subjugation of nature.

While the men have to negotiate their passage between domestic and wild, between independence and community, the women are essentially confined to domestic subservience. Thursday's wife is limited to the home, while the 'wild' Julie moves from being a domestic drudge to cleaning Ben's temporary accommodation, even as he turns her from ugly duckling to tame swan. Her double domestication makes her an eminently suitable mate.

2 For a discussion of the gendered nature of the western and the way it is used to re-establish male hegemony, see Tompkins (1989).

Considered alongside Thursday's initial anxieties over his wife and Mabel's destructive behaviour, it would also suggest that there is a significant anxiety about women at the heart of this story of 'strong' men.

The swamp is a place rich with meanings some of which have already been suggested. A testing ground for manhood and a natural resource ripe for economic entrepreneurship, it is also a place where Keefer finds himself closer to God and comes to terms with human failings by recognising their reflection in the natural world. Like society and human 'nature,' the swamp is both murderous and duplicitous and truthful and nurturing. To these multiple meanings which feed off a complex inherited discourse about the wilderness, I would like to add a further dimension by suggesting that the swamp can be seen as a female space, a space that encapsulates some of the dangers and attractions of the feminine in the film.[3] The film's small community is a patriarchal one dominated by the fathers and their laws. The swamp is a place where these laws do not apply, a place that, like a mother, offers nourishment and protection, but which also threatens to engulf or swallow up the males who seek to linger there, retaining them forever in a state of infancy outside of adult society. Ultimately, this threat of the engulfing maternal is defused by a masculine narrative of conquest and exploitation of nature that closely parallels the domestication of the women in the community.

Having explored a series of tensions within and between foundational American myths and institutions, *Swamp Water* ultimately achieves ideological closure by reaffirming their posi-tive qualities and displacing conflict onto scapegoats. The strong and potentially destructive male is domesticated without losing his masculinity. The community is re-established as a centre of

3 Short (1991) explores the rich discursive inheritance associated with wilderness. He tells us that the wilderness becomes a place of fear with the emergence of settled agriculture, but that in the nineteenth century, romanticism produces a pantheistic counter-discourse associating untamed space with the divine presence in nature, so that wilderness becomes a place of communion with God and with a truer self. He very usefully shows how European settlers used the notion of transforming the wilderness into a garden as a justification for their presence in America (Short 1991: 8–22 and 92–9).

pastoral virtue and the family unit is stabilised as the potentially explosive sexual tensions within it are safely defused. Economic entrepreneurship is shown to be socially cohesive rather than productive of egotistical individualism. The ultimate ideological conservatism of the film, its affirmation of continuity rather than revolt, is clearly revealed by the implicit pact between the two fathers and the son that is sealed when Keefer gives his daughter to Ben, thus allowing the latter to reproduce the patriarchal family of his father. However, it should also be noted that concurrently with the reaffirmation of foundational myths, we also see a softening of them, a negotiation of their meanings rather than a simple restatement of them.

This negotiation needs to be viewed in terms of the interplay of Renoir's specific situation, the influence of Hollywood and the socio-historical conjuncture, an interplay whose complexity makes it naïve to seek to identify any simple relationship between cause and effect. While one can see why a newly arrived Renoir might find it easier to explore key American myths rather than overturn them, the heavy hand of Zanuck might also help to explain the ideological conservatism of the film. Its tempering of economic individualism by family and community is more broadly understandable in a climate of economic depression (when *laissez-faire* capitalism has been substantially delegitimised), and in a period of impending war when community solidarity becomes imperative. The return to foundational values is typical of periods of crisis.

The Southerner (1945), seen by Renoir and many others as his most successful Hollywood film, is in some ways much less interesting than *Swamp Water*, taking far less time to explore tensions before reaffirming key myths in the way noted by Christopher Faulkner (1986: 145–61). Essentially it tells the story of Sam Tucker and his family who decide, following the advice of the dying 'uncle Pete' to stop working for others on a cotton plantation and to start their own farm. There follows a tale of trials and tribulations at the hands of a malevolent neighbour and the destructiveness of nature. The Tuckers come through due to the mutual support of husband and wife, help from the local community and the loyalty of a distant city 'cousin', Tim.

The film is fascinating for its fleeting evocation of major social conflicts and of a counter-mythical America. The first scene suggests a gritty social realism in the manner of classic Depression-era films such as *The Grapes of Wrath* (1940). The uncle's death highlights the back-breaking labour in the plantation while the migration towards the north of a Latino cotton-worker and the cousin's preference for steady wages in a factory evoke the long agricultural depression which forced many off the land and the more general transformation of a society increasingly dominated by the city. The southern plantation itself hints at two things: first, the dark side of America's origins, the mass exploitation of slave labour and the system of apartheid that was far from dead when Renoir arrived in America; second, the triumph of capitalist production in a country that had always celebrated the independent farmer. Yet none of this rich potential for social criticism is built upon. A director who had centred *Toni* on the experience of immigrants in France, cast a black character in a supporting role in *La Grande Illusion* and alluded to the rescue of a Negro from a lynch mob in *Le Crime de Monsieur Lange,* could find no significant place for oppressed minorities in a film set in the American south.

Instead, after its initial hint of something very different, *The Southerner* reinvigorates American myths in a conservative manner; the conquest of a wild land by the small farmers whose independence and strong-mindedness made them the backbone of American democracy; the centrality of the family as foundation of society; the goodness of small rural communities; the key role of religion. The borrowed, rickety lorry that takes the Tuckers to the abandoned shack on a deserted farm at once evokes the voyages of the pioneers to new lands and reverses the traumatic voyage from (apparent) independence to capitalist exploitation experienced by the Joads in *The Grapes of Wrath.* The Tuckers thus undertake a journey back in time to a seemingly more innocent and socially cohesive America. In the process, Sam lives up to the exacting standards set by the grandmother for previous generations of Tucker men.

As in *Swamp Water,* conflicts and tensions are displaced onto scapegoats. The principal villain of the piece is not the capitalist owner who can take Sam's land away on a whim but the Tuckers' new neighbour, Devers, a man soured by his own bitter struggle to become an independent farmer and by the loss of his wife. His selfish refusal to help and tyrannical domination of his own family are a counter-example to the neighbourly and mutually supportive Tuckers. Representing the unacceptable face of American values, he asserts that the poor must work for the wealthy and that there must be those who give orders and those who take them. His vision of a social bond dominated by inequality and purely financial ties associates venal egotism with one embittered man rather than with capitalism itself, while his eventual taming is a perfect example of the fictional resolution of real ideological tensions.

However, the chief source of the Tuckers' woes is the natural world. First, in the form of 'spring sickness' resulting from vitamin deprivation during the winter months. Second, when a storm and ensuing flood destroy the bumper crop of cotton which had seemed to confirm man's ability to make the wilderness flower. The family overcome the first problem with the help of Tim and the community and the second primarily through their own inner strength. The end sees them not triumphant but united, unbroken and indeed fortified by resistance to adversity.

The conflict with unpredictable natural forces gives the film an existential quality. It becomes a comment on the human condition rather than the work of social realism it seemed initially to promise. Its most striking images suggest an elemental struggle reduced to its most basic elements. The Tuckers' flimsy shack embodies the fragility of human enterprises, while the smoking stove and pot of hot coffee become symbols of human resilience that emerge in moments of adversity. Shots of Sam against the sky place him above all in a metaphysical context while those of the couple labouring together indicate determined solidarity in the face of overwhelming forces.

As in *Swamp Water*, closeness to nature generates a feeling of closeness to God that creates an interpretative framework that invites us to dehistoricise human behaviour. The vagaries and injustices of life are desocialised by location in a natural order that can be cruel as well as benevolent, destructive as well as nurturing.

It would not of course be difficult to argue that the 'natural' order in both films is produced for the especially conflictual and uncertain conjuncture of depression, social polarisation and war. The non-interventionist policy of the deity allows a moral framework to be maintained even in an apparently amoral natural order.

Unlike in *Swamp Water*, however, the principal family portrayed is not wracked by Oedipal tensions. The Tuckers are a model of internal harmony, self-abnegation, and mutual support.[4] Through their unselfish struggle with elemental forces, the desire to produce and sell becomes an act of moral rectitude and epic heroism. Their tight family bonds offer a model of social cohesion that extends to the broader community when Sam's widowed mother marries the local storekeeper. Tim, Sam's city friend and representative of the northern states and of urban America, is an adoptive family member. Interpersonal links thus hold together not only the local community but also the broader national one, spreading out from the family to embrace the nation, even at a time when the social bond was becoming increasingly abstract and impersonal in an ever more urbanised America.

The problematic and unequal relationship between the urban and rural and between large-scale capitalism and small producer is simply evaded. Through Tim, the city, the factory and capitalist production are presented simply as an alternative choice made by a friend, not as threats to Sam's status as independent producer. Sam's freedom in production is equated with Tim's freedom in consumption as the two men's friendship becomes a model for national cohesion. As the film ends, the debate about relative merits of the city and the country resolves with the conclusion that they are mutually supportive, that factories produce guns and tractors for the farmers while the latter produce food for the city.

Complementarity between city and country is matched by complementarity between men and women within the family although gender anxiety is again hinted at when Sam and Tim are driven comically out of a bar, not by the male owner, but by a

4 The only disharmony we see is used for comic effect and is produced by the defeatism and petty selfishness of grandma Tucker, someone who is always overruled by Sam and Nona, his wife.

bottle-throwing prostitute. Later, in another comic incident, Tim and Sam are knocked down by Nona and another woman. Earlier, at the beginning of the film, we had seen that cotton picking was carried out by men and women without gender differentiation. The small farm puts things back in their place. Although Nona is mentally and physically strong, buoying up the morale of her husband and working beside him, she never questions his role as head of the family. The tasks they carry out within and outside the home are complementary so that, for example, Sam hunts while Nona prepares the food. The rural family thus serves to promote yet contain a vision of female strength within a gendered social order.

What is one to make of *The Southerner*? Having seemed for a few minutes to promise a radical critique of cherished American myths, it then does a sharp about-turn, reaffirming visions of rural virtue and community and erasing social conflicts and oppression. The film can best be understood as a wartime film which polishes up American mythology for a time of crisis. The war promotes Manichaean thinking. It is seen as a conflict between good and evil, freedom and slavery, democracy and tyranny. Turning its back on the dark side of America, *The Southerner* produces a vision to suit this climate. War demands social unity. The film generates a picture of interdependence which spreads from the rural family, its pillar, to pull together north and south, city and country, capitalism and independent labour. The rural virtues of self-sacrifice, hard work and perseverance are precisely those needed in times of war. War required that American women participate actively in the economy and be strong. The film promotes such strength and participation while containing it safely within a traditional rural family.

Echoes of the Popular Front?

There is an astonishing contrast between the ideological conservatism of the two films we have just considered and the films Renoir made about France, *This Land is Mine* (1943) and *The Diary of a Chambermaid* (1946). The former was received with great hostility in France. It was seen as a Hollywood product that typified the threat to French cinema from across the Atlantic, a papier-mâché studio reconstruction of France, and worst of all, a melodramatic parody of the French Resistance from someone who had viewed the war from the safety of California. A star vehicle for Charles Laughton and Maureen O'Hara, it is a wartime propaganda piece with transparently didactic intentions, these being at their most flagrantly obvious when, in defiance of all verisimilitude, Laughton delivers a long courtroom speech denouncing the occupier and collaboration under the eyes of a watching German officer. The film's wordy speeches inevitably angered French critics who associated 'authentic' resistance with low-key, non-cinematic heroism. But there is perhaps another unexplored reason for French hostility to the film. Unlike the batch of resistance features that appeared after the war, Renoir's film links the wartime period to the internal struggles of the 1930s rather than producing a narrative structured around the fight against an external foe. Moreover, it dwells on the degree of collaboration in France as well as the distinctly non-heroic behaviour of a majority intent on survival, both aspects of the war that the French preferred to erase. Most scandalously, French anti-Semitism is clearly evoked in a scene where an entire class of schoolboys write the letter 'J' on the face of a Jewish child.

The film opens with a shot of a small town square labelled 'somewhere in Europe', but which is clearly meant to be France. We see the monument to the dead of the First World War. The crawling position of its stone soldier clearly evokes national humiliation. As the invaders pour forcefully into the town, the old mayor reluctantly shakes the German major's hand, clearly echoing the famous handshake between Pétain and Hitler. His policy of collaboration involves him in delivering a quiescent population to the occupiers and in economic cooperation which takes the form of increasing shipments of food to Germany. He rationalises his actions as a desire to protect the people of the town. More ideologically motivated collaboration comes from the middle-class Georges, a railway supervisor who has been an enemy of the Popular Front and its struggle for workers' rights. Laughton's character, Albert Lory, suggests that Georges's class are tempted by collaboration because they associate liberty with chaos and disorder. He adds that businessmen grow rich through collaboration and at the end of the war will own the town. Knowing that the Germans will make them slaves, the working class are immune from the temptation to collaborate. The heroic resister in the film, Paul Martin, is in fact a railway signalman. Intellectual leadership comes from Professor Sorel, the local headteacher and brains behind the clandestine newspaper. Both Sorel and Major von Keller, the German commander, mobilise the European cultural heritage in their struggle for hearts and minds. After Sorel's execution, Lory overcomes his cowardice. His final act of defiance is to read the *Déclaration des droits de l'homme et du citoyen* to his class.

The film clearly offers a Frontist reading of the occupation whereby capitalists and other ideological enemies betray France and the working class while the republican tradition and the Revolution are mobilised against Fascism. The typically Frontist alliance of intellectual and worker is at the core of resistance in the film. The narrative has, however, another less obviously political centre, the stifling of Albert Lory by an overprotective mother, which Faulkner with his narrow vision of the political cannot deal with other than by equating the timid Lory to Renoir himself and seeing the film in confessional terms (Faulkner 1986: 141–5).

Yet the occupation was often seen in gendered terms, as France's passive and supine position before the conquering occupier translated easily into a vision of a feminised or unmanned nation. The opening shots of the stone soldier on his knees illustrate this. When the film begins, Lory lives with his mother who dominates him entirely, telling him to have nothing to do with resistance pamphlets. She spoils him with black-market milk, using that maternal drink to maintain him in a state of infancy. She discourages his affections for Louise Martin, the sister of Paul and his colleague at the school, chasing away Louise's cat, the animal most associated with female sensuality. While Lory is terrified during air raids, she is unconcerned by them, her strength thus being directly associated with his weakness. When Lory becomes a 'man', finds the courage to oppose the Germans and declares his love for Louise, his mother is reduced to passive silence, as a 'proper' state of affairs is restored.

The school is an alternative centre of child-rearing to the home, one that is in the public domain, and thus controlled by men rather than women. It reminds the children of their correct gender roles. When there is a bombing raid, they are told, 'don't let the girls be better soldiers than the boys'. When a boy's father is taken away by the Germans, he is told 'you go home and comfort your mother, you're the man now'. At the end of the film, Lory reads the rights of man to a class made up entirely of boys and when he is led away by the Germans, Louise carries on for him, telling the next generation of men about the political rights that the Third Republic never thought to give her. A woman's strength and courage is again acceptable only if she plays a supporting role. When von Keller admits that the Germans would be worried about Louise if she were not to be married to Georges, a reliable man, it seems that the film endorses the attitudes of the occupier in one respect at least.

A castrating mother, an unmanned son and a strong woman whom the son loves are again the core of Renoir's next Hollywood French film, *The Diary of a Chambermaid*, (1946) loosely adapted from the celebrated and scandalous anarchist turn-of-the century novel by Octave Mirbeau. But, while *This Land is Mine* was an unsubtle and transparently didactic piece, *The Diary* returns us to the aesthetic complexity of *La Règle du jeu*, mingling elements of vaudeville, light pastoral, melodrama and sinister gothic to produce a challenging and difficult film. It collapses the novel's multiple episodes into one story, adapting it for an American audience and responding, albeit implicitly, to the French experience of the Second World War. With its deliberately incongruous and disturbing mix of elements, it could be described as a violent farce or sadistic fantasy. The action centres on a familiar story of masters and exploited servants. Mme Lanlaire, wealthy chateau owner and domestic tyrant, embodies counter-revolution and an entrenched hierarchical vision. Her husband's unending and ridiculous struggles with their apparently free-thinking but also cruel and violent neighbour, Mauger, would suggest the internal struggles of the French right, for, beneath the surface differences between the two groups, they share an attachment to inequality. Both hoard wealth, live in privilege and keep servants. More specifically, the Lanlaires' attachment to ancestral silver, which they only get out to mourn the Revolution, suggests a segment of French society unable to let go of the past or bury the hatchet. Captain Mauger can be tentatively linked to Bonapartism. A military man, he is happy to mingle with the populace unlike the élitist Lanlaire, while his pet squirrel, Kleber, carries the name of Napoleon's favourite general.

Pressure for change comes from two sources, Joseph, the butler and Célestine, the heroine, a new servant, who refuses from the start to accept subordination meekly and hesitates between individualism and a more collective vision of salvation, finally opting for the latter through her distribution of the stolen silver to the festive crowd celebrating 14 July. Joseph's alternative escape route from social subordination and economic inequality is to usurp the wealth of Mauger and the Lanlaires. Célestine is tempted to join with him but it is clear that she is very different from a coldly sadistic man who kills geese (and later Mauger) by slowly driving a long pin into their brains. Joseph's theft can be seen as a claiming of the anti-democratic inheritance of the French right by a violent outsider from the lower orders. He scorns the Republic, saying it is for weaklings.

Can we thus see the film as a thinly veiled comment on the wartime period? Costumes and the symbolic struggles over the newly institutionalised 14 July celebrations would seem to locate it in the *fin-de-siècle* period. Yet the novel's precisely situated refer–ences to social and political quarrels have been erased and replaced by the broadest of brush strokes. Gone is talk of Drumont, Barrès, Dreyfus and Déroulède. Gone too are anti-Protestantism, anti-Semitism and defence of the army. Because of this imprecision, the film can be linked to the period of war and liberation and, I would add, to the broad sweep of modern French history. One does not have to look very far into the Lanlaires' counter-revolutionary attitudes and Joseph's sadistic anti-republicanism to find Vichy and Fascism, while Célestine's description of 14 July as 'the day of our freedom' and the carnivalesque behaviour of the crowd clearly evoke the liberation. How could they not do so in 1946?

The film rewrites *La Règle du Jeu* in a way that is apparently more positive, repeating the interplay of servants and masters in a château but showing that the common people have not forsaken their attachment to liberty and do not share the vices of their masters as they had in the earlier film. A key narrative trajectory of *La Règle* is reversed, for while Marceau the previously free man had deliberately chosen domestic service, Célestine breaks out of it. In this respect, *Diary* provides the sort of optimistic vision that France so desperately needed in the immediate aftermath of the war. In other respects it is less comforting.

Having hated the film when he viewed it in terms of realism, Bazin reconciled himself with it by reconsidering it as a dream or a nightmare (Bazin 1989: 88–9). In this nightmare, the French people are stuck in a frozen historical struggle from which they cannot awake due to a privileged and reactionary minority's unwillingness to accept the common people's attachment to their freedom and to the Republic. By the end of the film, the childlike, good-natured populace has the blood of the Fascistic Joseph on its hands. If the 14 July celebrations are evidence of a Utopian wish for community, the symbolic and physical violence which runs through the action, are clear evidence of its failure. And if the liberty-loving, egalitarian crowd may be the image of themselves the French wished to see in 1946, the picture of indigenous counter-revolution and Fascism would have been less welcome.

The Diary is a key transitional film. It links back into the thirties by reviving elements of Renoir's Popular Front outlook, notably a clear alignment with the ordinary people against the privileged. But it also anticipates his later move away from any overt political position and search for a culturally defined national community. Although 14 July was traditionally associated as much with carnival pleasure as political commitment, the film's crowd seems singularly apolitical in the light of the historical conjuncture. They are more interested in dancing and the childish pleasures of the fairground than in radical social change. Indeed, with their capacity to move from childlike innocence to murder, they look forward to Renoir's disillusioned view of the masses in *Eléna et les hommes*, rather than backward to the politically mature revolutionaries of *La Marseillaise*. The film is none the less closer to those of the 1930s than those of the 1950s. The short-lived unity of pro-democratic parties and the euphoria of the liberation seem to have helped Renoir to adopt an overt left-of-centre political position for the last time.

A complicating factor is of course the possible need to water down the politico-historical content for an American public with little interest in or knowledge of French traditions. Indeed, one wonders whether some of the jarring moments in the film were not in fact a consciously engineered collision between Hollywood convention and the seriousness of the subject-matter. The pastoral naïvety of the villagers with their stories of wishing trees, the go-getting attitude of the heroine and the tacked-on romantic happy ending suggest mockery of the dream factory and its products.

In fact, the film has a double ending, showing first the republican crowd gathered round the dead Joseph and then Célestine's romantic departure with Georges. This conclusion brings out the film's unsettling complexity by reminding us of its inextricable interweaving of the collective political and the personal romantic. In the political narrative, Célestine's servant status and struggle for freedom enable her to represent socially subordinate classes in general. However, her oppression also takes on distinctly gendered aspects. She is expected to be a resilient domestic drudge (and there is still sufficient realism in this 'dreamlike' film for her physical efforts to be manifest), and to be attractive, decorative and available. Thus the film would seem to foreground the specific oppressions and contradictory demands visited upon women. Yet the final liberation of the film buries their specific unfreedoms in the more general equation of the republic with liberty, an equation that has its deep ironies given the Third Republic's denial of the vote to women.

The film's already ambivalent sexual politics grow murkier

when we turn to the second, romantic strand in which Célestine is a symbolic object representing liberty for the men, someone who will enable them to escape the juvenile status imposed upon them by the castrating domination of Mme Lanlaire or the (s)mothering of Rose, Mauger's housekeeper. 'Going to Paris' with Célestine comes to signify both escape and the enjoyment of denied adult sexual pleasure. Practising incest by proxy, Mme Lanlaire tries to use Célestine's attractiveness to keep Georges at home. She dresses her seductively and at one moment even sends her to his bedroom in her own nightgown with some hot broth, thus linking smothering, incestuous and castrating maternity together. Georges is too weak from tuberculosis to make the break with his mother, but draws strength from his relationship with Célestine and through fighting with Joseph over her. The other men in the Lanlaire household are repeatedly humiliated by the mistress of the house, to the point that the hen-pecked husband tries to hitch his personal revolt to the celebration of revolution and thus claim his independence from his wife's views, only to cave in at a word from her. What is one to make of this narrative of male humiliation? Most obviously one can link the unmanned males to the context of war and occupation. Like *This Land is Mine*, the film ties revolt against a dominating woman to the seizure of political liberty, with the unfortunate effect that liberty is equated with male autonomy and tyranny with female power.

One can only explain the film's bewildering ambivalence on gender if one assumes that it unreflectingly mobilises existing stereotypes and symbolic associations which are then inflected by the conjuncture and specific features of Mirbeau's story. To the degree that it is a realistic narrative centred on a female domestic, it brings out Célestine's gendered oppression. To the degree that it uses Célestine as representative of a class, it buries it. And to the degree that it links national humiliation with unmanning, it constructs a misogynistic narrative which again takes us back to the 1930s by recalling the unmanned father and tyrannical mother of *La Marseillaise*. It is surely no mere coincidence that, like Louis XVI, Lanlaire uses hunting as a flight from an oppressive situation.

A world turned upside down by war

Gender issues are again central in the next two films considered. In *The Woman on the Beach* (1946), gender disorder crystallises the characters' sense of disarray, while in *The River* (1950), questioning of western values suggests that traditional views of masculinity must be reconsidered. Both films feature physically and psychologically damaged males.

The Woman on the Beach recalls *La Bête humaine* by its sombre, shadowy *mise-en-scène* and exploration of murderous passion. In the earlier film, a small group of characters destroy each other against the social background of a class-ridden society where working-class solidarity is unable to save the doomed hero. In the latter, clear class demarcations are gone, and the stable normality that cannot prevent the drama takes the shape of a small community, something by now familiar from Renoir's American work, but in this case barely sketched in. *The Woman on the Beach* is a *film noir* and in true *noir* fashion explores the dark depths of passion and violence beneath the thin surface of convention. However, it moves the genre away from its usual terrain of the shadowy, rain-swept underside of the city to an elemental setting of clifftop, beach and sea. The décor at once conveys danger, passion and the murky depths of the human psyche within a context of isolation at the very edge of the social world.

The film shows two men who follow very different but strangely parallel trajectories. The central character, Scott, is tormented by nightmares from the war, specifically a sinking ship. He is trying to manage his return from wartime exceptionalism to peacetime normality and in the process must move out of the comforting world of homosocial bonding associated with representations of men in combat. The other male lead, Tod, is a famous artist who has been blinded and has withdrawn from the dizzying social whirl of high society. He cannot adapt to his new quiet life nor to his blindness. Clinging to his last paintings as proof of his powers, he too is tormented by the past. The two men evoke different dimensions of male power. Tod's creativity shaped the world to his artistic will, while Scott, a uniformed officer and virile figure, patrols the coast on horseback. Yet both are effectively paralysed by their inability to deal with the past and thus to face the future. The woman who sets them at each other's throats is played by Joan Bennett, often cast as *femme fatale* at this time.

The violence of war and the disruption it causes to conventional gender roles are tied together from the start by Scott's recurring nightmare in which a blonde woman dressed in bridal white approaches a sunken ship only for flames to burst out and for the blonde woman to be replaced by a dark one. In an attempt to escape from his torments, Scott tries to advance his marriage to his blonde fiancée, Eve, only to find that she refuses. In the absence of both her father and brother, Bill Gedden senior and junior, and the breaking of the smooth patriarchal continuity suggested by the shared name, she has to run the boatyard. She wears trousers and has moved away from conventional models of femininity. In the absence of a conventional mate, someone who can allow him to return to pre-war 'normality', Scott falls prey to the attractions of the *femme fatale* who lingers on the beach by the hulk of a sunken ship, gathering timber from its smashed lifeboats for firewood.

Although the war is, at first sight, responsible for Eve's unavailability, we later learn that her brother in fact enlisted following a fight with Tod over Peggy. It would seem that the dark woman is the prime cause of disorder, or rather, that she is to bear the burden of the disruption caused by the war. But, paradoxically, she is the more domestic of the two women, looking after her helpless husband and cooking for guests. Her domesticity would suggest that the home itself has ceased to be a place of safe conventionality, that even there woman's active sexual desire can cause disruption. Blinded accidentally in a domestic quarrel by his wife, Tod is not only stripped of his power to master the world through art, he is also unable to control her. At one highly symbolic moment of the film, he goes to show a nude of her to Scott, only to discover that she has hidden the painting away, thus claiming the right to control her own bodily image.

Tod initially seeks the friendship of Scott but, in the face of sexual jealousy, homosociality loses its power to cement men together. Scott does not believe that the older man's blindness is genuine and leads him to the clifftop only to realise his error as he falls over the edge, escaping with severe bruising. Peggy instigates a sea-fishing trip that brings matters to a head when Scott begins to sink the fragile rowing boat. The men struggle and end up in the water but then draw back from homicidal struggle over the woman. Tod burns his paintings, setting himself and Peggy free from the past. They leave together and he promises to release her if she still wishes it.

The ending may seem anticlimactic, but, in fact, it is more interesting than the conventional outcome that would have seen one of the men murdering the destructive woman, or one man murdering the other. The characters are able to draw back from the edge and liberate themselves from the crushing weight of the past and their own inner demons. In the light of this, Peggy tends to take on another significance. Her burning of the wreckage at the start of the film suggests a character who faces the past but will not be tied down by it. The fire she is associated with is thus liberatory as well as destructive and the lesson she teaches is picked up by Tod when he burns his paintings. The passion she unleashes in men teaches them about themselves as well as setting them against each other and her implied sexual encounter with Scott in the hull of the beached wreck suggests a triumph of life over death.

Starting with *Nana*, and continuing with *Madame Bovary*, *La Chienne* and *La Bête humaine*, Renoir's *femmes fatales* had either died gruesomely or been murdered, having first wreaked destruction around themselves. With Peggy, he finally breaks the pattern, although the strong woman is not yet given full subject status. The film's dramatic centre is still monopolised by a male-identity crisis so that women's refusal of conventional roles signals disorder in the men's world rather than authentic narrative enfranchisement. Certainly, the open ending means that the easy solution of a return to convention is denied. The images of harmonious community and the domesticated women of an older generation are out of reach of the main characters who have to learn to live in a less reassuring world. But the break from convention is only partial. By the end of the film, the men have reclaimed agency as Scott abandons Eve and Tod frees himself and Peggy from the past. Tod will become a writer and thus recapture his ability to shape and interpret the world. Having been his model, Peggy now becomes his typist.

Although strictly limited in its challenge to dominant representations of gender, *The Woman on the Beach* moves away from the ideological closure of *Swamp Water* and *The Southerner* with their comforting evocation of foundational myths. As in the 1920s films, *Charleston* and *Le Bled*, the undefined but broad-reaching disarray of a post-war period crystallises around gender disorder.

A key question is how much the film should be eased into an account of Renoir's evolution and how much it should be seen as a more or less typical example of *film noir*. Several of its key aspects coincide closely with more general descriptions of *noir* cinema (Kaplan 1980). The challenge of the female characters to conventional roles, their ambivalent moral status and their crystallisation of broader anxieties are all typical features of *noir*, while the absence of the families that would normalise and stabilise the gender order is also a familiar characteristic of the genre. *Noir's* prevailing mood of paranoia and sense of the past looming over the present come through strongly in Renoir's film. *The Woman on the Beach* is perhaps atypical in the survival of all the characters, their ability to transcend the past and the presence of contrastingly disruptive women. But in other ways it could clearly be located in the genre that is best seen to express the post-war malaise and the impossibility of returning to the apparently stable values of the pre-war world.

Shot in newly de-colonised India, *The River* (1950) is usually seen by critics as a key stage in Renoir's career, marking the emergence of a new philosophy of acceptance. Yet, as in the case of *Woman on the Beach*, there is a strong case for analysing it as an exemplar of a collectively produced discourse rather than as a purely personal statement. Nandi Bhatia does just this. Suggesting that critics, including those of the left, have failed to deal with its connection with colonialism, she locates it amongst orientalist portrayals of India accusing Renoir of reproducing 'the simplistic dichotomy of the mysterious and spiritual East versus the materialistic West' (Bhatia 1996: 52). A picturesque, exotic and homogenised India is divested of its socio-historical specificity and its own concerns silenced. Because it is shown as a haven and as a place of spiritual healing for the materially decayed West, it is removed from the flow of history, thus erasing the exploitation and economic domination that continues after decolonisation. The film naturalises hierarchical relationships between the whites and native people and neglects women's 'attempts to dismantle patriarchal and colonial structures', choosing rather to show them as 'meek and passive' (Bhatia 1996: 59).

Accusing Renoir of 'benevolent paternalism', and 'a celebration of imperialism', Bhatia suggests that he may have shied away from a critique of colonialism to avoid accusations of left-wing sympathy during the McCarthyite period of hysterical American anti-Communism. Even less flatteringly, she suggests that he produced *The River* as a 'standardised product' for a Hollywood audience (Bhatia 1996: 59–61).

While this account provides a very helpfully contextualised analysis of the film that helps to counterbalance the individualising excesses of the *auteurists*, it can itself be criticised on several points. Bhatia tends to homogenise the 'orientalist' discourse that she accuses of homogenising and dehistoricising India. Although it undoubtedly recycles exotic stereotypes, Renoir's film clearly engages with its historical moment and thus does not simply reproduce that which has already been said. It certainly occludes various forms of oppression, but it does not celebrate imperialism as Bhatia suggests. The pretensions of the colonialists are instead viewed with deep irony, for the apparent timeless and tranquil domination assumed by the English characters in the film must be placed in the context of India's recently won independence. The one-legged Captain John and the passive Mr John are hardly models of conquering colonial manhood. Renoir's film is about the post-war spiritual crisis of the West rather than about colonialism or neo-colonialism. While it is right to see it as Eurocentric and point out its regressive stereotyping, it would be reductionist to call it colonialist.

The story begins in classical fashion with the disruption of an apparently stable world by a stranger, in this case an American who has lost his leg in the war. This world centres on an English family who live very comfortably while tended by their Indian servants who, with the exception of the nanny, Nan, are mute and largely excluded from the action of the film. The father runs the local jute mill while the mother remains at home watching over her many daughters and one son, Bogey. The voice of Harriet, the eldest daughter, provides a distancing retrospective narration on a story which is essentially that of her own coming of age. Harriet has two friends of roughly similar age, the mill-owner's daughter, the wilful and beautiful Valerie, and Melanie, the Anglo-Indian daughter of Mr John, a neighbour who has been absorbed by India. The three girls become rivals for the attention of Captain John and although their adolescent infatuations come to nothing, the episode marks the end of childhood innocence and the passage into adulthood. Bogey dies from a snake bite and, shortly afterwards, a baby girl is born. Captain John returns to America having accepted his disabled state.

The family garden, with its protective wall and watchful maternal eyes, is tightly associated with this childhood innocence. The turmoil of the external world is kept at bay and the safe daily routine of the family seems to promise an endless return of the same. While the garden is associated with freedom, play and domesticated nature, the father's daily departure takes him to the broader world of discipline and productivity of the jute factory where he supervises the anonymous Indian labourers in their exacting toil and the brutal subjugation of nature by the machine. This harsher world also embraces the recent war and its unhealed wounds. The barrier separating the two worlds is not intact however, as the wall is breached symbolically by a tree which allows the dangers of the outside to penetrate into the inside in the form of the snake that takes Bogey's life.

The film clearly builds on a Judeo-Christian myth of origins. The garden suggests the toil-free, timeless world from before the Fall, while the outside world represents the mortality, toil and knowledge that succeeded it. The snake precipitates the Fall, its destructive presence being associated not only with death but with the girls' loss of spiritual innocence as sexual awakening takes them out of childhood.

Leaving the characters stranded between the illusory safety of the garden and the fallen world outside, western mythology seems to provide no way out. However, Renoir's mythologised India does offer a way forward by locating humanity in a cosmos that encompasses life and death, beginnings and endings, work and idleness in a cyclical order where good and evil are locked in eternal struggle. This dynamic cyclicality is crucially different from the apparently timeless return of the same in the garden, being based not on an illusory shutting out of toil and mortality but encapsulating them in a disorder containing order. The river of the title is at the centre of the cosmos, suggesting perpetual mutability and endless recurrence by its constant flow. Harriet finally comes to terms with her part in the death of her brother when she throws herself in it, only to be fished out again, dying a little to be born again a wiser character. Bogey's death is balanced in the cycle of life and death by the birth of a child.

While the western order comes to terms with the fall from grace by repressing man and subjugating nature, Indians accept their place within the natural order. This difference of attitude is represented in the film by the noisy machinery and sweating bodies of the jute mill on the one hand and the unhurried work of Indians on and around the river on the other. The mill implies constant struggle. The activities around the river suggest an unhurried harmony with natural rhythms that means that no rigid boundaries need separate production, contemplation and collective celebration. The steps of riverside temples descend into the water, joining the human order to the natural one rather than fighting against it.

However, at this stage it is worth returning to the key point made by Bhatia. This is an essentialised and dehistoricised India that is being used to give a lesson in life to the West. Despite appearances to the contrary, the film is part of the West's ongoing monologue with itself. The only Indian character of any significance is the Eurasian, Melanie. Her struggle to define an identity for herself and eventual choice of the Indian half of herself, of stereotypical eastern acceptance over western revolt, is used to show the way forward to the western characters, not to explore the explicit dilemma of a Eurasian woman at a particular historical conjuncture (Bhatia 1996: 51). In a similar way, the considerable amount of documentary footage fails to engage with contemporary India by suggesting an unhurried, unchanging world integrated with the order of the cosmos through a recurring cycle of festivals. The canalisation of these shots for the film's didactic purposes is clearly revealed by the voice-over of the mature Harriet that accompanies them.

It is no accident that the central voice of the film is that of a woman. If it is implied that the West in general has followed the wrong path, it is men in particular who are most in question because of their control of the world of toil outside the garden. Significantly it is the boy-child who is killed, his death saving him from the traumatic abandonment of childhood enjoyment of instinct and nature that is required to reach adult masculinity. Captain John's portrayal suggests that it is primarily men who bear the scars of the war. His identity crisis springs from a rejection of the official world of parades, flags and heroism and his refusal to accept his own unwholeness as a man. One woman, Valerie, forces him to face his own diminished stature by physically humiliating him in a game of catch, and another, Melanie, teaches him a lesson of acceptance. His namesake, Mr John, finds peace by abandoning the western desire for ever greater prosperity in favour of a life of contemplation, thus renouncing the domination of self and of nature which is at the heart of western manhood.

The women are faced with less polarised choices. Their socially constructed identity makes them appear closer to nature and thus they can more easily reintegrate into the 'natural'. Their enclosure in the endless repetition of the domestic, their exclusion from the public world of historical change, and, most importantly, their role in reproduction all make them more open to the cyclical repetition of the cosmic order. Harriet's mother in particular suggests a path to wisdom through acceptance of woman's 'natural' role. Growing, she tells Harriet, is getting ready for motherhood which itself is 'the meaning of a woman'. Labour pains, she adds, make woman think and feel. Women are thus firmly located in natural cycles and their knowledge that life means pain primes them for a philosophy of acceptance.

However, this 'naturalisation' of women brings out a tension at the heart of the film for beneath their apparent acceptance of their place in the order of things, there are the remnants of a very different story, one more prominent in the novel, that of Harriet's struggle to make a name for herself as an artist. As control of the story passes from Rumer Godden (author of the novel and Renoir's collaborator on the script), Harriet's story of determined striving is subsumed by the story of acceptance. One episode in particular illustrates this well. In the novel, Harriet is given a kite which, after many failures, she succeeds in flying on her own (Godden [1946] 1991: 102–5). In the film, she can only fly the kite with the help of Captain John and so her fight for independence and public recognition is overwritten by a romance in the private sphere.

Harriet tells one story in the film that goes to the heart of things. Using the deeply problematic real-life story of Melanie as a starting point, she creates a tale of endless, naturalised repetition. Melanie becomes a young Indian girl whose parents had prayed for a boy but who none the less loved her and saved for her dowry. She loves a young man, but it is her father who will choose her mate. The father's choice is the man she loves. They have a child, another girl, and the story will start again unvarying and thus perfectly circular.

Is the story suggesting that women are compensated for their social inferiority by their centrality in the life cycle? Is Renoir holding up the formal perfection of art against the imperfections and unhappiness of life as some critics have suggested? If so, it almost begs to be read against the grain. Harriet's narrative resolution of unresolvable real-life contradictions would seem to offer a textbook example of the ideological function of art. It is more interesting and more plausible if one sees it as bearing the same relationship to the broader narrative of the film as does the garden to the cosmos. The garden can only appear to be innocent and timeless by excluding the mutability and conflict of the broader world beyond. Harriet's story likewise only generates an apparently conflict-free world by excluding complexity. But Renoir's own story encapsulates pain and struggle within its cosmic vision. The male director retains narrative mastery in a world where men struggle to survive, and in the process holds on to his power to define racialised and gendered others.

The River is perhaps best seen as a post-war film, one like The Woman on the Beach in which gender becomes a terrain to explore a more general sense of crisis and men have difficulty fitting into a new world, leading in some ways to a similar conclusion that they must accept their physical or psychological weaknesses in order to move on. Yet while the earlier film showed an unrepaired crack in the ideology of domesticity, The River replaces women in wholly traditional roles. Like The Diary of a Chambermaid it positions a woman at the heart of the narrative, but what had held a promise of female assertiveness again ultimately fails to deliver. Yet The Diary is different in a crucial way for it still takes the side of the social inferior against the superior, while The River, as Bhatia has shown, is more intent on aestheticising the 'timeless' qualities of Indians and turns its back on social oppression. The key change is that Renoir has moved from denunciation of material inequality to a broad condemnation of materialism and productivism. Moving towards a belief that western civilisation as a whole is alienating and repressive, he no longer seems able to focus on specific oppressions. Indeed, as he stands the dominant values of the West on their head, those with least and who live closest to nature seem most to be envied.

Melanie is perhaps the faultline where the film's cracks show through. It suggests that she has a simple choice between two separate halves of herself, the eastern and the western, as if the two had somehow existed in her side by side, each in its pure state. But even on its own evidence the film suggests that any notion of an unproblematic untangling of east and west is Utopian. The Indians on the river may seem to be in harmony with nature's rhythms in ways that have not changed for thousands of years, but the presence of the jute mill clearly demonstrates that indigenous agriculture, transportation and bodily labour are willy-nilly participating in a westernised economy, even if their relegation to labouring roles makes it seem as if their work is somehow unchanged from the manual toil of pre-industrial societies.

The River must in the end be read as a moral piece, a telling of how things should be and how individuals with free choices should behave. But individual choices are always constrained by social and historical contexts as well as personal circumstances. So, as Renoir's cinema takes on a new breadth, driven by the war to a critique of western civilisation, it loses or renounces its capacity to address inequality and suggest a way out of it. Moral lessons will now take the place of political projects. The critical edge is not lost even though the targets change, but rather than showing people coming together to transform social structures, Renoir locates his Utopia in alternative spaces be they in India or, as we shall see in the next chapter, Parisian music halls.

Conclusion

Renoir's American output shows no consistent direction but is not without pattern. Those films set in rural America explore tensions within that country's foundational myths, but ultimately in a conservative manner that fails to engage with social struggles and exclusions. Those that look back to France, show a lingering Frontist outlook, but one that is fading by the time of *The Diary of a Chambermaid*. *The Woman on the Beach* and *The River* both address the confusion of the post-war world, the former more open endedly, the latter moving towards a philosophy of acceptance by locating struggle and pain in a cosmic order and thus dehistoricising it in a way clearly foreshadowed in *The Southerner*.

The films feed off Frontist ideology, American mythology, the conventions of *film noir* and orientalist stereotype, inflecting them for the specific conjuncture of post-Depression and wartime America and a post-war world where decolonisation has begun. While it would be absurd to seek to insert them into a story of directorial self-expression in light of their shaping by historical, ideological and institutional contexts, it also seems absurd to exclude the director from the equation. His earlier commitment to the Front, exile status and emergent critique of the West's Promethean striving and materialism must surely be a key element in any analysis of the films, but one whose precise contribution it would be naïve to expect to disentangle from the complex web of intermingled influences.

References

Bazin, A. (1952), 'Renoir français', *Cahiers du Cinéma*, 2(8): 9–29.

Bazin, A. (1989), *Jean Renoir*, Paris, Lebovici.

Bhatia, N. (1996), 'Whither the colonial question? Jean Renoir's *The River*' in Sherzer, D. ed. *Cinema, Colonialism, Postcolonialism*, Austin, University of Texas Press, 51–64.

Durgnat, R. (1974), *Jean Renoir*, Berkeley, University of California.

Faulkner, C. (1986), *The Social Cinema of Jean Renoir*, Princeton, Princeton University Press.

Godden, R. ([1946] 1991), *The River*, London, Pan.

Kaplan, E. A. ed. (1980), *Women in Film Noir*, London, BFI.

Koppes, K. R. and Black, G. D. (1988), *Hollywood Goes to War*, London, I. B. Taurus.

Renoir, J. (1952a), 'On me demande', *Cahiers du cinéma*, 2(8): 5–8.

Renoir, J. (1952b), 'Quelque chose m'est arrivé', *Cahiers du cinéma*, 2(8): 31–2.

Renoir, J. (1984), *Lettres d'Amérique*, (trans. Annie Wiart), Paris, Presses de la Renaissance.

Renoir, J. (1994), *Letters*, (eds L. LoBianco and D. Thompson), London, Faber & Faber.

Schérer, M. (1952), 'Renoir américain', *Cahiers du cinéma*, 2(8): 33–40.

Serceau, D. (1985), *La Sagesse du plaisir*, Paris, Editions du Cerf.

Shindler, C. (1996), *Hollywood in Crisis, Cinema and American Society, 1929–1939*, London, Routledge.

Short, J. R. (1991), *Imagined Country: Environment, Culture and Society*, London, Routledge.

Tompkins, J. (1989), 'West of everything', in Longhurst, D. ed. *Gender, Genre and Narrative Pleasure*, London, Unwin Hyman, 10–30.

6

Late Renoir

In 1951, after an absence of more than ten years, Renoir returned to a France that was changing fast. Explosive economic growth was not new, but its sustained nature in the post-war era was. It turned French society upside down. The state-led charge for growth demolished the old republican 'compromise' whereby a balance had been preserved between rural and urban interests, small and large business, salaried and independent labour, and dynamic and traditional sectors. The new France would be dominated by the urban and by large-scale capitalism. At the same time, France's international role was also undergoing radical change. Having had the world's second largest colonial empire, it now underwent rapid and at times traumatic decolonisation while at the same time beginning the process of European integration.

The United States would remain Renoir's permanent home. He was a semi-detached figure in this new France, making films in and about a fast-changing country (and continent) where he no longer had his roots and in whose struggles he no longer participated. Hostile critics suggested that he was simply out of touch. Friendly ones defended him, suggesting that his work had taken on a new dimension with greater breadth and depth replacing the sharp focus on the burning issues of the day that had characterised the films of the Popular Front. Certainly, the outlook was different.

He became a more active critic of his own work than before. In the *Cahiers* interviews and elsewhere, he increasingly looked back on the totality of his work, seeking retrospectively to give it a shape and direction that it had not always seemed to have. His new films were also mobilised to give a sense of coherence to his output. Some of them would portray the world of spectacle and thus comment implicitly on his role as a cinematographer and his relation with the public. Most would echo earlier works, pushing us to read them in terms of personal evolution and thematic consistency. Thus *Eléna et les hommes* clearly reworks *La Règle du jeu*, while *French Cancan* echoes *Nana*, and *Le Caporal Epinglé* returns us to the prisoner-of-war camps of *La Grande Illusion*. *Le Petit théâtre de Jean Renoir*, the last film, is a self-conscious conclusion to all that has gone before. Foregrounding Renoir's creative presence, it reassembles actors from earlier films and evokes the broad sweep of the 'œuvre', from *La Petite Marchande d'allumettes* to the more recent *belle époque* films.

The later films are also more consistent in tone than the disparate body of work that had gone before. Comedy is the prevailing mood. *Le Caporal Epinglé* and *Le Testament du Docteur Cordelier* have a markedly darker surface mood, but the former ends in upbeat manner while the latter is a moral fable told with a good deal of ironic distance. Indeed, it could be said that the later films generally see the world and its failings with mocking irony, preferring a dispassionate moral vision to a tragic or political one.

The surface lightness created by comic plots can help us to understand the frequent comment that Renoir's work has become quietist and turned its back on injustice and oppression. The apparent retreat from the present in most of the later films only serves to strengthen this feeling. The reaction of Georges Sadoul, the celebrated Communist critic, to *Le Carosse d'or*, provides an excellent example. He compares the film unfavourably with the play by Mérimée (*Le Carosse du Saint-Sacrement*) on which it was based, accusing Renoir of emptying it of subversive content. Finding that the film camouflages a lack of content with theatricality and formal perfection, he concludes that the director has fled his country, reality and contemporary problems. Yet his damning reading is undermined from within, for the film clearly makes him think of anti-colonial struggles even as he accuses it of being escapist and empty. He writes for example, 'Le scénariste a pensé sans doute à peindre, à travers l'ancien Pérou, les colonies modernes et leurs indiens révoltés ... Qu'on n'aille pas y voir une allusion, si lointaine soit-elle, au Viet-nam' (Sadoul 1953).[1]

A more recent account of the apparent political quietism of later Renoir comes from Janet Bergstrom who highlights the exiled director's need to regain acceptance in his native land. Bergstrom suggests that Renoir had been deeply wounded by French critics' response to *La Règle du jeu* in 1939, to the American films when they were seen after the war, and indeed to *Le Carosse d'or*. To gain public acceptance, he created a simple and positive image of France, which drew on the *belle époque* to avoid the deep internal divisions that hung over from the war and had been exacerbated by the Algerian conflict (Bergstrom 1996: 478–81). Significantly, Bergstrom makes her case by stopping before *Eléna et les hommes*, a film whose sharp critical edge she might have found much harder to fit into her account.

Comments Renoir made in 1952, suggest an alternative way to see his later work, while partially undermining Bergstrom's analysis and beginning to explain Sadoul's contradictory feelings. The director explains an outlook that had changed fundamentally since his politically partisan films of the 1930s:

> Avant la guerre, ma manière à moi de participer à ce concert universel, était d'essayer d'apporter une voix de protestation ... Aujourd'hui, l'être nouveau que je suis réalise que le temps n'est plus pour le sarcasme et que la seule chose que je puisse apporter à cet univers illogique, irresponsable et cruel, c'est mon 'amour'. Evidemment il y a dans cette attitude l'espoir égoïste d'être payé de retour. (Renoir 1952: 31)[2]

---

1 'The scriptwriter doubtlessly thought about using historical Peru to depict the revolt of Indians in modern colonies ... Let nobody make out that there is an allusion no matter how distant to Vietnam'.

2 'Before the war, my personal way to join in this universal concert was to try to add a voice of protest ... Today, I am a new person who realises that sarcasm is no longer called for and that the only thing that I can bring to this illogical, irresponsible and cruel universe is my love. This attitude obviously includes the selfish hope that I will be paid back in kind.'

While an initial glance might focus on the easy benevolence so often associated with Renoir's 'maturity', closer scrutiny reveals a much darker outlook. The tension between apparent warmth and underlying severity suggests that we should look beyond the escapist surface of films that hide their more serious intent beneath a frivolous surface. Their layered attempt to appeal in different ways to an 'élite' and a mass public helps to explain the sometimes violent reactions they generate. Detecting allusions to colonial struggles, dictatorship or the capitalist colonisation of popular culture, critics are disgusted to find these issues treated with the apparent lightness of vaudeville or musical comedy.

We will now turn to the films themselves. The first three (*Le Carosse d'or*, *French Cancan*, *Eléna et les hommes*), are all historically set costume dramas and form a natural group. The next two (*Le Testament du Docteur Cordelier*, *Le Déjeuner sur l'herbe*) are contemporary fantasies and were shot in the same innovative way. They too form an obvious pair. The last two films do not have the same obviously shared features. They will be considered separately.

Flights into the past?

For many, *Le Carosse d'or* (1952), *French Cancan* (1954), and *Eléna et les hommes* (1956) represent the pinnacle of Renoir's post-war work. All three are set in the past, the first in eighteenth-century Peru, the others in *belle époque* France. Attempting no realistic period recreations, they proclaim in various ways their lack of interest in rooting their characters in a convincing social or historical context. They make a deliberately unrealistic use of colour (be it the pastel court costumes and the primary colours given to the actors in *Le Carosse d'or*, the bright-red sky of *Eléna*, or the appropriation of the national colours in *French Cancan*). They disclaim any immediate access to history by foregrounding their dependence on other cultural forms for the evocation of the past. *Le Carosse d'or*, for example, draws constantly on the music of Vivaldi as a way of evoking both Italy and a classical aesthetic. *Eléna* and *French Cancan* proclaim their nature as spectacle by engaging with pre-existing representations of the *belle époque*. They evoke Paris by focusing on favourite Impressionist motifs such as the entertainment industry, military pageantry, the festive crowd or the dance rehearsal. All three make deliberate use of stock types such as the macho bullfighter (*Le Carosse d'or*), the dashing soldier and the beautiful foreign princess (*Eléna*) or the romantic foreign prince and the *femme fatale* (*French Cancan*).

Their anti-realism is reinforced by their comic form. Situations are deliberately clichéd and endings manifestly contrived as the action follows the predictable patterns of farce, vaudeville and musical comedy (hidden lovers discovered, circular chases through interlinked rooms, comic fights, the disruption of public events by affairs of the heart). We are never allowed to take the characters too seriously and stand back and judge them, knowing that nothing too serious can befall them.

This anti-realism was not pre-programmed. Renoir's letters reveal clearly that he would have liked to shoot at least some of *Le Carosse d'or* on location in South America where he would have been able to explore the collision and interaction of Spanish and Indian cultures (Renoir 1994: 264–8). Even when he accepted that he would have to shoot in Italy, he still hoped to use establishing shots taken in Latin America. His film's overt theatricality can initially be seen as a response to enforced studio shooting rather than an aesthetically motivated shift in direction. However, having accepted that it would not be realistic, Renoir exploits its artificiality to explore the relationship between social life and theatre. The title sequence with its theatrical curtain and the opening shot which takes us through a proscenium arch are both clear indications of the centrality of the theatrical theme. Theatre is used to explore a series of false images and self-deceptions, revealing the seedy reality behind the grandiose décor of colonial Spain, the empty seduction of power and the misuse of spectacle to hold the public in thrall. A film that has been seen as a celebration of the consolations of theatre and thus of art in a debased world is better seen in terms of its use of theatre for social critique.

It begins with the destabilising arrival in colonial Peru of the golden coach ordered by the Spanish viceroy to enhance his personal prestige. The coach is accompanied by Camilla, an Italian actress, who will set the viceroy, a bullfighter and a young Spanish nobleman at each others' throats as they vie for her favours. Their rivalry is laid over and exacerbates existing tensions between the viceroy and the court. The backdrop to this comic chaos (and what so irritated Sadoul in an apparently frivolous context) is the rebellion that threatens the gold and silver mines from which the colony derives its wealth. Matters are brought to a head when the viceroy offers the coach to Camilla. The nobles withdraw financial support for the war against the Indians and attempt to depose him. Having lost her lovers by seeking to have all three, Camilla then saves the situation and restores order by giving the coach to the Archbishop who will use it to take the last rites to the poor. She will henceforth seek her happiness through the exercise of her art.

The theatre troupe's arrival in the colony brings together two contrasting dimensions of western Europe, a common cultural inheritance and a history of global ambition and exploitation. The troupe comes from Italy, the country Renoir saw as the heart of western civilisation, bringing with it the *commedia dell'arte*, an Italian form which had a profound influence on European theatre and was thus part of a shared culture. On the other hand, Peru's mines encapsulate the thirst for wealth and power behind imperial expansion and, despite Sadoul's comments, it seems impossible not to see the links between Spain's struggles to retain them and France's doomed attempt to deny Vietnam its independence. More broadly, the sharp historical decline of the Spanish empire has obvious parallels with Europe's diminishing post-war influence. The continent is at a crossroads and must choose between its cultural inheritance and the pursuit of wealth and power.

Camilla's vacillation between theatre and glittering but hollow rewards is exemplary of the choices Europe faces. Her different love affairs illustrate the various temptations that must be overcome while her final renunciation and achievement of self-knowledge shows a way forward.

Initially, she wishes to conquer the crowd and considers romantic alliance with Ramon the bullfighter who exercises a hypnotic power over it. But the anonymous mass only knows her theatrical persona so its love is inevitably transient and illusory. The viceroy, a rival suitor, embodies the sophistication and power of the court, but its elegance is a theatrical décor that masks its true nature. It is rent by internal rivalries and sustained by oppression and exploitation. At one telling moment, the viceroy takes Camilla to the palace balcony promising to show her the splendid view. He points to an off-screen cemetery and prison, fleetingly but tellingly punctuating the witty interplay of ruler and actress with a reminder of the dark side of the imperial splendour of the court.

The golden coach Camilla covets encapsulates her other temptations by embodying the seduction of wealth and courtly elegance and being an impressive symbol of power that helps to perpetuate the docility of the masses. The viceroy's remark that he had always wanted 'une voiture étrangère' (a foreign coach/car), again suggests a reference to the contemporary period when the motor car was the consumer commodity *par excellence*. Yet the coach causes discord among those who covet it and frustration among those who are denied it. Its disruptive power is only tamed when Camilla gives it to the church, thus restoring the proper hierarchy between the spiritual and the material.

Camilla's exemplary pursuit of the egotistical satisfactions of wealth, power and popular adulation leads only to alienation as all that she covets only brings satisfaction through the eyes of others. To achieve any authentic happiness, she must first know herself and this she can only do by losing her ego through her acting. By extension, Europe must shed an inflated (and unsustainable) image of itself based on oppression and materialism masquerading as civilisation.

The story of Felipe, Camilla's first jilted lover, contains a critique of the West in typical telegraphic form, while also revealing the limits of the film's vision. Having joined the Spanish army, he is captured by insurgents but treated with a kindness and generosity that is singularly lacking in the Europeans. He informs Camilla that there would be no room for her precious golden coach on the narrow paths used by the Indians, who by implication are not tainted by materialism. This stereotype of the innocent and happy savage is typical of a Eurocentric outlook that instrumentalises non-Europeans to generate positive or negative visions of the West. The film focuses not on the oppressed but on the unhappiness and alienation of the oppressors. At no stage does it give a voice to the insurgents, nor indeed to the black servants at the court or the Indian spectators to Camilla's performances. Like *The River* before it, it uses the colonised to generate a moral rather than a political critique of Europe.

The voiceless spectators are part of a more general picture of a populace subjugated by the spectacle of power, violence and material wealth. They applaud indifferently the viceroy's golden coach, the hypnotic spectacle of the bullfight and the acting of Camilla. The theatre, it is implied, can be part of a system that feeds off mass passivity. Camilla's turning to a theatre of self-discovery and renunciation of her initial desire to captivate her public is indicative of art's need to retain its critical, moral function. It is also a pointer to how we should read the film. On the surface an escapist piece for a passive public, it invites those who dig further to question their civilisation.

The *belle époque* lends itself perfectly to a similar playing off of seductive spectacle and more serious intent. A retrospectively imagined period of innocence and harmony before the torments of the twentieth century began in earnest in 1914, it is a key moment for the invention of a rose-tinted vision of Frenchness in which images of festivity and harmonious community are prevalent (Rearick 1985: 220). Feeding off the brilliant surface of Impressionism, it exploits Paris's reputation as world capital of pleasure, love and uninhibited sensuality. But it is also a time of xenophobic nationalism, social strife, political instability and increasing external tensions, negative aspects which have been mobilised to produce a dark counter-image of the period. Rather than opting for the dark image or the nostalgic myth, Renoir plays one against the other, perfecting an aesthetic of conflicting moods, of light surface and dark undertone. This complex layering allows his *belle époque* films to keep a sometimes bitter critical edge while at the same time salvaging Utopian elements that hold a message of sensual pleasure and restored community.

French Cancan is not short of Utopian elements. It evokes the entertainment industry that was central to the production of images of 'gay Paris'. It also evokes Montmartre, that bohemian centre of opposition to both Catholic morality and bourgeois sobriety. Finally, and most obviously, it revolves around the cancan, a symbol of gaiety and revolt of which Charles Rearick writes: 'Identified with the lower classes since revolutionary times, the dance both attracted and disturbed other classes, while government and police tried to restrain its irreverent kick from going too high' (Rearick 1985: 49).

The film recounts the founding of the *Moulin Rouge* by Danglard, an impresario in constant financial difficulties and thus dependent on the backing of wealthy investors. He is proprietor of the *Paravent Chinois*, a place where exotic spectacle is offered to the bourgeoisie. The opening shots show his mistress, la Belle Abbesse, performing an erotic, orientalist dance before a crowd of black-suited men. After the performance, Danglard takes the Abbesse and her other lover Walter (who is also his backer) to the Place Blanche where, mixing with the popular classes, they dance a cancan. It is here that he discovers Nini who will become his new lead dancer and mistress. His interest in her provokes the jealousy both of Paulo, her baker lover, and the Abbesse thus destabilising existing relationships and prompting Walter to withdraw his financial backing. Thereafter, cancan rehearsals mix with scenes of love and jealousy, although Danglard still has time to look for new talent on the streets of Montmartre. An eastern European prince attempts suicide when he realises that Nini is in love with Danglard, but recovers and gives her the deeds to the Moulin Rouge, thus saving the show. On the opening night, she sees Danglard with his newest discovery and refuses to dance. He tells her that she doesn't own him and that they must above all devote themselves to the public. She emerges to lead the final triumphant cancan which brings together all the main actors of the drama as social divisions and sexual jealousy are transcended in the joyous abandon of the dance and the black suits of bourgeois seriousness are sucked into the vibrant primary colours of the cancan dancers.

Danglard's key role brings out some of the ambiguities of the film. It invites us to enjoy 'low' culture and the everyday by celebrating French popular song and dance, the life of the street, even the way of walking of a young laundry maid. But this invitation comes from an exceptional individual and creator in a high-cultural mould who sees the untapped beauty around him and possesses the vision to bring it to public attention. Constant implicit references to the celebrated French artists who have shaped our perception of the period also suggest that the popular and the everyday can only truly be appreciated when filtered through the prism of high cultural forms. Although the film can be seen as operating a Utopian fusion of high and popular culture, it does so in a way that preserves cultural hierarchies.

Apparently wallowing in nostalgia, it also addresses itself to the transformation of France in the 1950s. It shows us a Montmartre where rural and urban overlap, capitalist enterprise and *petits commerçants* mingle, streets are paved over and prices rise due to property speculation. This sense of an old and new France in uneasy and unstable juxtaposition clearly suggests the early years of what we now know as the *Trente Glorieuses* as well as the *belle époque*. The title's linkage of English language and something quintessentially French (the cancan) evokes the fears of American cultural hegemony and loss of cultural identity that so marked the post-war period. More specifically, the dynamiting of La Reine blanche, which had been a centre of autonomous popular culture with links to nineteenth-century revolutionary activity, and its replacement by the Moulin Rouge, a capitalist enterprise, suggests the taming and incorporation of the popular classes by the culture industries and by implication by consumerism, a process which was a dominant trait of the post-war period.

This taming of the popular can be interpreted in two radically different ways (one deeply pessimistic, one more optimistic) that can be approached by examining what happens to Nini, the leading cancan dancer. She originally dances for her own pleasure with people of similar humble social background. Under the supervision of Danglard, her body is disciplined and, following a choreography that is no longer her own, she becomes a public spectacle. The alienation of her image, her body and her pleasures is compounded by the fact that Walter, Danglard's backer, is fully conscious of the social value of illusion and knows that he and his partners will profit financially. Unbridled, autonomous popular culture is thus doubly co-opted. First, for profit. Second, as a tame spectacle that promotes social pacification in the interest of the wealthy and the powerful.

Yet the film ultimately overrides the pessimistic interpretation which it itself proposes. It suggests that Danglard can use Nini and her fellow dancers to make an irreverent, sensual and collective popular spirit explode into mass culture, challenging both the bourgeois attachment to seriousness, appearances and property and the *petit bourgeois* ethic of self-reliance, hard-work and respectability which is expressed in the film by Paulo, Nini's baker lover. This challenge is limited in its scope. Danglard does not encourage revolt against the status quo but keeps an alternative, Utopian set of values alive by preserving the spirit of popular culture within a commodified spectacle.

The film's challenge to convention overflows into the terrain of sexual behaviour. Walter's bourgeois attachment to appearance means that he cannot accept a public display of infidelity by his mistress. Paulo's *petit bourgeois* possessive individualism leads to a proprietorial attitude to Nini's body and a refusal to let her dance for the pleasure of others. Danglard refuses respectability and possessiveness. His cancan unrestrainedly flaunts the body, affirming a preference for immediate and concrete enjoyment that casts restraint and repression to the wind. His sexual morality follows similar lines. He invites his partners to enjoy the moment with him, only to move on when another partner presents herself.

The film's attack on repressive moralities is part of a broader search for an alternative Frenchness. The notion of a shared political culture has conventionally been central to definitions of national identity. However, the republic's failure to unite the French is comically illustrated when a minister comes to open the Moulin Rouge and the assembled public dissolve into private and then general quarrels despite the omnipresence of the *tricolore* and the playing of 'La Marseillaise'. The film suggests that community can be found in the sharing of the French art of living and the sensuous enjoyment of the everyday. Its self-conscious reorientation of nation is underlined by the prominence accorded to the national red, white and blue during the final cancan.

It would also seem to be making a statement about the relationship between an artist and a national culture that is particularly relevant to Renoir's own semi-detached relationship to France. The erotic, orientalist dance of the beginning of the film is a purely escapist spectacle with no grounding in French culture. The music hall's manifestly foreign name Le Paravent Chinois underlines this. The production of the explicitly national cancan in the Moulin Rouge expresses a need to reroot culture in a French context. If Danglard's work is to avoid pure escapism, it has to be able to open his audience's eyes to what is around them, and to do this, it must be embedded in their lives.

As Bergstrom suggests, *French Cancan* is a clear attempt by Renoir to re-establish contact with a French audience by making a film which celebrates Frenchness. However, her suggestion that it avoids anything potentially contentious is not entirely fair. It is Utopian but not escapist. It does not close its eyes to capitalist exploitation, class and political differences or the consumerisation of culture. But it does suggest that art, even in the consumer age, can keep alternative values alive and have a liberatory function.

The opposition of a divisive political tradition with a unifying cultural Frenchness is only sketched in *French Cancan*. It will be the main theme of *Eléna et les hommes* (1956) which starred Ingrid Bergman and is a thinly disguised version of the story of General Boulanger. Boulangism was a political force in the 1880s that managed to gain support from those on the left and right who rejected the only recently installed Third Republic. Maximising popular mobilisation by rattling the French sabre at Germany over a relatively minor incident, it briefly threatened to usher in a more authoritarian regime before petering out with a whimper. The republic survived, tension with Germany was defused and, having failed to win power democratically or mount a *coup d'état*, Boulanger went into exile and committed suicide on the tomb of his mistress.

Boulangism can be said to inaugurate the modern era in French politics by showing the power of the media (in this case the press) to manipulate a mass public (see Winock 1987: 118). More centrally from our point of view, it manifests certain negative, recurrent features of French history. First, the thirst for *grandeur* and the nationalism that repeatedly led France into war. Second, the failure to unite around a democratic regime. Third, and relatedly, the reiterated Bonapartist temptation which saw the First and Second Republics swept away by members of the Bonaparte family and the Third by Pétain's Vichy regime. The Boulangist episode thus provided Renoir with a perfect vehicle to explore his nation's self-repeating and turbulent past in a non-tragic context.[3] A vision of French history as tragi-comic repetition inevitably echoes the comments of Karl Marx on the rise of Napoleon III, the second of the Bonaparte dynasty to seize power. Marx observed that all the great events and characters of history occur twice, 'the first time as high tragedy, the second time as low farce'. He added some famous lines which, after a little editing, could serve as an exegesis of Renoir's film: 'Tradition from all the dead generations weighs like a nightmare on the brain of the living ... They nervously summon up the spirits of the past, borrowing from them their names, marching orders, uniforms, in order to enact new scenes in world history but in this time-honoured guise and with this borrowed language' (Marx 1996: 31–2).

Renoir kept the major contours of the Boulanger story but strengthened the love interest by introducing a Polish princess, Eléna, (played by Ingrid Bergman) and a dilettante aristocrat, Henri, who falls in love with her. Eléna's beauty kindles desire in the men she meets, including Rollan, the Boulanger figure, but instead of satisfying their passion, she turns their libidinal energies outwards to worldly ambitions. Her suitors include a composer, a shoe magnate and the general himself, evoking between them the triple temptations of fame, wealth and power that lay at the heart of *Le Carosse d'or*. A sub-plot involves the rivalry between the magnate's son and a soldier for the affections

3 Daniel Serceau, one of the few critics to discern the critical edge beneath the surface *bonhomie* of late Renoir, suggests that the director uses *Eléna* to lay bare the ideological contradictions of the French (Serceau 1985: 98).

of a maidservant. The mid-section of the film directly echoes *La Règle du jeu* as masters and servants engage in comic pursuits, seductions and fights in the rooms and corridors of a château. This time no murder ensues. The finale brings the triumph of love in a small provincial town and dispatches the general and his mistress, not to Paris, the city of history and revolution, but to the south of France. One character's concluding comment that a country where love is so important is immune to dictatorship is at once dripping with irony, given France's long-term and recent past, and indicative of a possible way to escape from a destructively self-repeating history.

It is surely no accident that the film begins with Bastille-day celebrations that evoke the possibility of harmonious community and innocently shared pleasure yet serve as a reminder that history and politics can only divide the French. The deeply ambivalent representation of the 14 July crowd takes up where *The Diary of a Chambermaid* laid off, but this time without the disturbing murder of the anti-republican butler. Analysis of the crowd helps to bring out the film's multiple historical resonances. As it surges around Paris, the populace clearly suggests the revolutionary crowd so prominent in French history ('Is that how you took the Bastille?' asks Eléna), while its easy informality and pleasure in shared festivity feed off a tradition of rose-tinted representations of the common people. Its capacity for irrational swings of mood evoke late nineteenth-century visions of the mob. The easily manipulable masses of the twentieth century are also suggested by a populace that is stirred up by the press, prey to fads and finally only tamed by music and spectacle. Sober, impersonal republicanism – represented significantly by a sombrely dressed and isolated individual – has no purchase on the volatile crowd which falls in love with the brightly coloured uniforms of the military pageant and the dashing general. This portrayal is a world removed from the Popular Front films and more specifically *La Marseillaise* where the people's active political consciousness made them progressive and mature historical actors. No progressive vision on history can be built on the capricious and gullible crowd of *Eléna*.

If history is not progressive, it is best escaped from. The film suggests that the French can bring down the curtain on their tragi-comic history by channelling their libidinal energies into sensual pleasure rather than political struggle or the pursuit of grandeur. This solution emerges from a struggle between two principal characters, Eléna and Henri, to direct the story. Eléna, the beautiful Polish princess, is an energising heroine. She has multiple suitors but refuses to accede to their or her own desires, instead spurring them on in pursuit of worldly ambition so that libidinal energy is repressed or displaced, turned away from private satisfaction and outwards to public activity and conflict. The aristocratic Henri is an anti-Promethean apostle of laziness, *légèreté* and sensual pleasure. He eventually wrests narrative control from Eléna and directs libidinal energy into its proper channels, turning the French away from the repressive programme offered by Rollan supporters ('*sobriété, moralité, autorité, l'ordre, un chef*') and towards the satisfaction of their own desires. Playing the part of Rollan, he kisses Eléna by a window, producing a seductive and calming cinematic spectacle for the assembled crowd below.

The spectacle's location between a brothel and a gypsy encamp-ment suggests the radical shift of values that needs to take place. Community cannot be based on political values, history or nationalism because they inevitably set the French against out-siders or each other. Nor can it spring from a crowd whose warmth turns too easily to hate. But, as Henri's *mise-en-scène* reveals, the turbulent French can come together in a loose and peaceful community of shared values, based around French *joie de vivre*, the shared sensuous enjoyment of immediate pleasures. Interestingly, Freud suggests a similar possibility in *Civilisation and its Discontents* where, having noted that it seems impossible to bind large human communities together in love without directing their aggression outwards to other groups, he suggests that it is possible to 'imagine a cultural community consisting of double individuals ... who, libidinally satisfied in themselves, are connected with one another through the bonds of common work and common interests' (Freud 1991: 298). If one replaced work and interests with idleness and pleasure this might serve as the moral of Renoir's film.

Eléna pursues Renoir's concern with the masses in his post-war cinema, taking a line somewhere between the passive public of *Le Carosse d'or* and the relatively positive image of the festive crowd of *French Cancan*, but adding an element of unruly bellicosity absent from the other two films. Spectacle's sensual appeal is the main form of influence upon this non-reflective mass. When it takes the form of a dashing general and a military parade, it brings out the worst in the crowd. But, as the finale suggests, it can also be used to tame it. The film is highly ambivalent. It suggests that libidinally satisfied people are good-natured and peaceful but it also shows how they are infantile, fickle and manipulable (and thus always subject to the influence of less benign spectacles). The general's élitist mistress expresses her scorn for the crowd while Eléna expresses a populist love of it. The film plots a middle path between these two extremes by espousing a disabused paternalism.

The close association of Eléna and the crowd is unsurprising. Classically seen as fickle and irrational, the crowd was perceived as possessing stereotypically feminine traits. Both crowd and woman need the intervention of a lucid Henri to transcend their destructive tendencies. The film reinforces retrograde gender stereotypes in this respect, but is also deeply critical of the 'masculine' pursuit of power and wealth which is seen as a destructively mistaken misuse of human energy. Its ultimate failure to develop this potentially radical critique of dominant masculinities into a broader questioning of gender stereotyping reveals an underlying conservatism.

Such also is the conclusion of Burch and Sellier who use *Eléna* as proof that French light comedy of this era is particularly favourable ground for the expression of misogyny. They see *French Cancan* in the same light, noting how it centres upon the patriarchal viewpoint of Danglard, to whose genius Nini must submit even when he betrays her openly in public. In refreshingly anti-*auteurist* mode, they view the two films as proof that great film-makers do not escape from the prejudices of their period (Burch and Sellier 1996: 264–25). They could indeed have taken their analysis further by showing how the relationship between the male artist (the creative mind), and the female dancer (the body to be moulded), reproduces one of the central structuring binaries of western art and civilisation.

In contrast, they see *Le Carosse d'or* as an overt challenge to the gender status quo noting that it privileges the woman's point of view and gives her full subject status. They note too how it exposes prevalent double standards as Camilla finds that the men unite against her when she tries to pursue several relationships simultaneously, whereas infidelity is accepted in men. She comes to realise that the different forms of seduction employed by men (virile domination, power and wealth or tender protectiveness) are all masks for the same possessiveness. She even challenges the public–private divide that helps to maintain male domination by repeatedly breaking into the viceroy's council of state. Burch and Sellier do, however, express some doubts about their feminist appropriation of Camilla. They suggest that, beyond a character's gender, one must also consider what they represent symbolically. Any account of gender relationships must take into account the film's implied message that art (Camilla) must distance itself from domination (the men) (Burch and Sellier 1996: 290–5). Pushing the implications of what they say beyond the point where they leave it, one might suggest that when men monopolise power in the public sphere, any critique of domination will necessarily target them without necessarily leading to a deliberate questioning of gender inequality. Besides, Camilla is something of an unlikely heroine for any consciously feminist narrative, motivated as she is by the same desire for power and wealth as the men, and almost precipitating disaster before she comes to her senses.

Flight into fantasy?

Turning to Renoir's next two films, Burch and Sellier detect a critique of how 'masculine' rationality seeks mastery of the world through repression of the body, producing Fascistic behaviour when the repressed returns (Burch and Sellier 1996: 265). These remarks provide a useful introduction to the films in question (*Le*

Testament du Docteur Cordelier (1959) and *Le Déjeuner sur l'herbe*, (1959)) which continue to probe the founding dualisms of western modernity (mind–body; culture–nature; intellect–instinct) while offering only a limited challenge to the gender stereotypes that feed off and into them.

Both revolve around scientists who seek to control what one might call human nature – one seeks to repress 'evil' by the use of drugs, the other to improve the species by scientific control of procreation. They show in very different ways the ultimate vanity of these attempts. While one (*Le Testament*) is a dark fable shot in black and white in depressingly bare Paris locations, the other (*Le Déjeuner*) is an apparently light comedy, shot in colour and set in the idyllic landscape of Provence. The former is almost immediately recognisable as an adaptation of Stevenson's story of Jekyll and Hyde. The other, as its title suggests, pays clear homage to Impressionist painting, being shot in a landscape where Auguste Renoir used to paint and where Renoir himself had lived as a child.

The two films break with the three we have just considered by their contemporary setting and location shooting. However, each has a renowned theatrical actor at its centre (Jean-Louis Barrault in *Le Testament* and Paul Meurisse in *Le Déjeuner*) and plays highly non-realist plots against the authenticity of their locations.

The earlier of the two, *Le Testament du Docteur Cordelier*, revolves around four central figures: Cordelier, a psychiatrist who seeks to repress his own instincts by chemical means; Maître Joly, a notary, who is an old and loyal but also deeply conventional and unimaginative friend of Cordelier; Opale, the monster that Cordelier unleashes from within himself; Séverin, another psychiatrist whose materialist rationalism is deeply at odds with Cordelier's belief in the existence of the soul. The dominant viewpoint for most of the film is that of Joly, whose bourgeois conformism makes him incapable of comprehending what is happening.

The mystery begins when Cordelier dictates a new will to Joly leaving all his money to the monstrous Opale and is resolved by a tape-recorded confession delivered to the same horrified man, just before Opale, unable to become Cordelier again, puts an end to his life. The movement from will to confession is symptomatic of a broader shift from the factual details of Opale's crimes to the psychological and moral complexity behind them.

Cordelier, a high-society psychiatrist, reveals that he was tormented by the conflict between repressive social norms and his instinctual desire for pleasure. The conflict was initially manifested by his refusal to give in to his desire for his eminently attractive and willing German maid and continued when he refused to respond to the desire he aroused in a female patient. However, having sedated the same woman, he had sex with her without her consent and did the same with other women clients. Thus his turning to pure research and attempt to control 'base' instincts by different cocktails of mind-altering drugs. However, rather than freeing him of his urges, his experiments unleash them in pure form in the shape of Opale. The latter is younger in appearance and more vigorous in his movements than the stiff and middle-aged Cordelier and his initial experience of a debauched guilt-free life is liberatory and exhilarating. However, the release of repressed instincts is accompanied by acts of violence in the shape of sadistic sex with prostitutes, an attack on a little girl (which begins the film), on a woman with a baby and then the murder of an old man.

We may initially react, as does Joly, and consider that the respectable Cordelier needs protecting from the animalistic Opale. However, as the final confession unfolds, we are forced to go beyond this conventional response. Cordelier is, after all, a rapist, even if his victims' unconsciousness preserved his veneer of respectability. Opale is already there within him. His belief that he can modify his mind through drugs is symptomatic of the megalomania of modern science and it is made clear that he is motivated by the wish to prove his professional rival wrong, not by any thirst for pure knowledge. In any case, Opale is not 'pure' instinct, but a product of repression and hypocrisy. His public outrages are directed at those society designates as weak or innocent and are challenges to social taboo not presocial acts. Guilt thus shifts from the criminal to the repressive society which produced him. More specifically, it shifts to Joly, Séverin and Cordelier who embody different and sometimes competing outlooks that none the less come together in the repression of the instincts.

Joly is the voice of bourgeois respectability that demands the denial of desire and truth about self for the sake of appearances. Modern science finds expression in Séverin's search for purely rational behaviour which suppresses instinctual drives and separates mind and body. His chain smoking, nervous tics and sudden outbursts are clear signs that irrationality and disorder will inevitably undermine the desire for mastery of self. While endorsing Séverin's splitting of the mind and the body, Cordelier locates himself within a Manichaean western moral tradition which sees the world in terms of good and evil and associates the drive for sexual pleasure with the latter. In the epilogue that closes the film, Renoir suggests that Cordelier has the best role. Rather than seeing this as some form of endorsement of what he represents, we should perhaps see it as a comment on his recognition of the mind's complexity as compared to the one-dimensional viewpoints of Séverin and Joly.

Stevenson's story is above all a moral tale about scientific hubris and our inevitably dual nature. While substantially following the storyline of the original, Renoir's film shifts the emphasis to the harmful effects of the different forms of repression prevalent in western society. It also adds a tone of mocking irony that invites us to be amused as well as horrified by events. Cordelier's quest, for example, is undermined by the rather ridiculous refusal of healthy sexual pleasure that motivated him in the first place.

Stevenson's story shows a London split between respectable houses and dismal and disordered back streets, a city whose combination of opposites mirrors the splitting of the main character himself. Renoir's film splits Paris similarly. Cordelier's large house in an eerily empty *banlieue* reveals his self-inflicted social isolation, while the contrast between the respectable façade and the horrors that go on inside are a physical manifestation of social hypocrisy. Opale's sadistic practices in a dingy room on *rue Pigalle* suggest that the red-light district is an unhealthy product of the repression and marginalisation of the instincts by scientific rationality, bourgeois respectability and Christian morality. The city-centre location of Séverin's modern office indicates the social dominance of the scientific rationality he represents. Notable by their absence are more positive images of Paris. The little girl scurrying alone in the dark sets the tone. Later, the presence of a single kissing couple in the dark streets only emphasises the general gloom while evoking the loss of the Paris of lovers. The comment of an American diplomat, that he is happy to return to a joyful capital, is deeply ironic in this context. It is as if the repressive value systems of the leading characters had produced a joyless, divided and empty city.

If *Le Testament du Docteur Cordelier* suggests that there is something wrong with the values at the heart of the country, *Le Déjeuner sur l'herbe* finds an antidote on its southern margins and more specifically within the rural world that the France of 1960 was increasingly leaving behind.

The story is as preposterous as that of *Le Testament,* but this time has no literary predecessor to help to render it acceptable. It begins with a televised broadcast that introduces the key character, Etienne Alexis, a scientist who seeks to replace haphazard sexual reproduction with the scientifically controlled renewal of the species in order to produce humans fit to live in a world transformed by technology. He is the leading candidate to be president of Europe and is engaged to his cousin Marie-Charlotte, a German scout leader. Both are from the same powerful and wealthy European dynasty and their marriage will help to cement the union of France and Germany's chemical industries thus serving powerful financial interests. The couple agree via the television screen to meet in Provence for a picnic in the countryside. At the same time, a group of ordinary French workers who have seen the same broadcast set off for a camping holiday in the same area. The explosive cocktail of characters is complete when we add the family of Provençal wine growers, and principal among them, the younger daughter, Nénette, who, despairing of the men she knows, but drawn towards motherhood, wants a test-tube baby.

Initially everything goes to plan. However, as Alexis's party picnic in the shelter of the temple of Diana (previously the goddess of pregnant women, we are told), Gaspard, an old goatherd and healer, plays his pipe to summon a wind which disperses the picnickers and unleashes repressed sexual drives. Alexis accidentally sees Nénette bathing naked and is carried away by his instincts. The couple later join the workers' informal picnic. Confused by what has happened, Alexis hides out at Nénette's house, but his companions track him down and take him back to marry Marie-Charlotte so that their political and financial plans can go ahead. Chance throws Nénette back into his path and, learning she is pregnant by him, he marries her instead. His wedding speech will be about 'the union of nature and science'.

The film looks to France and Europe's future and recent past, inviting spectators to consider the present in a broader context. The evocation of European presidential elections clearly refers to the then very recent establishment of the European Economic Community (1957), but also looks to the future. The name given to the central character seems a clear reference to Alexis Carrel, the famous French eugenicist, whose desire to control reproduction fed off and into racist and Fascist ideologies. Marie-Charlotte's nationality, Aryan appearance and paramilitary uniform recall the Nazi period, albeit in a light, mocking manner while Nénette's rustic existence evokes the rural world that had been central to France's identity but which was quickly marginalised after 1945. Finally, Gaspard's role as goatherd, sorcerer and healer, and his Dionysian unleashing of disorder suggest an era that precedes religion's repression of sexuality and scientific rationality's devaluing of the body and the instinctive.

The association of Alexis and Marie-Charlotte with the era of Fascism is clearly meant to disturb by pointing to the totalitarian potential of a world run by even benevolent technocrats. Alexis's wish to control the human reproductive process is highly symbolic. It would imply state invasion of the most intimate spheres of the private world and scientific control of the very nature of the human species. His justificatory argument, that human beings have not changed while science has transformed the world, is itself indicative of the increasing mismatch between human beings and the demands of modern society. His regressive solution is to make humans fit the needs of the technocratic machine.

The workers watching Alexis's televised broadcast are far from passive. Some of them agree uncritically with what he suggests. One women declares her support by expressing her attachment to her motor scooter and record player, implying that the workers may accept technocratic rule in exchange for material prosperity. Others evoke the dangers of science, citing the atomic bomb and the dangers of radioactive pollution. Choice polarises around a wholesale rejection of technological change and an unquestioning acceptance of it. The lively debate shows that this is not the passive crowd of *Le Carosse d'or* nor the infantile mass of *Eléna*. It is a public that is not simply manipulated by the powerful through the media. But its naïvety suggests that, if it is to offer a way forward, it is to be through its actions rather than its thoughts.

When Alexis joins the workers' picnic, he escapes the stultifying formality of his class. He learns from them the spontaneous enjoyment of simple things such as sitting on the grass, drinking red wine or singing a song with a group of friends, activities enjoyed for their own sake and not put to the service of political or financial ends. He also learns from them a different use of the machine. While prestigious, chauffeur-driven cars separate him from nature, the scooter he borrows from the workers allows him to ride pressed up against Nénette and feel the wind in his hair. This machine, a symbol of youthful informality, is thus at the service of human pleasure.

The film would seem to suggest that even as France turns its back on its rural past, the ordinary people may show the way to place sensual enjoyment of the concrete world at the centre of civilisation through their spontaneous use of the emerging leisure culture. If living in the country is no longer an option for most people, then eating lunch on the grass, swimming in a river or camping in the open air may be acceptable ways to keep in contact with nature and the senses. A more pessimistic vision would suggest that leisure, itself a prime site for capitalist colonisation, is simply one of the ways modern society buys the acquiescence of the populace.

Whether the workers show a potential way forward or are simply dupes of the system, it is clear that the rich and powerful are their own principal victims. Alexis and his companions avoid direct contact with nature. During their formal picnic, they maintain strict control over what they eat so that their self-image intervenes between themselves and the simplest of pleasures. One woman, the wife of an important businessman, can never eat what she wants because she must always look good. She is thus multiply alienated from her own pleasure, having to conform to a public image for the sake of someone else's career. The presence of the press at the picnic underlines the alienation of this group by showing that each of their bodily gestures has to be calculated for the way it may be publicly received.

The disciplining of the body and its subjection to the dictates of the mind is taken to its limit by Marie-Charlotte whose mode of contact with nature is through the paramilitary activity of scouting. The imprisonment of her body in a stiff, high-collared uniform is a visual representation of her repressive attitude, her denial of pleasure to herself and others. The contrast between this stiff, blond, northern European and Nénette, the dark-haired, southern woman underlines their markedly different attitudes to the body and to pleasure. It is through the latter that Alexis will rediscover his senses.

Initially it seems that the peasant woman should learn from the technocrat. However, once the goatherd has created the liberating chaos that dissolves the repressive established order, he becomes her pupil even if she expresses no awareness of her role. The first stage in his re-education is when they make love. Shots of the wind in the trees, of running water, even of bees, seem a rather clichéd way of indirectly communicating what has happened. What is suggested, however, is that through spontaneous love-making, Alexis reopens himself more generally to sensual enjoyment of the natural world.

Although the film clearly has some elements of pastoral (the idealisation of the rural as a repository of alternative values to the modern or the urban) Nénette's family is not set up as a model of harmony. Her sister Ninette is constantly run off her feet looking after her four children and doing the work of an idle husband whose drinking has to be restricted by his father-in-law. Renoir was perhaps conscious of the reactionary connotations of the glorification of the rural and of the large family and wanted to distance himself from them. His film is an apologia for sensualist hedonism and an attack on the technocratic control of society, not simply a piece of conservative traditionalism.[4]

However, where the film is solidly traditional is in the characterisation of the heroine. Her principal characteristic is her desire to have a baby, biology seemingly defining her destiny. She is further defined by her physical attractiveness, and it is through her body that Alexis comes to rediscover his senses. When the film evokes Impressionism, she is cast in stereotypical manner as the female nude, as the object whose beauty, along with that of nature, is to be revealed by the male subject. She is unashamedly non-intellectual and admits to being more impressed by what men say when she doesn't understand it. Alexis's rediscovery of the pleasure of idleness requires that she wait on him hand and foot. Although Renoir's film is a challenge to the hierarchical binary divisions that structure western perceptions of the world (mind–body; science–nature; the intellect–the senses) it reinforces the stereotypical association of women with the 'inferior' term of each pair. Nénette is never allowed to reverse Alexis's trajectory and reclaim access to the intellect through him.

Le Testament du Docteur Cordelier follows a similar pattern despite the near absence of women. The German maid who offers sensual satisfaction to Cordelier is an embryonic Nénette figure. Cordelier's female patients are mere objects of temptation while the prostitutes whom Opale mistreats are bodies to be used and abused. The privileges of intellectual and spiritual torment are confirmed as male preserves.

4 This does not prevent Oms using the film to confirm his view that Renoir has always been a reactionary. Seeing it as an apologia for a return to the land, he then finds a similar underlying message in a cluster of films reaching back into the period of the Popular Front (Oms 1962: 44–7).

The return of the political?

Le Caporal épinglé, one of the most underestimated of all Renoir films, was made in 1962. Perhaps realising the limitations of an apologia for sensual pleasure and laziness in the face of the massive state-promoted and capitalist-driven transformation of France, it moves away from cultural definitions of nation and back towards a more 'political' Frenchness, centred on the need to fight for freedom. This shift is not a break, as a concern with the repressiveness of the modern world remains central.

A prisoner-of-war drama set in the Second World War, it has echoes of *La Grande Illusion* of which it is sometimes simplistically seen as a pale imitation. Like the earlier film, it is doubly historically inscribed, representing the past but also responding to the present, depicting French defeat by Germany in 1940 but also responding to the need to reinvent Frenchness in the midst of the radical transformations of the *Trente Glorieuses*. The two films are very different despite their shared focus on prisoners of war. *La Grande Illusion* is essentially a politically committed anti-war film that weighs class identity against national affiliation. *Le Caporal*'s central concern is the need to be free in order to live an authentic life. It signals its difference from its predecessor when the escaping hero, (the corporal of the title), meets a Frenchman who has decided to stay and work the land with a German war widow, thus echoing the desire of Maréchal to stay with Else in the earlier film. The corporal understands this choice but goes on to Paris to fight for personal and national freedom. Although the earlier film has not been rejected, the struggle this time is different.

Le Caporal begins with newsreel shots of the collapse of France in 1940. We see the Germans marching past the Arc de Triomphe, symbol of past French military victories, claiming the centre of France and effacing French greatness. We see also the signing of the armistice in the railway compartment at Rethondes where French triumph had been sealed in 1918 but which is now a site of national humiliation. France has lost itself, its centre and any link with a positively connoted national past. The French are reduced to a disorganised rabble. When the newsreel shots give way to the feature film proper, we see remnants of their army held captive in a muddy field. Its bedraggled, chaotic state is a visual reflection of the moral state of the nation. Individual soldiers are left with nothing but their own inner resources and the friendship of their comrades. Collective identity must be rebuilt from scratch.

The corporal and his friends initially seek to deny the reality of defeat and subservience by improvising an escape, but are immediately captured and punished. By the final, successful escape, the corporal is aware that he cannot be free in a country that is unfree. His increasingly conscious struggle for freedom (*liberté*) builds on the non-hierarchical homosocial bonding of the camp (*égalité, fraternité*) to restore the link with the republican past and tie the personal struggle for freedom into a national narrative.[5]

Like *La Grande Illusion*, the film takes masculinity to the verge of disintegration before retreating to gender conservatism. Male insecurities and repressed desires are unleashed by a prison-camp story of subordination and close confinement and anxieties again crystallise around women, despite their almost complete absence from the film. We hear of their sexual infidelity and of how they take the jobs of absent men. Intense homosocial bonding sees the men nurture, tend and cry for each other, even begging to share the same bunk. Gender hierarchy and roles are stabilised by the struggle for freedom. A German dentist's daughter, the only woman who plays a part of any significance, falls for the hero because he is not 'a slave'. Her love consigns her to the private realm of emotions while rewarding the man for his refusal of subordination. Later, on a bridge in Paris, in the symbolic heart of the nation, the corporal vows to continue the fight against the occupying army with his adoring friend Pater after a visit home to his wife. Intense male bonding is thus directed outwards into the fight for autonomy and control of public space that is essential to adult masculinity while women are again interned in domestic space.

5 I am indebted to Serceau for this recognition of *Le Caporal*'s appropriation of the national trinity of values (Serceau 1985: 213). Serceau, needless to say, neglects the gendered dimension of their use.

The film explores the administered unfreedom of the modern world through the rigidly ordered prisoner-of-war camp. The imposition of German labour discipline on the captive French with the collaboration of a French NCO cannot help but evoke the post-1957 Franco-German economic axis and France's state-sponsored drive for economic growth. Significantly, the prisoners are overwhelmingly salaried workers and thus representative of the accelerated disappearance of independent labour in post-war France. Together they evoke a world of bureaucracy, subservience and surveillance. One reads gas meters while another character checks tickets in the metro. One is a waiter and another an insurance agent.

Refusing to acknowledge their fundamental unfreedom, the prisoners fall back on a hollow affirmation of their place and importance in the economy or on French sociability and archetypal cultural values such as love of food, *douceur de vivre*, or individualistic resistance to the system. Yet the ever-present barbed wire, hut walls and German soldiers will not let us forget the captive status that prevents them building an authentically positive sense of self. One character illustrates how this tangible wartime unfreedom parallels the less overt servitude of peacetime. As he talks proudly of how he used to wear a uniform and make holes in metro tickets, his mocking friend points out to him that he is still wearing a uniform and digging holes for the Germans.

Ballochet, the corporal's closest friend, is the clearest example of this attempt to build a positive sense of self on a denial of the reality of one's condition. His projected superiority depends on a denial of his position as a gas-meter reader, a cog in a bureaucratic machine, a denial which continues when he refuses to face up to his cowardice. He establishes a very French superiority by obtaining access to luxury foods and even has a German soldier doing his bidding. When shaken out of his complacency by the corporal, he attempts to escape in a way that simply confirms that he is a slave to his image. In the tradition of French theatre, he bangs thrice on the floor to summon the audience he needs to demonstrate how a superior being escapes. When he is machine-gunned at the perimeter wire, he pays the absolute price for valuing appearances above reality.

As in other late Renoir' films, theatricality is presented negatively when associated with deception or self-deception. Although the film has been seen as an attack on heroism and its destructiveness, it would be better to see it as a rejection of heroism as self-conscious performance. The corporal's single-minded pursuit of freedom is conveyed through an anti-heroic aesthetic which punctuates his dramatic escapes with comedy, as when a bystander is shot in the knee and falls into his arms. This uneasy mixing of the comic and the serious, also typical of late Renoir, prevents absorption in the immediacy of the action. The film requires a reflective audience.

In some ways, *Le Caporal épinglé* can be seen as a typical film about the Second World War, one perfectly suited to the period when General de Gaulle, one of the chief architects of the myth of a freedom-loving France, had just returned to power. While the self-preservation of the mass of the prisoners and the active collaboration of the NCO might not be seen as a flattering image, the focus on a character who fights for personal and national freedom offers a satisfying image of France at war. The film's reverberations are much more complex if one sees it as a coded message about the need to defend liberty in a society where people are increasingly the tools of the productive machine. Read in this second way, it can be seen to turn the Gaullist founding myth of a liberty-loving France against the unfreedom and subordination that follow from the drive for productivity and economic modernisation that the Gaullist state so wholeheartedly supported. While the film sends clear signals that push us towards this latter, more radical interpretation, the model of revolt it proposes is tied to the Second World War. Certainly, it places a liberty that must be fought for at the heart of Frenchness, but at no time does it suggest what form such a fight might take.

The film breaks to a degree with its predecessors. It recognises that the individual cannot be free in an unfree society and thus reinstates the need for action and accompanying hardship in a cinema that had increasingly celebrated sensual pleasure and inactivity. However, in its failure to suggest a concrete way to realise the values it proposes, it conforms to the pattern of the earlier films. Its apparent reactivation of core French political values does not in the end signify a return to a political vision. The film makes no link to contemporary political struggles.

Little revolutions

Renoir's final film, *Le Petit Théâtre de Jean Renoir* (1969), was made the year after the students' and workers' revolt of 1968 which was partly directed against productivism, consumerism and the repressive nature of traditional sexual morality. One might have expected him to respond positively to the events and establish connections between his own preoccupations and the concerns of the demonstrators, but although *Le Petit Théâtre* recounts little revolutions in two of its four sketches, it never overtly seeks to build a bridge to a broader political movement. It is better seen as an attempt to effect a synthesis between *Le Caporal*'s affirmation of the need for struggle and its predecessors' turning away from history and towards a cultural definition of Frenchness.

The four sections of the film are as follows: *Le Dernier Réveillon*, a 'fairy story' tribute to Hans Christian Andersen; *La Cireuse électrique*, a domestic 'opera' complete with singing chorus; *Quand l'amour meurt*, a *belle époque* song performed by Jeanne Moreau; *Le Roi d'Yvetot*, a realist fable shot in Provence. The sections are linked together by Renoir himself, who presents each piece as he stands next to a tiny theatre whose curtains the camera will lead us through. The film is initially notable for its bringing together of a range of cultural forms that Renoir has used before (popular song, theatre, fairy story). To these it adds opera, a genre he briefly engaged with when he began to make *La Tosca* in 1940. Studio shooting is juxtaposed with location work, colour with black and white, high with popular cultural forms. It is as if, referring back to his own work, Renoir were exploring the possibilities of cinema, its complex relation to other forms, its ambivalent status between art and mass culture, and its ability to combine realism and spectacle.

The first studio-shot piece is a fairy story set on Christmas Eve that constitutes a fable about alienation in a materialist society. Gontran, a wealthy cynic, enters a restaurant with a group of friends, and, identifying in a tramp a perfect specimen of hunger (a clear reference to *Boudu*), pays him to stand outside the window and watch the wealthy eat. Like his fellow diners, Gontran takes pleasure only from having things that other people do not have. When he orders *vin ordinaire* not champagne, it is not because he enjoys simple things but because he needs to assert his superiority to those around him by what he consumes. The other guests are driven away, unable to face the truth about their world. One or two even try to salvage their self-image by giving luxury coats to the tramp. The restaurant owner persuades the tramp to move on by offering him a luxury meal, but, part of a society in thrall to images, the tramp insists on the best champagne. He too wishes to distinguish himself by what he consumes.

The tramp returns to his cold and hungry companion but, instead of using the coats and the food to satisfy their immediate physical needs, they lose themselves in an imagined past when they were young and wealthy. Affirming their undying love, they curl up together and freeze to death, their meal still untouched. Two rather more earthy tramps arrive and help themselves to the food, remarking how happy the couple appear in death.

The story is somewhat ambivalent. Certainly, one could read it in positive terms as a celebration of the refusal of the tramps to accept the position society assigns to them, of the triumph of the spirit over matter, or of love over death. But, my own interpretation, and one that essentially echoes that of Serceau, is that the film is a critique of a society that places hollow images between itself and its pleasures, a society where everyone, from the top to the bottom, is alienated from their own desire by the need to affirm their social status (Serceau 1985: 243–53). If satisfaction comes from having what others don't have, it is never a response to an authentic personal need.

The second vignette, *La Cireuse électronique*, is a discordant blend of opera and realism. Set among newly built blocks of flats, and showing crowds of similarly dressed commuters leaving and entering the metro, it is a piece about the new France of the 1960s, a France of consumer goods, of urban monotony and of salaried labour. A France too, the setting suggests, whose identity is disappearing in the anonymous concrete spaces of modern urbanism. The archetypally French *baguettes* that are carried by various groups in the film seem designed to highlight the lack of cultural specificity of the décor.

The piece begins with a mixed chorus emerging from the underground, singing of 'métro, boulot, dodo' (metro, work, sleep). This bored chorus takes a voyeuristic interest in the domestic tragi-comedy that constitutes the centre of the section. The story focuses on narcissism, alienation and object fetishism within a couple. The husband is absorbed by his work and bases his self-esteem on his recent promotion to second clerk, so that what he values most is determined not by himself but by his place in the world of salaried labour. His wife, on the other hand, is obsessed by her home, and above all her polished wooden floor. The moment when she narcissistically contemplates her own image in the shiny wood demonstrates that her self-worth is dependent on the social prestige attached to objects.

As in much of late Renoir, the drama revolves around the denial of libidinal satisfaction. After they have quarrelled, the couple are about to seal their reconciliation and escape temporarily from their self-absorption by making love. However, a neighbour interrupts them. He sells electric floor polishers and will carry out a demonstration for the wife. In the new France, the world of marketing and advertising thus penetrates into the heart of the home. Private space has been colonised by consumer capitalism. Later, the wife will lovingly caress and sing a love song to the new floor polisher that becomes a sexual object for her in a way that highlights both advertising's eroticisation of consumer goods and its ultimate absurdity.

The immediate result of the polisher's arrival is that the husband slips on the gleaming floor and cracks his head. At the ensuing funeral, the wife rediscovers an old flame whom she marries. The drama is ready to begin again. However, the second husband is firmer. He tolerates the constant noise of typewriters during the day but insists his home be a haven of peace. Supported by winks and smiles from the dead husband's photograph, he insists that the polisher not be used while he is in the apartment, eventually throwing it off the balcony when his wife refuses to give in. She herself jumps off the balcony and dies holding the broken machine, a gesture which prompts the conformist chorus to sing that machines are sacred and human beings replaceable. Within the 'operatic' context the plunge from the balcony inevitably evokes the similar suicide of Puccini's Tosca, but Puccini's heroine was motivated by love and resistance to tyranny, not by narcissism and conformism.

The film's critique of consumerism feeds off gender stereotypes. Firmly locating the husbands in the world of work and production, it encloses the woman in the world of domesticity and consumption. Her attempts to assert her identity through the exercise of autonomy in the space she has been relegated to are presented in purely negative terms. In a world lacking in communication and where voyeurism has replaced community, the only solidarity in evidence is generated by the two husbands in their struggle for domestic authority.

The third (very short) part of the film presents a song from the *belle époque* sung by Jeanne Moreau, one of the favourite actresses of the *nouvelle vague*. It is simplicity itself. Moreau is shot front on to camera, on a bare stage, in front of a simple backcloth. The camera tracks forward to a medium shot then tracks out again on the same axis to show the whole stage. At the formal level it seems to be both a tribute to the stage and a demonstration of the specificity of the cinema. The simple track forward radically changes what we see, giving us an intimate closeness to the actress's face that the spectator in the theatre is denied. The song's title, Quand l'amour meurt (When love dies), recalls the two preceding vignettes, for in the first the lovers die, while in the second love itself is 'killed' by materialism and consumerist narcissism. It would thus seem to offer a provisional conclusion to the film, one that seems to be deeply pessimistic. Building on the earlier focus on an alienating present, its association of the *belle époque* with loss suggests a vision dominated by nostalgia for the director's childhood and for a (mythical) time of national innocence. This 'conclusion' is then counterbalanced (but not completely over-written) by the life-affirming hedonism of the final vignette wherein, refusing a tragic or nostalgic outlook, an old man lives for present pleasures.

The final vignette sets off a tightly knit community in Provence against the Parisian scenes of the first two pieces, thus marking a return to the contrast between the southern French idyll of *Le Déjeuner sur l'herbe* and the Parisian nightmare of *Le Testament du Docteur Cordelier*. It also has strong echoes of Pagnol's celebrated cinematic representations of this part of France. The opening game of boules is almost certainly a reference to a parallel scene in Pagnol's *Fanny* (1932). The central opposition between happiness and honour is also at the heart of Pagnol's Marseilles trilogy (1931–36) although Renoir finds a decidedly more unconventional way to allow for the triumph of the former. This overt intertext-uality would seem to be a signal that Renoir is consciously playing a Utopian rural south against the urban dystopia of the first two vignettes.

Duvallier, the central character of the story, initially has every reason to be happy with his lot. As a retired naval commander he can divide his time between boules and aperitifs with his friends in the village, and eating and idling in his garden with his attrac-tive young wife. This apparently perfect happiness is disturbed by Maître Joly, the local notary, who is the church-going voice of convention and someone who refuses to join in with the lazy sociability of the village. Joly (whose destructiveness is a clear pointer to how we should judge the character of the same name in *Le Testament du Docteur Cordelier*) points out the contrast between Duvallier's age and his wife's youth and sows initial seeds of doubt in his mind. The doubts are confirmed when his wife complains of '*chatouillements*' (itches). A new local vet proves to be a kindred spirit for Duvallier, sharing his love of good food and an easy life, but he is also attracted to Duvallier's wife who returns his feelings. A new equilibrium emerges as the wife finds sexual fulfilment with the younger man while Duvallier is enchanted with his new friend and his wife's rediscovered contentment. When he discovers her infidelity, he is faced with a dilemma about what to do. One villager says he must kill them both to save his honour, thus sacrificing concrete pleasures for a socially generated image. The vet rather absurdly proposes a duel, intending to give his friend a loaded gun and himself an empty one. Duvallier himself solves the problem when he decides that all three must stay together as they need each other to be happy. They go to the village where everyone is by now aware of the situation. In the course of a game of boules, Duvallier's old friend calls him '*cocu*' (cuckold) and after initial embarrassment, all the village shares in the laughter, marking the triumph of shared pleasure and tolerance over honour and convention. Even Joly joins in this final image of Utopian community that brings down the curtain on Renoir's little theatre.

This final vignette provides a positive model to orientate our diagnosis of the social ills shown in the earlier pieces. Its ideal society is based neither on having what others do not have nor on monotonous labour. It does not let images come between itself and its happiness and refuses to bow to repressive moral codes or to stultifying convention. The neglected food of the first story and the abandoned love-making of the second are replaced in this final vignette by sexual satisfaction and the shared sensual pleasure of eating. If the second story suggested that France was losing its specificity, this story's celebration of good eating, boules and the sociability of the southern village square, suggests that the French can find a better way of life by selecting wisely from their traditions.

The location of the film's Utopia in a rural village might suggest a purely nostalgic vision. However, its rejection of certain repressive traditions (the macho cult of honour, the Catholic belief in self-denial) means that it cannot simply be seen as backward-looking, even if it is overwhelmingly critical of an alienating present. It was, indeed, in an earlier version to have been called 'Vive la Révolution' which might suggest not a nostalgic Renoir but one ready to return to a belief in wholesale and cataclysmic social change (Renoir 1981: 341–98). But the revolutions that are presented in the film that emerged are against convention and conformism not concerted assaults on capitalism or the state. In the end, it suggests how individuals might reorder their lives not how groups with concrete political projects might change the status quo. Its apparent synthesis of political and cultural French-ness (and of pre- and post-war Renoir) by the importation of revolution into everyday life masks a failure to suggest mechan-isms for the achievement of collectively directed social change.

Conclusion

The lack of a political project in the Renoir films of the post-war era should not be mistaken for detachment. On the contrary, the films engage consistently with their socio-historical context bringing a sharp critical edge to bear on the fast-changing face of France, Europe and the West more generally. This edge is easily missed by readings that focus on the surface of the films. The light, often comic and antirealist plots can suggest frivolity at worst and an ingratiating desire to please at best, while the repeated 'flight' into history can easily be read as avoidance of controversy or reactionary celebration of tradition. The fore-grounding of spectacle can be viewed as a clichéd affirmation of the superiority of 'art' over 'reality', or at least a turning inwards of Renoir's cinema upon itself. Such readings are not simply wrong, as evidence can clearly be mustered in support of them, but they do fail to engage with the complexity of the later films. Their lightness is real but must be weighed against their evocation of the darker side of the past and the oppressive face of the post-war present. Frivolity placed alongside seriousness is meant to disturb as well as entertain, to celebrate pleasure but also to highlight the obstacles to its realisation. The turning to the past is similarly complex. Used to expose the recurrent patterns of history and to root repression in the project of western modernity, it is also a repository of alternative, potentially Utopian modes of being. The turning 'inwards' is a symptom of a self-conscious search for a critical art that refuses the sedative seduction of spectacle yet still celebrates sensual pleasure.

It is unsurprising that critics of the left have failed to engage with the critical and Utopian dimensions of late Renoir. There is too much that turns them away. The focus on the generally oppressive nature of western modernity leads to a neglect of specific oppressions, notably those of class. The left's preferred agents of historical transformation, the working class, or, more broadly, the common people are unrecognisable in Renoir's depiction of passive, fickle or at best childlike masses. The turning away from history has no appeal for a left generally wedded to the notion of progress while the return of struggle or revolt in the last two films only highlights their lack of a political project and the gulf that separates Renoir's defence of everyday revolutions from the revolutionary traditions of the left that he once espoused.

References

Bergstrom, J. (1996), 'Jean Renoir's return to France', *Poetics Today*, 17, 453–89.

Burch, N. and Sellier, G. (1996), *La Drôle de guerre des sexes du cinéma français (1930–1956)*, Paris, Nathan.

Freud, S. (1991), *Penguin French Library, 12. Civilization, Society and Religion*, (trans. Richards, A.), London, Penguin.

Marx, K. (1996), *Late Political Writings*, (trans. Carver, T.), Cambridge, Cambridge University Press.

Oms, M. (1962), 'Renoir, revu et rectifié,' *Premier Plan*, 22/23/24, 44–51.

Rearick, C. (1985), *Pleasures of the Belle Epoque: Entertainment and Festivity in Turn of the Century France*, New Haven, Yale University Press.

Renoir, J. (1952), 'Quelque chose m'est arrivé', *Cahiers du cinéma*, 1952, 2(8): 31–2.

Renoir, J. (1981), *Œuvres de cinéma inédites*, (Gauteur, C. ed.), Paris, Gallimard.

Renoir, J. (1994), *Letters*, eds, Thompson, D. and LoBianco, L., London, Faber & Faber.

Sadoul, G. (1953), 'Sous de brillantes couleurs', *Les Lettres Françaises*, 5 March.

Serceau, J. (1985), *Jean Renoir. La sagesse du plaisir*, Paris, Editions de Cerf.

Winock, M. (1987), *La Fièvre hexagonale. Les grandes crises politiques de 1871 à 1968*, Paris, Seuil.

7

Conclusion

Renoir's work defies any easy summing-up. Or rather, it should do. Produced with a range of different collaborators, in widely varying circumstances and production contexts, it must also be located in a world undergoing massive and often traumatic change, one rent by competing ideologies and war. Rather than seeking some impossible synthesis, it is better to trace its evolution, identifying periods of relative consistency and crucial turning points that gave it a new direction.

The silent period is one when the films rely on a largely conventional content to explore the possibilities of the medium. They are more interesting for their technical innovation and visual inventiveness than for their consciously conventional content. Their stylistic diversity is striking.

The early 1930s are dominated by adaptations of novels and boulevard theatre and take from them a critique of the bourgeoisie that is at times gentle and at times acerbic but always inward-looking. They also derive from them a more general critique of the repressive and mercenary nature of modern society. More rarely, they engage directly with their time, either because they overflow their source (*Boudu sauvé des eaux*), because the source itself engages with the contemporary (*La Nuit du carrefour*), or because they leave literary adaptation behind (*Toni*). During this period a relatively consistent style emerges. Composition in depth and a mobile panning and tracking camera links characters spatially to a broader world, even if those links sometimes lack social density.

Toni moves Renoir's cinema towards political engagement, affirming an open vision of nation at a time of rising xenophobia, shifting the common people to centre stage, and focusing on the solidarity that arises from shared labour. It paves the way for the clear but varying left-wing line adopted by Renoir's films during the Popular Front, when, plunging fully into the political battles of that period, they bring classes into conflict (and alliance) and claim the nation and its symbols for the left. Moving away from literary adaptations that foreground the bourgeoisie, they seek to build a bridge between the popular and the political. At times closely dependent on a received Communist Party line (*La Vie est à nous, La Marseillaise*), at other times their stance is more open (*La Grande Illusion, Les Bas fonds*) while still inflected by Frontist values. Due to the unevenness of their engagement their politics cannot simply be read off from those of the Front which was in any case an uneasy and unstable alliance marked by internal ideological struggle and negotiation. They are better seen as conditioned but active interventions in a conflictual terrain.

Those few films of the early 1930s that engage with their time register change but project no sense that history is shaped by struggle. The Frontist films engage fully with a contemporary which itself is located in ongoing historical struggle. When the Front fails and faith is lost in the transformatory potential of the working class, the sense of history remains but takes a tragic turn (*La Bête humaine*) or a tragi-comic one (*La Règle du jeu*). A Frontist sensibility returns in those of Renoir's American films that look back to France, *This Land is Mine* and *The Diary of a Chambermaid*, manifestly so in the former, more ambivalently in the latter. *The Diary* signals the final farewell of the Renoir of the left, somewhat later than is usually recognised.

The remainder of Renoir's Hollywood output explores tensions in American mythology to a limited degree without ever subverting it (*Swamp Water, The Southerner*). The wartime context helps explain this essentially conservative engagement by a man who was able to be far more critical of his old country than his new one. *Woman on the Beach* opens a period when his cinema addresses the disruption of the war and embarks on a broader questioning of the values at the heart of western civilisation. The critique of productivism and the accompanying quest for the domination of inner and outer nature dominates Renoir's post-war output, which achieves a degree of continuity that his earlier career manifestly lacked.

Continuity does not mean uniformity. Renoir moves from a broad focus on the West (*The River*, *Le Carosse d'or*) to a more narrow concentration on his home country which is at times celebratory (*French Cancan*) and at times acerbically critical (*Eléna et les hommes*). Having promoted a left-wing vision of France's revolutionary tradition in the Frontist period, he now seeks an alternative anti-political Frenchness that would allow the country to escape from a turbulent history by an embrace of *joie de vivre*, sensuality and laziness. This Frenchness feeds off popular culture (*French Cancan*), myths of the south (*Déjeuner sur l'herbe*) and the French aptitude for love (*Eléna*). *Le Caporal Epinglé* goes against the grain by showing the need for active revolt against the bureaucratic and productivist prison of the modern world.

Although engaging with different oppressions and repressions at different times, Renoir's cinema is never able or never seeks to combine a broad critique of materialism and productivism with a critique of specific oppressions. The early 1930s focus largely on the bourgeoisie's self-repression and hypocrisy but neglect that class's exploitative relationship to other groups. The Frontist films focus on class oppression but move away from the critique of repression. Post-war Renoir shows how the West's Promethean striving requires self-repression, but it loses sight of inequality and feeds off or aestheticises regressive stereotypes of colonised peoples (*The River*) and women (*Déjeuner sur l'herbe*, *Eléna et les hommes*). 'Renoir américain' connives in American mythology's erasure of the oppression of African and Native Americans.

A focus on class oppression identifies the Frontist period as the peak of Renoir's radicalism. An approach that considers the various oppressions, repressions and exclusions explored by the films produces a more nuanced analysis that recognises the critical dimension of other periods and the sometimes regressive elements of the Frontist films. We might note, for example, how a pre-Frontist film (*Toni*) and a Frontist one (*La Grande Illusion*), come together to project an anti-essentialist and open vision of nation that contrasts with the whiff of xenophobia in *La Marseillaise*. We might also note that, of the trio of 1930s films that explore or challenge women's subordination (*Une Partie de campagne, Toni, Le Crime de M. Lange*), only one is usually considered Frontist.

If indeed one privileges gender over class as an axis of analysis one develops a very different vision of the work with a general but evolving pattern of marginalisation and female stereotyping being punctuated by the more progressive representations that we found in the mid-1930s. First emerging in contrast to the passive victims of melodrama, the destructive *femme fatale* runs through the pre-war silent and sound films (*Nana, La Chienne, Madame Bovary, Les Bas-fonds, La Bête humaine*) recurring in *Woman on the Beach* and in lighter mode in *Eléna et les hommes*. *La Marseillaise* and *La Vie est à nous*, two of Renoir's key Frontist works, largely exclude women from political participation and the making of the nation, an exclusion that is reiterated in *Le Caporal Epinglé*. Castrating mothers are used to figure the unmanning of men in *This Land is Mine* and *Diary of a Chambermaid*. These films' use of destabilised gender relations to crystallise the disruption of war recurs less regressively in works as diverse as *Charleston, The River* and *La Grande Illusion*. Alternating between representations of women as whores and virtuous mothers, *La Grande Illusion* none the less takes masculinity to the verge of disintegration. In similar mode, *The River* places stereotypes of women alongside a radical questioning of 'masculine' Promethean striving. The critique of masculine domination of self and nature will continue in the post-war films without leading to a parallel questioning of stereotypes of women. Instead, essentialised gender differences provide stability even as other features of our civilisation are placed in question. Women continue to serve as domestic to man's public (*Le Caporal Epinglé*), nature to man's culture (*Déjeuner sur l'herbe*), and consumer to man's producer (*Le Petit Théâtre de Jean Renoir*).

While the representation of gender in Renoir cannot be considered independently of specific conjunctures (such as war) and broader evolutions in outlook, it undeniably feeds off and continues dominant patterns within French and western culture and as such is the perfect corrective to those *auteurist* readings that see the individual creator as the point of origin of the films' meanings. This does not mean that we should then revert to the opposite extreme, see the films as the simple expression of socially generated ideologies or discourses, and deny the possibility of the intervention of the individual or collective creator in the process of meaning generation. Renoir's films feed off a range of 'discourses', at times simply reproducing them, at times inflecting them for a specific conjuncture, and at times engaging with them actively.

The complex and evolving nature of this interaction helps explain the attractions of *auteurism* and radical anti-*auteurism*. Privileging extremes of conscious creativity and unconscious passivity, they evacuate the key terrain in between upon which individuals and groups in specific institutional frameworks engage reflexively with social and ideological contexts to generate meanings. Rather than simply being denounced as ideological mystification, the later Renoir's *auterist* self-invention needs to be analysed and contextualised. Feeding off a deeply embedded discourse of individual creativity, it was more specifically a response to the specific context of film viewing and reception that prevailed in the post-war period, as well as a form of resistance to the perceived consumerist uniformity generated by sustained post-war prosperity.

Whatever its roots, Renoir's connivance in the rewriting of his output did it a disservice by detaching it from the contexts that allow it to resonate fully and by downplaying the discontinuity that is at the root of its rich diversity. Faulkner (1986) suggested that Renoir had two maturities. One might alternatively suggest that he had multiple careers, each marked by specific personal, institutional and socio-historical contexts that must be taken into account if we are to begin to understand his work. Such an understanding will always inevitably be partial, not least because our reading of Renoir is inevitably inflected by the sedimented critical readings that have accrued around his films. This should not necessarily be taken negatively. Renoir's other career as object of critical analysis is also a fascinating one. As the most valuable prize in the French cinematic pantheon, his films have been at the centre of debates which may have distorted our perception of his work but which have certainly cast light on struggles within French film criticism.

References

Faulkner, C. (1986) *The Social Cinema of Jean Renoir*, Princeton, Princeton University Press.

Filmography

Films are listed by the date shooting was completed. Direction is by Renoir unless otherwise indicated and only completed, major projects are included. Release dates if different are given in brackets. American titles of French films are likewise in brackets. Lengths for silent films are approximate.

Silent films

La Fille de l'eau 1924 (release 1925)

75 min., b/w
Production: Films Jean Renoir, Maurice Touzé, Studio films
Screenplay: Pierre Lestringuez
Adaptation: Jean Renoir
Photography: Jean Bachelet, Alphonse Gibory.
Principal actors: Catherine Hessling (Virginia), Pierre Philippe (Uncle Jeff), Harold Lewingston (Georges Raynal)

Nana 1926

120 min., b/w
Production: Films Jean Renoir
Screenplay: Pierre Lestringuez, from the novel by Emile Zola
Adaptation: Jean Renoir
Photography: Edmond Crown, Jean Bachelet
Editing: Jean Renoir
Principal actors: Catherine Hessling (Nana), Werner Krauss (Count Muffat), Jean Angelo (Count de Vandeuvres), Pierre Philippe

(Bordenave), Pierre Champagne (la Faloise), Raymond Guérin-Catelain (Georges Hugon), Claude Autant-Lara (Fauchery)

Charleston or *Sur un air de charleston* 1926 (release 1927)

20 min., b/w.
Production: Néo-film (Pierre Braunberger)
Screenplay: Pierre Lestringuez from an idea by André Cerf
Photography: Jean Bachelet
Music: Clément Doucet
Principal actors: Catherine Hessling (the dancer), Johnny Huggins (the explorer), André Cerf (the ape)

Marquitta 1927

100 min., b/w
Production: Artistes Réunis
Screenplay: Pierre Lestringuez
Adaptation: Jean Renoir
Photography: Jean Bachelet, Raymond Agnel
Principal actors: Marie-Louise Iribe (Marquitta), Jean Angelo (Prince Vlasco)

La Petite Marchande d'allumettes (*The Little Match Girl*) 1928

29 min., b/w
Production: Jean Renoir, Jean Tedesco
Directors: Jean Renoir, Jean Tedesco
Screenplay: Jean Renoir, from the story by Hans Christian Andersen
Photography: Jean Bachelet
Principal actors: Catherine Hessling (Karen, the little match girl), Jean Storm (young man, wooden soldier), Manuel Raaby (policeman, death)

Tire-au-flanc 1928

95 min., b/w.
Production: Néo-film (Pierre Braunberger)
Screenplay: Jean Renoir, Claude Heymann, André Cerf, from the play by André Mouézy-Eon and A. Sylvane
Photography: Jean Bachelet
Principal actors: Georges Pomiès (Jean Dubois d'Ombelles), Michel Simon (Joseph), Fridette Faton (Georgette), Félix Oudart (Colonel Brochard), Jean Storm (Lieutenant Daumel), Kinny Dorlay (Lily),

Maryanne (Madame Blandin), Zellas (Muflot), Jeanne Helbing (Solange)

Le Tournoi or *Le Tournoi dans la cité* 1928

120 min., b/w
Production: Société des Films Historiques
Screenplay: Henry Dupuy-Mazuel, André Jaeger-Schmidt
Photography: Marcel Lucien, Maurice Desfassiaux
Editing: André Cerf
Principal actors: Also Nadi (François de Baynes), Jackie Monnier (Isabelle Ginori), Enrique Rivero (Henri de Rogier), Blanche Bernis (Catherine de Medicis), Suzanne Després (Countess de Baynes), Manuel Raaby (Count Ginori)

Le Bled 1929

100 min., b/w
Production: Société des Films Historiques
Screenplay: Henry Dupuy-Mazuel, André Jaeger-Schmidt
Photography: Marcel Lucien, Léon Morizet
Principal actors: Jackie Monnier (Claude Duvernet), Enrique Rivero (Pierre Hoffer), Diana Hart (Diane Duvernet), Manuel Raaby (Manuel Duvernet), Alexandre Arquillière (Christian Hoffer)

Sound Films

On purge bébé 1931

60 min., b/w
Production: Braunberger–Richebé
Screenplay: Jean Renoir, from the play by Georges Feydeau
Photography: Théodore Sparkuhl, Roger Hubert
Editor: Jean Mamy
Set: Gabriel Scognamillo
Music: Paul Misraki
Sound: D. F. Scanlon
Principal actors: Jacques Louvigny (M. Follavoine), Michel Simon (Chouilloux), Marguerite Pierry (Julie Follavoine), Fernandel (Horace Truchet), Sacha Tarride (Toto Follavoine)

La Chienne 1931

100 min., b/w
Production: Films Jean Renoir, Braunberger–Richebé
Screenplay: Jean Renoir, André Girard, from the novel by Georges de la Fouchardière
Dialogue: Jean Renoir
Photography: Théodore Sparkuhl
Editor: (initially) Denise Batcheff, Paul Fejos (then) Marguerite Renoir, Jean Renoir
Set: Gabriel Scognamillo
Music: Eugénie Buffet, Toselli
Sound: Joseph de Bretagne, Marcel Courme
Principal actors: Michel Simon (Maurice Legrand), Janie Marèze (Lulu), Georges Flammant (Dédé), Magdaleine Bérubet (Adèle Legrand), Pierre Gaillard (Alexis Godard)

La Nuit du carrefour (*Night at the Crossroads*) 1932

80 min., b/w
Production: Europa Films
Screenplay: Jean Renoir and Georges Simenon, from the novel by Georges Simenon
Photography: Marcel Lucien, Georges Asselin
Editor: Marguerite Renoir
Set: William Aguet
Sound: Joseph de Bretagne, Bugnon
Principal actors: Pierre Renoir (Inspector Maigret), Winna Winfried (Else Andersen), Georges Koudria (Carl Andersen)

Boudu sauvé des eaux (*Boudu Saved from Drowning*) 1932

83 min., b/w
Production: Société Sirius (Films M. Simon)
Screenplay: Jean Renoir, from the play by René Fauchois
Photography: Marcel Lucien
Editors: Marguerite Renoir, Suzanne de Troyes
Set: Jean Castanier, Hugues Laurent
Music: Raphael, Johann Strauss
Sound: Igor B. Kalinowski
Principal actors: Michel Simon (Boudu), Charles Granval (Edouard Lestingois), Marcelle Hainia (Madame Lestingois), Séverine Lerczinska (Anne-Marie)

Chotard et cie 1933

83 min., b/w
Production: Films Roger Ferdinand
Screenplay: Jean Renoir, from the play by Roger Ferdinand
Photography: Joseph-Louis Mundwiller
Editors: Marguerite Renoir, Suzanne de Troyes
Set: Jean Castanier
Sound: Igor B. Kalinowski
Principal actors: Fernand Charpin (François Chotard), Georges
    Pomiès (Julien Collinet), Jeanne Boitel (Reine Chotard)

Madame Bovary 1933 (release 1934)

120 min., b/w
Production: Nouvelle Société du Film (Gallimard)
Screenplay: Jean Renoir, from the novel by Gustave Flaubert
Photography: Jean Bachelet
Editor: Margeurite Renoir
Set: Robert Gys, Eugène Lourié, Georges Wakhevitch
Music: Darius Milhaud
Sound: Marcel Courme, Joseph de Bretagne
Principal actors: Valentine Tessier (Emma Bovary), Pierre Renoir
    (Charles Bovary), Max Dearly (M. Homais), Daniel Lecourtois
    (Léon Dupuis), Fernand Fabre (Rodolphe Boulanger), Robert Le
    Vigan (Lheureux)

Toni 1934

85 min., b/w
Production: Films d'Aujourd'hui
Screenplay: Jean Renoir, Carl Einstein, from a true story recorded by
    Jacques Mortier
Photography: Claude Renoir
Editor: Marguerite Renoir, Suzanne de Troyes
Music: Paul Bozzi, Joseph Kosma
Sound: Bardisbanian
Principal actors: Charles Blavette (Toni), Jenny Hélia (Marie), Celia
    Montalvan (Josefa), Max Dalban (Albert), Edouard Delmont
    (Fernand)

Le Crime de Monsieur Lange *(The Crime of Mr Lange)* 1935 (release 1936)

85 min., b/w
Production: Obéron
Screenplay: Jacques Prévert, Jean Renoir, from a story by Jean Castanier
Photography: Jean Bachelet
Editor: Marguerite Renoir
Set: Jean Castanier, Robert Gys
Music: Jean Wiener, Joseph Kosma
Sound: Guy Moreau, Louis Bogé, Roger Loisel, Robert Teisseire
Principal actors: Jules Berry (Batala), René Lefèvre (Amédée Lange), Florelle (Valentine), Nadia Sirbirskaia (Estelle), Maurice Baquet (Charles)

La Vie est à nous 1936 (first commercial showing, 1969)

66 min., b/w
Production: Parti Communiste Français
Directors: Jean Renoir, Jacques Becker, André Zwoboda, Jean-Paul Dreyfus (Le Chanois)
Screenplay: Jean Renoir, Paul Vaillant-Couturier, Jean-Paul Dreyfus, André Zwoboda
Photography: Louis Page, Jean-Serge Bourgoin, Jean Isnard, Alain Douarinou, Claude Renoir, Nicholas Hayer
Editor: Marguerite Renoir
Music: 'The Internationale', Shostakovich, Chorale Populaire de Paris.
Principal actors: Jean Dasté, Max Dalban, Charles Blavette, Jacques Brunius, Nadia Sibirskaia, Jacques Becker, Jean-Paul le Chanois, Gaston Modot and (as themselves) Marcel Cachin, André Marty, Maurice Thorez, Jacques Duclos

Une Partie de campagne *(A Day in the Country)* 1936 (release 1946)

40 min., b/w
Production: Films du Panthéon, Films de la Pléiade (Pierre Braun-berger)
Screenplay: Jean Renoir, from the story by Guy de Maupassant
Photography: Claude Renoir
Editor: Marguerite Renoir
Set: Robert Gys
Music: Joseph Kosma

Sound: Marcel Courme, Joseph de Bretagne
Principal actors: Sylvie Bataille (Henriette Dufour), Jane Marken (Madame Dufour), Gabriello (Cyprien Dufour), Georges Darnoux (Henri), Jacques Brunius (Rodolphe), Paul Temps (Anatole)

Les Bas-fonds (The Lower Depths) 1936

90 minutes, b/w
Production: Albatros Films (Alexandre Kamenka)
Screenplay: Eugène Zamiatine, Jacques Companeez, from the play by Maxim Gorki
Adaptation: Jean Renoir, Charles Spaak
Photography: Jean Bachelet, Fedote Bourgassof
Editor: Marguerite Renoir
Set: Eugène Lourié, Hugues Laurent
Music: Jean Wiener
Sound: Robert Ivonnet
Principal actors: Jean Gabin (Pépel), Louis Jouvet (the Baron), Vladimir Sokoloff (Kostilev), Gabriello (Police inspector), Suzy Prim (Vasilissa), Junie Astor (Natacha)

La Grande Illusion 1937

113 min., b/w
Production: RAC (Réalisation d'Art Cinématographique)
Screenplay: Jean Renoir, Charles Spaak
Photography: Christian Matras
Editor: Marguerite Renoir
Set: Eugène Lourié
Music: Joseph Kosma
Sound: Joseph de Bretagne
Principal actors: Jean Gabin (Maréchal), Pierre Fresnay (de Boieldieu), Erich von Stroheim (von Rauffenstein), Marcel Dalio (Rosenthal), Julien Carette (Cartier, the actor), Dita Parlo (Elsa)

La Marseillaise 1937 (release 1938)

135 min., b/w
Production: CGT (Conféderation Générale du Travail) then Société de production et d'exploitation du film La Marseillaise
Screenplay: Jean Renoir, with Carl Koch and Nina Martel-Dreyfus
Dialogue: Jean Renoir
Photography: Jean-Serge Bourgoin, Alain Douarinou, Jean-Marie Maillols, Jean-Paul Alphen, Jean Louis

Editors: Marguerite Renoir and Marthe Huguet
Music: Joseph Kosma, Sauveplane, Rouget de L'Isle, Mozart, etc.
Sound: Joseph de Bretagne, Jean-Roger Bertrand, J. Demède
Principal actors: Pierre Renoir (Louis XVI), Lise Delamare (Marie-Antoinette), Andrex (Arnaud), Edmond Ardisson (Bomier), Nadia Sibirskaia (Louison), Edouard Delmont (Cabri)

La Bête humaine (The Human Beast) 1938

105 min., b/w
Production: Paris Film Production (Robert Hakim)
Screenplay: Jean Renoir, from the novel by Emile Zola
Photography: Curt Courant
Editors: Marguerite Renoir and Suzanne de Troyes
Set: Eugène Lourié
Music: Joseph Kosma
Sound: Robert Teisseire
Principal actors: Jean Gabin (Jacques Lantier), Simone Simon (Séverine), Fernand Ledoux (Roubaud), Julien Carette (Pecqueux), Jacques Berlioz (Grandmorin), Jean Renoir (Cabuche)

La Règle du jeu (The Rules of the Game) 1939

112 min., b/w
Production: Nouvelles Editions Françaises
Screenplay: Jean Renoir with Carl Koch
Photography: Jean Bachelet
Editor: Marguerite Renoir
Set: Eugène Lourié, Max Douy
Music: Joseph Kosma, Mozart, Saint-Saëns, etc.
Sound: Joseph de Bretagne
Principal actors: Marcel Dalio (Robert de La Chesnaye), Roland Toutain (André Jurieux), Nora Grégor (Christine de La Chesnaye), Mila Parély (Geneviève), Paulette Dubost (Lisette), Jean Renoir (Octave), Julien Carette (Marceau), Gaston Modot (Schumacher)

Swamp Water 1941

86 min., b/w
Production: Twentieth Century-Fox
Screenplay: Dudley Nichols, from the story by Vereen Bell
Photography: Peverell Marley, Lucien Ballard
Editor: Walter Thompson

Set: Thomas Little, Richard Day

Music: David Rudolph

Principal actors: Dana Andrews (Ben Ragan), Walter Huston (Thursday Ragan), Mary Howard (Hannah Ragan), Walter Brennan (Tom Keefer), Ann Baxter (Julie Keefer)

This Land is Mine 1943

103 min., b/w.

Production: RKO

Screenplay: Jean Renoir, Dudley Nichols

Photography: Frank Redman

Editor: Frédéric Knudtsen

Set: Eugène Lourié, Albert d'Agostino, Walter Keeler

Music: Lothar Perl

Sound: Terry Kelum, James Stewart

Principal actors: Charles Laughton (Albert Lory), Una O'Connor (Mrs Lory), Maureen O'Hara (Louise Martin), Kent Smith (Paul Martin), George Sanders (George Lambert), Walter Slezack (Major von Keller)

The Southerner 1945

92 min., b/w

Production: Robert Hakim, David Loew

Screenplay: Jean Renoir, Hugo Butler, from the novel *Hold Autumn in Your Hand* by George Sessions Perry

Photography: Lucien Andriot

Editor: Gregg Tallas

Set: Eugène Lourié

Music: Werner Janssen

Sound: Frank Webster

Principal actors: Zachary Scott (Sam Tucker), Betty Field (Nora Tucker), Beulah Bondi (Grandma), J. Carroll Naish (Devers, the neighbour), Charles Kemper (Tim)

The Diary of a Chambermaid 1946

91 min., b/w

Production: Benedict Bogeaus, Burgess Meredith

Screenplay: Jean Renoir, Burgess Meredith, from the play by Heuze, de Lord and Norès, itself adapted from the novel by Octave Mirbeau

Photography: Lucien Andriot

Editor: James Smith
Set: Eugène Lourié
Music: Michel Michelet
Sound: William Lynch
Principal actors: Paulette Goddard (Célestine), Burgess Meredith (Captain Mauger), Hurd Hatfield (Georges Lanlaire), Judith Andersen (Mme Lanlaire), Reginald Owen (M. Lanlaire), Francis Lederer (Joseph)

The Woman on the Beach 1946 (release 1947)

71 min., b/w
Production: RKO
Screenplay: Jean Renoir, F. Davis, J. Hogan from the novel *None so Blind* by Mitchell Wilson
Photography: Harry Wild, Leo Tover
Editors: Roland Gross, Lyle Boyer
Set: Albert d'Agostino, Walter E. Keller
Music: Hans Eisler
Sound: Jean L. Speak, Clem Portman
Principal actors: Joan Bennett (Peggy Butler), Robert Ryan (Scott Burnett), Charles Bickford (Tod Butler), Nan Leslie (Eve)

The River 1950 (release 1951)

99 min., col.
Production: Oriental International Films inc., Theatre Guild
Screenplay: Jean Renoir, Rumer Godden, from the novel by Rumer Godden
Photography: Claude Renoir
Editor: George Gale
Set: Eugène Lourié
Music: Traditional Indian, Weber
Sound: Charles Paulton, Charles Knott
Principal actors: Patricia Walters (Harriet), Nora Swinburne (mother), Esmond Knight (father), Arthur Shields (Mr John), Thomas E. Breen (Captain John), Radha Sri Ram (Melanie), Adrienne Corri (Valerie)

Le Carosse d'or (*The Golden Coach*) 1952 (release 1953)

100 min., col.
Production: Panaria Films, Hoche Productions (Franco-Italian co-production)

Screenplay: Jean Renoir, Renzo Avenzo, Giulio Macchi, Jack Kirk-
land, Ginette Doynel, from the play *Le Carosse du Saint-Sacrement*
by Prosper Mérimée
Photography: Claude Renoir, Ronald Hill
Editors: Mario Seranderi, David Hawkins
Set: Mario Chiari
Music: Vivaldi, Corelli, Olivier Mettra
Sound: Joseph de Bretagne, Ovidio del Grande
Principal actors: Anna Magnani (Camilla), Duncan Lamont (the
Viceroy), Riccardo Rioli (Ramon), Paul Campbell (Felipe)

French Cancan 1954 (release 1955)

97 min., col.
Production: Franco London Films, Jolly Films
Screenplay: Jean Renoir, from an idea by André-Paul Antoine
Photography: Michel Kelber
Editor: Borys Lewin
Set: Max Douy
Music: Georges von Parys and songs from *café-concert* repertory
Sound: Antoine Petitjean
Principal actors: Jean Gabin (Danglard), Maria Félix (la belle abbesse),
Françoise Arnoul (Nini), Jean-Roger Caussimon (Baron Walter),
Gianni Exposito (Prince Alexandre)

Eléna et les hommes (*Paris Does Strange Things*) 1956

95 min., col.
Production: Franco London Films, Les Films Gibé, Electra
Compagnia Cinematografica
Screenplay: Jean Renoir, Jean Serge
Photography: Claude Renoir
Editor: Borys Lewin
Set: Jean André
Music: Joseph Kosma, Georges Van Parys
Sound: William Sivel
Principal actors: Ingrid Bergman (Eléna), Jean Marais (General
Rollan), Mel Ferrer (Henri de Chevincourt), Pierre Bertin (Martin-
Michaud), Juliette Greco (Gypsy singer)

Le Testament du Docteur Cordelier 1959 (release 1961)

100 min., b/w
Production: RTF, Sofirad, Compagnie Jean Renoir
Screenplay: Jean Renoir, from the novel *The Strange Case of Dr Jekyll and Mr Hyde* by Robert Louis Stevenson
Photography: Georges Leclerc
Editor: Renée Lichtig
Set: Marcel-Louis Dieulot
Music: Joseph Kosma
Sound: Joseph Richard
Principal actors: Jean-Louis Barrault (Dr Cordelier/Opale), Teddy Billis (Maître Joly), Michel Vitold (Dr Séverin)

Le Déjeuner sur l'herbe (*Picnic on the Grass*) 1959

92 min., col.
Production: Compagnie Jean Renoir
Screenplay: Jean Renoir
Photography: Georges Leclerc
Editor: Renée Lichtig
Set: Marcel-Louis Dieulot
Music: Joseph Kosma
Sound: Joseph de Bretagne
Principal actors: Paul Meurisse (Professor Etienne Alexis), Catherine Rouvel (Nénette), Fernand Sardou (Nino), Ingrid Nordine (Marie-Charlotte), Charles Blavette (Gaspard)

Le Caporal épinglé (*The Elusive Corporal*) 1962

105 min., b/w
Production: Films du Cyclope
Directors: Jean Renoir, Guy Lefranc
Screenplay: Jean Renoir, Guy Lefranc, from the novel by Jacques Perret
Photography: Georges Leclerc
Editor: Renée Lichtig
Set: Eugène Herrly
Music: Joseph Kosma
Sound: Antoine Petitjean
Principal actors: Jean-Pierre Cassel (the Corporal), Claude Brasseur (Pater), Claude Rich (Ballochet), Cornelia Froeboess (Erika)

Le Petit Théâtre de Jean Renoir (*The Little Theatre of Jean Renoir*)
1969

100 min, col. and b/w.
Production: Son et Lumière, RAI, Bavaria, ORTF
Screenplay: Jean Renoir
Photography: Georges Leclerc, Antoine Georgiakis, Georges Liron
Editor: Geneviève Winding
Set: Gilbert Margerie
Music: Jean Wiener, Joseph Kosma, Octave Crémieux
Sound: Guy Rolphe
Principal actors: (*Le Dernier Réveillon*) Nino Formicola and Milly-
    Monti (tramps), Roland Bertin (Gontran); (*La Cireuse électrique*)
    Marguerite Cassan (Emilie), Pierre Olaf (Gustave), Jacques Dynam
    (Jules); (*Quand l'amour meurt*) Jeanne Moreau (the singer); (*Le Roi
    d'Yvetot*) Fernand Sardou (Duvallier), Françoise Arnoul (Isabelle),
    Jean Carmet (Feraud)

Select bibliography

Books and special numbers of periodicals

Bazin, A. (1989), *Jean Renoir*, (ed.) F. Truffaut, Paris, Lebovici. A book published using Bazin's notes after his death and clearly incomplete. Notable for its brilliant insights into *mise-en-scène* and its thinness on almost everything else.

Cahiers du cinéma (1952), 2(8). The first stage in *Cahiers'* appropriation of Renoir for *auteurism*. Contains key articles by Bazin, Schérer (Rohmer) and Renoir himself.

Chardère, B. (1962), *Premier Plan* (special number on Renoir), 22–4. An enormously useful book because of its compilation of the range of responses to Renoir's films.

Faulkner, C. (1979), *Jean Renoir: a Guide to References and Resources*, Boston, Hall. Essential guide to available material on Renoir, usefully supplemented by R. Viry-Babel (1989) *Jean Renoir: Films, textes, références*, Nancy, Presses Universitaires de Nancy.

Faulkner, C. (1986), *The Social Cinema of Jean Renoir*, Princeton, Princeton University Press. Despite limitations rooted in its Althusserian analytical framework, this is a clear, incisive analysis, especially when dealing with Renoir's films of the 1930s. The best left-wing account available.

Persistence of Vision: Politics and the Cinema of Jean Renoir, (1996), 12/13. A special number of the journal devoted essentially to Renoir's 1930s output. It contains a number of important articles that relocate Renoir's films in the context that others seek to detach them from.

Poulle, F. (1969), *Renoir 1938 ou Jean Renoir pour rien?*, Paris, Editions du Cerf. Politically committed and passionate. A key post-1968 account.

Renoir, J. (1974), *Ecrits, 1926–1971*, Paris, Belfond. This contains the important journalistic writings of the 1930s and provides a very useful overview of the evolution of Renoir's thought.

Renoir, J. (1989), *Renoir on Renoir*, (trans. C. Volk), Cambridge, Cambridge University Press. This contains some of Renoir's most important interviews with *Cahiers du Cinéma*. It is fascinating for the insights it provides into how *Cahiers* and Renoir 'rewrote' the pre-war films.

Serceau, D. (1981), *Jean Renoir, l'insurgé*, Paris, Le Sycomore and Serceau, D. (1985b), *La Sagesse du plaisir*, Paris, Editions du Cerf. An *auteurist* account that locates an ongoing philosophical quest at the heart of Renoir's films (and thus to be distrusted), it provides incisive readings of the films and develops (in the later volume) by far the most persuasive analysis of post-war Renoir. For a much more compact but rather telegraphic version of Serceau's analysis one can turn to: Serceau, D. (1985a), *Jean Renoir*, Paris, Edilig.

Sesonske, A. (1980), *Jean Renoir. The French Films, 1924–1939*, Cambridge, MA, Harvard University Press. Overlong, but by far the most thorough account of the *mise-en-scène* of Renoir's pre-war films.

Viry-Babel, R. (1994), Paris, Ramsay. An eminently clear and beautifully illustrated introduction to Renoir's films.

Studies of individual films

Recent years have seen a lack of overviews of Renoir's output but, by means of compensation, there has been a succession of studies of individual films. The following are worth looking at:

Boston, R. (1994) *Boudu Saved from Drowning*, London, BFI. A personal but stimulating account of the film.

Curchod, O. (1994), *La Grande Illusion*, Paris, Nathan. Clear and informative.

Curchod, O. (1995), *Partie de campagne*, Paris, Nathan. Informed, detailed analysis.

Leutrat, J.-L. (1994), *La Chienne*, Crisnée (Belgium), Editions Yellow Now. A brilliant account of the film. The most impressive of these single-film analyses.

Vanoye, F. (1989), *La Règle du jeu*, Paris, Nathan. The best of several short studies of the film.

Index

Page numbers in italics refer to illustrations while 'n.' after a page reference indicates the number of a note on that page